GALIT SHMUELI

ERIC BERGER

PRACTICAL TIME SERIES FORECASTING WITH PYTHON

A HANDS-ON GUIDE

AXELROD SCHNALL PUBLISHERS

PUBLISHED BY AXELROD SCHNALL PUBLISHERS

ISBN-13: 978-0-9978479-6-3

ISBN-10: 0-997-8479-6-4

For further information see `www.forecastingbook.com`

First Edition, August 2025

Contents

To Boaz Shmueli, who made the production of the Practical Analytics book series a reality

Preface

The purpose of this textbook is to introduce the reader to quantitative forecasting of time series in a practical and hands-on fashion. Most predictive analytics courses in data science and business analytics programs touch very lightly on time series forecasting, if at all. Yet forecasting is extremely popular and useful in practice.

From our experience, learning is best achieved by doing. Hence, the book is designed to achieve self-learning in the following ways:

- The book is relatively short compared to other time series textbooks, to reduce reading time and increase hands-on time.

- Explanations strive to be clear and straightforward with more emphasis on concepts than on statistical theory.

- Chapters include end-of-chapter problems, ranging in focus from conceptual to hands-on exercises, with many requiring running software on real data and interpreting the output in light of a given problem.

- Real data is used to illustrate the methods throughout the book.

- The book emphasizes the *entire forecasting process* rather than focusing only on particular models and algorithms.

- Cases are given in the final chapter, guiding the reader through suggested steps, but inviting self-solution. Working on the cases helps integrate the information and experience gained.

Software

The free and open-source software *Python* (www.python.org) is used throughout the book to illustrate the different methods and procedures. This choice is good for students who are comfortable with some computing language, but does not require prior knowledge of Python. We provide code for figures and outputs to help readers easily replicate our results while learning the basics of Python.

In particular, this edition uses the Python sktime package.[1] Python developers worldwide have contributed over 500,000 packages that can be freely accessed.[2] Many of these packages are devoted to forecasting algorithms, but adopt different conventions for how to use them. One of the goals of the sktime package is to provide a layer above these different algorithms, allowing for a uniform way to employ them. The Python ecosystem is also dominant in machine learning, and the Python package sklearn (also known as scikit-learn) plays a significant role. The sktime package was designed as an extension of sklearn, leveraging the many tools and models in sklearn for those focused on time series. To mention two examples, one can create a custom component, such as the transformation of raw data into a new feature, and then incorporate this transformation in a machine learning pipeline.[3]

[1] www.sktime.net/en/stable

[2] See the Python Package Index at www.pypi.org

[3] For a brief introduction, see www.sktime.net/en/stable/get_started.html

For data visualization, we advocate also using interactive visualization software for exploring the nature of the data before attempting any modeling, especially when many series are involved. One can create interactive graphics within Python using the plotly package.[4] Two standalone packages, not involving Python, are Tableau[5] and TIBCO Spotfire.[6] We illustrate the power of such packages in Chapter 2.

[4] www.plotly.com/python

[5] www.tableau.com

[6] www.spotfire.com

Supporting Materials

Datasets and Python code used in this book are available at github.com/gshmueli/ptsf-Python. Additional supporting materials are available at www.forecastingbook.com.

Using Python for Forecasting

The free and open-source software *Python* (`www.python.org`) is used throughout the book to illustrate the different methods and procedures. In particular, we use the *sktime* package, (`www.sktime.net/en/stable/`) which we described in the previous section.

We also rely on a set of Python packages that provide needed functions, such as those for manipulating and plotting data. Specifically, we use the following packages:

matplotlib	scipy	scikeras
numpy	seaborn	sklearn
pandas	sktime	tensorflow
rpy2	statsmodels	

There are a variety of ways to install Python packages and to run Python code. One can run code locally, or use an online tool such as Google Colab. While teaching this material, we have seen that certain setups require special treatment. See setup instructions at www.forecastingbook.com.

If you are new to installing Python packages, consult with an LLM for guidance, specifying your operating system and the list of packages you want to install.

Install the packages in the rightmost column only if you plan to use deep learning (see Chapters 8 and 9).

Course Plan

The book was designed for a forecasting course at the graduate or upper-undergraduate level. It can be taught in a mini-semester (6-7 weeks) or as a semester-long course, using the cases to integrate the learning from different chapters. A suggested schedule for a typical course is:

Week 1 Chapters 1 ("Approaching Forecasting") and 2 ("Data") cover goal definition, data collection, characterization, visualization, and pre-processing.

Week 2 Chapter 3 ("Performance Evaluation") covers data partitioning, naive forecasts, measuring predictive accuracy and uncertainty.

Weeks 3-4 Chapter 4 ("Forecasting Methods: Overview") describes and compares different approaches underlying forecasting methods. Chapter 5 ("Smoothing Methods") covers moving average, exponential smoothing, and differencing.

Weeks 5-6 Chapters 6 ("Regression Models: Trend and Seasonality") and 7 ("Regression Models: Autocorrelation and External Information") cover linear regression models, autoregressive (AR) and ARIMA models, and modeling external information as predictors in a regression model.

Optional Week Chapter 8 ("Neural Networks") introduces neural networks for forecasting time series. It covers ordinary neural networks as well as deep learning. We recommend covering deep learning in more advanced courses.

Optional Week Chapter 9 ("Forecasting Binary Outcomes") expands forecasting to binary series, introducing appropriate visualization, performance metrics, benchmarks, and models (logistic regression and neural networks).

Optional Week(s) One or more cases from Chapter 11.

Final week Chapter 10 ("Communication and Maintenance") discusses practical issues of presenting, reporting, documenting and monitoring forecasts. This week is a good point for providing feedback on a case analysis from Chapter 11.

Team project A team project is highly recommended in such a course, where students work on a real or realistic problem using real data.

Cases

Chapter 11 ("Cases") offers three cases that integrate the learning and highlight key forecasting points.

Case 11.1 (forecasting public transportation demand) covers visualization and exploration of time series patterns and exceptions, multiple seasonal cycles, non-standard time periods (15-minute counts during work-hours), performance evaluation, and the range of forecasting methods.

Case 11.2 (forecasting tourism activity) focuses on forecasting a large number of series, including visualization and exploration, data partitioning and performance evaluation (addressing zero counts with MAPE and MASE), computing naive benchmarks, and fitting a variety of forecasting models, including ensembles.

Case 11.3 (forecasting stock price movements) covers binary series. This includes suitable visualization and exploration, performance measures (confusion matrix, ROC, and AUC), logistic regression and neural networks, and inclusion of external predictors.

Acknowledgments

We thank Rob Hyndman for his generous and varied contributions to both the forecasting and the open source communities. While Rob and his team have directly contributed software to the R ecosystem, many of their ideas and algorithms have been incorporated into Python packages.

We thank Franz Kiraly for his vision and dedication to the `sktime` project and for his encouragement and advice on the specific issues that we raised. We are grateful to the entire family of contributors to the `sktime` package (and to the packages on which they rely).

Thanks to Kenneth C. Lichtendahl, Ravi Bapna, Peter Bruce, and Jan Trommelmans for their useful feedback and suggestions on previous editions. Special thanks to Noa Shmueli for her meticulous editing of this and earlier editions. Kuber Deokar and Shweta Jadhav from UpThink Edutech Services Pvt. Ltd. provided valuable feedback on the book problems and solutions.

Lastly, we thank multiple readers who have shared comments that helped improve the various editions and the supporting website.

1 Approaching Forecasting

In this first chapter, we look at forecasting within the larger context of where it is implemented and introduce the complete forecasting process. We also briefly touch upon the main issues and approaches that are detailed in the book.

1.1 Forecasting: Where?

A time series is a series of measurements taken on an object over time. Examples include monthly sales, daily restaurant occupancy, and hourly traffic. Time series forecasting is performed in nearly every organization that works with quantifiable data. Retail stores forecast sales. Energy companies forecast reserves, production, demand, and prices. Educational institutions forecast enrollment. Governments forecast tax receipts and spending. International financial organizations such as the World Bank and International Monetary Fund forecast inflation and economic activity. Passenger transport companies use time series to forecast future travel. Banks and lending institutions forecast new home purchases, and venture capital firms forecast market potential to evaluate business plans.

1.2 Basic Notation

The amount of notation in the book is kept to the necessary minimum. In particular, we use four types of symbols to denote time periods, data series, forecasts, and forecast errors:

$t = 1, 2, 3, \ldots$	An index denoting the time period of interest. $t = 1$ is the first period in a series.
$y_1, y_2, y_3, \ldots, y_n$	A series of n values measured over n time periods, where y_t denotes the value of the series at time period t. For example, for a series of daily average temperatures, $t = 1, 2, 3, \ldots$ denotes day 1, day 2, and day 3; y_1, y_2, and y_3 denote the temperatures on days 1,2, and 3.
F_t	The forecasted value for time period t.
F_{t+k}	The k-step-ahead forecast when the forecasting time is t. If we are currently at time period t, the forecast for the next time period $(t+1)$ is denoted F_{t+1}.
e_t	The forecast error for time period t, which is the difference between the actual value and the forecast at time t, and equal to $y_t - F_t$ (see Chapter 3).

1.3 *The Forecasting Process*

As in all data analysis, the process of forecasting begins with defining the goal. Data is then collected and cleaned, and explored using visualization tools. A set of potential forecasting methods is selected, based on the nature of the data. The different methods are applied and compared in terms of forecast accuracy and other measures related to the goal. The "best" method is then chosen and used to generate forecasts.

Of course, the process does not end once forecasts are generated, because forecasting is typically an ongoing goal. Hence, forecast accuracy is monitored and sometimes the forecasting method is adapted or changed to accommodate changes in the goal or the data over time. A diagram of the forecasting process is shown in Figure 1.1.

Note the two sets of arrows, indicating that parts of the process are iterative. For instance, once the series is explored one might determine that the series at hand cannot achieve the required goal, leading to the collection of new or supplementary data. Another iterative process takes place when applying a forecasting method and evaluating its performance. The evaluation often leads to tweaking or adapting the method, or even trying out other methods.

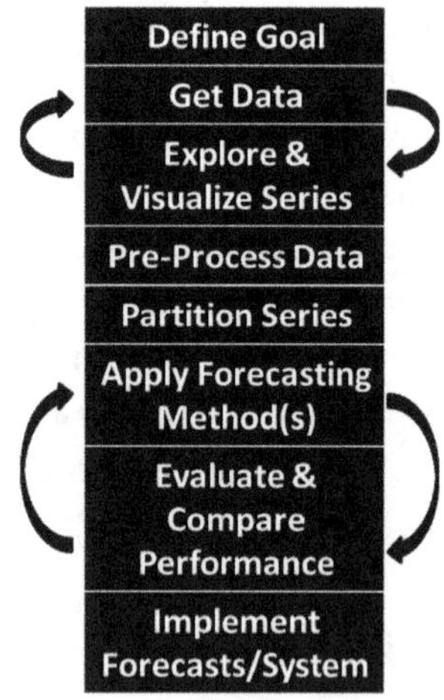

Figure 1.1: Diagram of the forecasting process

Given the sequence of steps in the forecasting process and the iterative nature of modeling and evaluating performance, the book is organized according to the following logic. In this chapter we consider the context-related goal definition step. Chapter 2 discusses the steps of data collection, exploration, and preprocessing. Next comes Chapter 3 on performance evaluation. The performance evaluation chapter precedes the forecasting method chapters for two reasons:

1. Understanding how performance is evaluated affects the choice of forecasting method, as well as the particular details of how a specific forecasting method is executed. Within each of the forecasting method chapters, we refer to evaluation metrics and compare different configurations using these metrics.

2. A crucial initial step that allows the evaluation of predictive performance is data partitioning. This means that the forecasting method is applied only to a subset of the series. It is therefore important to understand why and how partitioning is carried out before applying any forecasting method.

The chapters on forecasting methods (Chapters 5-8) are followed by Chapter 10 ("Communication and Maintenance"), which discusses the last step of implementing the forecasts or forecasting system within the organization.

Before continuing, let us present an example that will be used throughout the book for illustrative purposes.

Illustrative Example: Ridership on Amtrak Trains

Amtrak, a U.S. railway company, routinely collects data on ridership. Our illustration is based on the series of monthly Amtrak ridership between January 1991 and March 2004 in the United States.

The series was originally part of a forecasting competition focused on transportation data and was available on the now-defunct `predicitonprinciples.com`. A copy of the data[1] is available at `www.forecastingbook.com`.

[1] The archived data is available at `web.archive.org/web/20160216212143/http://www.forecastingprinciples.com/`. Click on *Data*, then *Transportation time-series data* to download `MHcompl.xls`. Open the file, switch to the Monthly worksheet, and find series M034.

1.4 *Goal Definition*

Determining and clearly defining the forecasting goal is essential for arriving at useful results. Unlike typical forecasting competitions,[2] where a set of data with a brief story and given set of performance metrics are provided, in real life neither of these components are straightforward or readily available. One must first determine the purpose of generating forecasts, the type of forecasts that are needed, how the forecasts will be used by the organization, what costs are associated with forecast errors, what data will be available in the future, and more.

[2] For a list of popular forecasting competitions see the "Data Resources and Competitions" pages at the end of the book.

It is also critical to understand the *implications* of the forecasts to different stakeholders. For example, The National Agricultural Statistics Service (NASS) of the United States Department of Agriculture (USDA) produces forecasts for different crop yields. These forecasts have important implications:

> [...] some market participants continue to express the belief that the USDA has a hidden agenda associated with producing the estimates and forecasts [for corn and soybean yield]. This "agenda" centers on price manipulation for a variety of purposes, including such things as managing farm program costs and influencing food prices. Lack of understanding of NASS methodology and/or the belief in a hidden agenda can prevent market participants from correctly interpreting and utilizing the acreage and yield forecasts.[3]

[3] From farmdocdaily blog, posted March 23, 2011, `farmdocdaily.illinois.edu/2011/03/usda-corn-and-soybean-acreage-1.html`; accessed Aug 7, 2025.

In the following we elaborate on several important issues that must be considered at the goal definition stage. These issues affect every step in the forecasting process, from data collection through data exploration, preprocessing, modeling, and performance evaluation.

Descriptive vs. Predictive Goals

As with cross-sectional data,[4] modeling time series data is done for either descriptive or predictive purposes. In descriptive modeling, or *time series analysis*, a time series is modeled to determine its components in terms of seasonal patterns, trends, relation to external factors, and the like. These can then be used for decision making and policy formulation. In contrast, *time series forecast-*

[4] Cross-sectional data is a set of measurements taken at one point in time. In contrast, a time series consists of one measurement over time.

ing uses the information in a time series (possibly alongside additional information) to forecast future values of that series. The difference between descriptive and predictive goals leads to differences in the types of methods used and in the modeling process itself. For example, in selecting a method for *describing* a time series or explaining its patterns, priority is given to methods that produce explainable results (rather than black-box methods) and to models based on causal arguments. Furthermore, description can be done in retrospect, while prediction is prospective in nature. This means that descriptive models can use "future" information (e.g., averaging the values of yesterday, today, and tomorrow to obtain a smooth representation of today's value) whereas forecasting models cannot use future information. Finally, a predictive model is judged by its predictive accuracy rather than by its ability to provide correct causal explanations.

Consider the Amtrak ridership example described at the beginning of this chapter. Different analysis goals can be specified, each leading to a different path in terms of modeling, performance evaluation, and implementation. One possible analysis goal that Amtrak might have is to forecast future monthly ridership on its trains for purposes of pricing. Using demand data to determine pricing is called "revenue management" and is a popular practice by airlines and hotel chains. Clearly, this is a predictive goal.

A different goal for which Amtrak might want to use the ridership data is for impact assessment: evaluating the effect of some event, such as airport closures due to inclement weather, or the opening of a new large national highway. This goal is retrospective in nature, and is therefore descriptive or even explanatory. Analysis would compare the series before and after the event, with no direct interest in future values of the series. Note that these goals are also geography-specific and would therefore require using ridership data at a finer level of geography within the United States.

A third goal that Amtrak might pursue is identifying and quantifying demand during different seasons for planning the number and frequency of trains needed during different seasons.

If the model is only aimed at producing monthly indexes of demand, then it is a descriptive goal. In contrast, if the model will be used to forecast seasonal demand for future years, then it is a predictive task.

Finally, the Amtrak ridership data might be used by national agencies, such as the Bureau of Transportation Statistics, to evaluate the trends in transportation modes over the years. Whether this is a descriptive or predictive goal depends on what the analysis will be used for. If it is for the purposes of reporting past trends, then it is descriptive. If the purpose is forecasting future trends, then it is a predictive goal.

The focus in this book is on *time series forecasting*, where the goal is to predict future values of a time series. Some of the methods presented, however, can also be used for descriptive purposes.[5]

[5] Most statistical time series books focus on descriptive *time series analysis*. A good introduction is the book . C. Chatfield. *The Analysis of Time Series: An Introduction*. Chapman & Hall/CRC, 6th edition, 2003

Forecast Horizon and Forecast Updating

How far into the future should we forecast? Must we generate all forecasts at a single time point, or can forecasts be generated on an ongoing basis? These are important questions to be answered at the goal definition stage. Both questions depend on how the forecasts will be used in practice and therefore require close collaboration with the forecast stakeholders in the organization. The forecast horizon k is the number of periods ahead that we must forecast, and F_{t+k} is a k-step-ahead forecast. In the Amtrak ridership example, one-month-ahead forecasts (F_{t+1}) might be sufficient for revenue management (for creating flexible pricing), whereas longer term forecasts, such as three-month-ahead (F_{t+3}), are more likely to be needed for scheduling and procurement purposes.

How recent are the data available at the time of prediction? Timeliness of data collection and transfer directly affect the forecast horizon: forecasting next month's ridership is much harder if we do not yet have data for the last two months. It means that we must generate forecasts of the form F_{t+3} rather than F_{t+1}. Whether improving timeliness of data collection and transfer is possible or not, its implication on forecasting must be identified at the goal definition stage.

While long-term forecasting is often a necessity, it is important to have realistic expectations regarding forecast accuracy. The further into the future, the more likely it is that the forecasting context will change and therefore uncertainty increases. In such cases, expected changes in the forecasting context should be incorporated into the forecasting model, and the model should be examined (and ideally updated) periodically to assure its suitability for the changed context.

When long-term forecasts are required, it is sometimes useful to provide periodic updated forecasts by incorporating new accumulated information. For example, a three-month-ahead forecast for April 2012 generated in January 2012 might be updated in February and again in March. This refreshing of the forecasts based on new data is called *roll-forward forecasting*.

All these aspects of the forecast horizon have implications on the required length of the series for building the forecast model, on frequency and timeliness of collection, on the forecasting methods used, on performance evaluation, and on the uncertainty levels of the forecasts.

Forecast Use

How will the forecasts be used? Understanding how the forecasts will be used, perhaps by different stakeholders, is critical for generating forecasts of the right type and with a useful accuracy level. Should forecasts be numerical or binary ("event"/"non-event")? Does over-prediction cost more or less than under-prediction? Will the forecasts be used directly or will they be adjusted in some way before use? Will the forecasts and forecasting method be presented to management or to the technical department? Answers to such questions are necessary for choosing appropriate data, methods, and evaluation schemes.

Level of Automation

The level of required automation depends on the nature of the forecasting task and on how forecasts will be used in practice. Some important questions to ask are:

1. How many series need to be forecasted?
2. Is the forecasting an ongoing process or a one-time event?
3. Which data and software will be available during the forecasting period?
4. What forecasting expertise will be available at the organization during the forecasting period?

Different answers will lead to different choices of data, forecasting methods, and evaluation schemes. Hence, these questions must be considered already at the goal definition stage.

In scenarios where many series are to be forecasted on an ongoing basis, and not much forecasting expertise can be allocated, automated solutions can be advantageous. A classic example is forecasting Point of Sale (POS) data for purposes of inventory control across many stores. Various consulting firms offer automated forecasting systems for such applications.

"Predict" or "Forecast"?

The terms *predict* and *forecast* are often used interchangeably in common language. In the world of data science, *forecast* is more common when referring to time series, whereas *predict* is popular in cross-sectional settings. In this book we mostly use *forecast*. We occasionally use predict-related terms (such as *prediction interval* or *predictors*) when those are the common terms used in practice.

1.5 Problems

Impact of September 11 on Air Travel in the United States: The Research and Innovative Technology Administration's Bureau of Transportation Statistics (BTS) conducted a study to evaluate the impact of the September 11, 2001, terrorist attack on U.S. transportation. The study report and the data can be found at `www.bts.gov/archive/publications/estimated_impacts_of_9_11_on_us_travel/index`. The goal of the study was stated as follows:

> The purpose of this study is to provide a greater understanding of the passenger travel behavior patterns of persons making long distance trips before and after September 11.

The report analyzes monthly passenger movement data between January 1990 and April 2004. Data on three monthly time series are given in the file *Sept11Travel.csv* for this period: (1) actual airline revenue passenger miles (Air), (2) rail passenger miles (Rail), and (3) vehicle miles traveled (Auto).

In order to assess the impact of September 11, BTS took the following approach: Using data before September 11, it forecasted future data (under the assumption of no terrorist attack). Then, BTS compared the forecasted series with the actual data to assess the impact of the event.

1. Is the goal of this study descriptive or predictive?

2. What is the forecast horizon to consider in this task? Are next-month forecasts sufficient?

3. What level of automation does this forecasting task require? Consider the four questions related to automation.

4. What is the meaning of $t = 1, 2, 3$ in the Air series? Which time period does $t = 1$ refer to?

5. What are the values for y_1, y_2, and y_3 in the Air series?

2
Time Series Data

2.1 Data Collection

When considering which data to use for generating forecasts, the forecasting goal and the various aspects discussed in Chapter 1 must be taken into account. There are also considerations at the data level which can affect the forecasting results. In this chapter we discuss several of these issues.

Data Quality

The quality of our data in terms of measurement accuracy, missing values, corrupted data, and data entry errors can greatly affect the forecasting results. Data quality is especially important in time series forecasting, where the sample size is small (typically not more than a few hundred values in a series).

If there are multiple sources collecting or hosting the data of interest (e.g., different departments in an organization), it can be useful to compare the quality and choose the best data (or even combine the sources). However, it is important to keep in mind that for ongoing forecasting, data collection is not a one-time effort. Additional data will need to be collected again in the future from the same source. Moreover, if forecasted values will be compared against a particular series of actual values, then that series must play a major role in the performance evaluation step. For example, if forecasted daily temperatures will be compared against measurements from a particular weather station A, forecasts based on measurements from station B should be compared to the measured temperatures at weather station A rather than B.

In some cases the series of interest alone is sufficient for arriving at satisfactory forecasts, while in other cases external data might be more predictive of the series of interest than solely its history. In the case of external data, it is crucial to assure that the same data will be available at the time of prediction.

Temporal Frequency

With today's technology, many time series are recorded on very frequent time scales. Stock ticker data is available on a minute-by-minute basis. Purchases at online and brick-and-mortar stores are recorded in real time. However, although data might be available at a very frequent scale, for the purpose of forecasting it is not always preferable to use this frequency. In considering the choice of temporal frequency, one must consider the frequency of the required forecasts (the goal) and the level of noise[1] in the data. For example, if the goal is to forecast next-day sales at a grocery store, minute-by-minute sales data is likely less useful than daily aggregates. The minute-by-minute series will contain many sources of noise (e.g., variation by peak and nonpeak shopping hours) that degrade its daily-level forecasting power. However, when the data is aggregated to a coarser level, these noise sources are likely to cancel out.

[1] "Noise" refers to variability in the series' values beyond patterns such as trends and seasonality. See Section 2.2.

Even when forecasts are needed on a particular frequency (such as daily), it is sometimes advantageous to aggregate the series to a lower frequency (such as weekly), and model the aggregated series to produce forecasts. The aggregated forecasts can then be disaggregated to produce higher-frequency forecasts. For example, the top performers in the 2008 *NN5 Time Series Forecasting Competition*[2] describe their approach for forecasting daily cash withdrawal amounts at ATM machines:

> To simplify the forecasting problem, we performed a time aggregation step to convert the time series from daily to weekly... Once the forecast has been produced, we convert the weekly forecast to a daily one by a simple linear interpolation scheme.

[2] R. R. Andrawis, A. F. Atiya, and H. El-Shishiny. Forecast combinations of computational intelligence and linear models for the NN5 time series forecasting competition. *International Journal of Forecasting*, 27:672–688, 2011

Series Granularity

"Granularity" refers to the coverage of the data. This can be in terms of geographical area, population, time of operation, etc. In the Amtrak ridership example, depending on the goal, we could look at geographical coverage (route-level, state-level, etc.), at a particular type of population (e.g., senior citizens), and/or at particular times (e.g., during rush hour). In all these cases, the resulting time series are based on a smaller population of interest than the national level time series.

As with temporal frequency, the level of granularity must be aligned with the forecasting goal, while considering the levels of noise. Very fine coverage might lead to low counts and possibly many zero counts. Exploring different aggregation and slicing levels is often needed for obtaining adequate series. The level of granularity will eventually affect the choice of preprocessing, forecasting method(s), and evaluation metrics. For example, if we are interested in daily train ridership of senior citizens on a particular route, and the resulting series contains many zero counts, we might resort to methods for forecasting binary data rather than numeric data (see Chapter 9).

Domain Expertise

While the focus in this section is on the quantitative data to be used for forecasting, a critical additional source of information is domain expertise. Without domain expertise, the process of creating a forecasting model and evaluating its usefulness might not achieve its goal.

Domain expertise is needed to determine which data to use (e.g., daily vs. hourly, how far back, and from which source) and to describe and interpret patterns that appear in the data, from seasonal patterns to extreme values and drastic changes (e.g., clarifying what are "after hours", interpreting massive absences due to the organization's annual picnic, and explaining a drastic change in trend due to a new company policy).

Domain expertise is also used to help evaluate the practical implications of the forecasting performance. As we discuss in Chapter 10, implementing the forecasts and forecasting system requires close linkage with organizational goals. Hence, the ability to communicate with domain experts during the forecasting process is crucial for producing useful results, especially when the forecasting task is outsourced to a consulting firm.

2.2 *Time Series Components*

For the purpose of choosing adequate forecasting methods, it is useful to dissect a time series into a systematic part and a non-systematic part. The systematic part is typically divided into three components: *level*, *trend*, and *seasonality*. The non-systematic part is called *noise*. The systematic components are assumed to be unobservable, as they characterize the underlying series, which we only observe with added noise. *Level* describes the average value of the series. *Trend* is the change in the series from one period to the next. *Seasonality* describes a short-term cyclical behavior that can be observed several times within the given series. While some series do not contain trend or seasonality, all series have a level. Lastly, *noise* is the random variation that results from measurement error or other causes that are not accounted for. It is always present in a time series to some degree, although we cannot observe it directly.

The different components are commonly considered to be either *additive* or *multiplicative*. A time series with *additive* components can be written as:

$$y_t = \text{Level} + \text{Trend} + \text{Seasonality} + \text{Noise} \tag{2.1}$$

A time series with *multiplicative* components can be written as:

$$y_t = \text{Level} \times \text{Trend} \times \text{Seasonality} \times \text{Noise} \tag{2.2}$$

Forecasting methods attempt to isolate the systematic part and quantify the noise level. The systematic part is used for generating point forecasts[3] and the level of noise helps assess the uncertainty associated with these point forecasts.

Trend patterns are commonly approximated by linear, exponential, and other mathematical functions. Illustrations of different trend patterns can be seen by comparing the different

[3] A *point forecast* is a single numerical value (e.g., 102), whereas a *prediction interval* (or *forecast interval*) is a forecast range that has an uncertainty level attached to it. See Section 3.3.

rows in Figure 2.1. For seasonal patterns, two common approximations are *additive seasonality* (where values in different seasons vary by a constant amount) and *multiplicative seasonality* (where values in different seasons vary by a percentage). Illustrations of these seasonality patterns are shown in the second and third columns of Figure 2.1. Chapter 6 discusses these different patterns in further detail, and also introduces another systematic component, which is the correlation between neighboring values in a series.

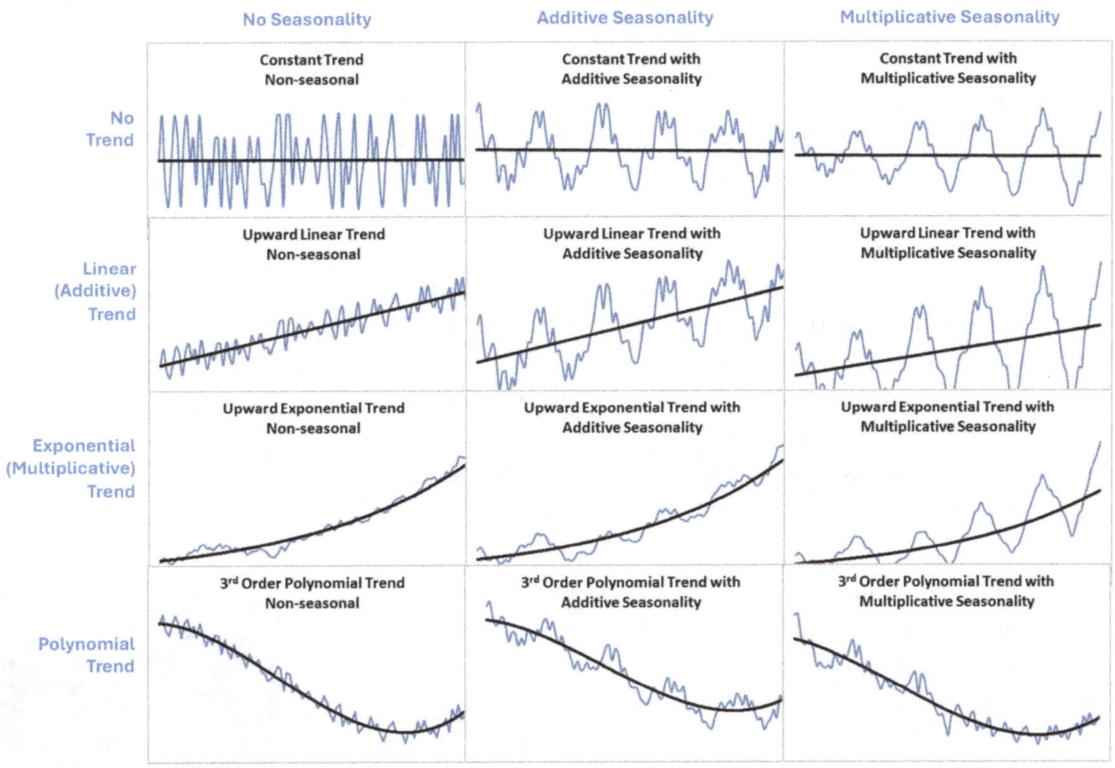

Figure 2.1: Illustrations of common trend and seasonality patterns. Image courtesy of Jim Flowers.

2.3 *Visualizing Time Series*

An effective initial step for characterizing the nature of a time series and detecting potential problems is data visualization. By visualizing the series, we can identify its components, detect initial patterns, and spot potential problems such as extreme values, unequal spacing, and missing values.

The Time Plot

The most basic and informative plot for visualizing a time series is the *time plot*. In its simplest form, a time plot is a line chart of the series values $(y_1, y_2, \ldots)$ over time $(t = 1, 2, \ldots)$, with temporal labels (e.g., calendar date) on the horizontal axis. To illustrate this, consider the Amtrak ridership example. A time plot for monthly Amtrak ridership series is shown in Figure 2.2. Note that the values are in thousands of riders. Looking at the time plot reveals the nature of the series components: the overall level is around 1,800,000 passengers per month. A slight U-shaped trend is discernible during this period, with pronounced annual seasonality. Peak travel occurs during the summer months of July and August.

A second step in visualizing a time series is to examine it more carefully. The following operations are useful:

Zooming in: Zooming in to a shorter period within the series can reveal patterns that are hidden when viewing the entire series. This is especially important when the time series is long. Consider a series of the daily number of vehicles passing through the Baregg tunnel in Switzerland.[4] The series from November 1, 2003 to November 16, 2005 is shown in the top panel of Figure 2.3. Zooming in to a four-month period (bottom panel) reveals a strong day-of-week pattern that is not visible in the initial time plot of the complete time series.

The Baregg tunnel, between Bern and Zurich, is one of the busiest stretches of motorways in Switzerland. Source: Wikimedia Commons

[4] Data is available in the same location as the Amtrak ridership data; series D028.

Changing the Scale: To better identify the shape of a trend, it is useful to change the scale of the series. One simple option is to change the vertical scale (of y) to a logarithmic scale. If the

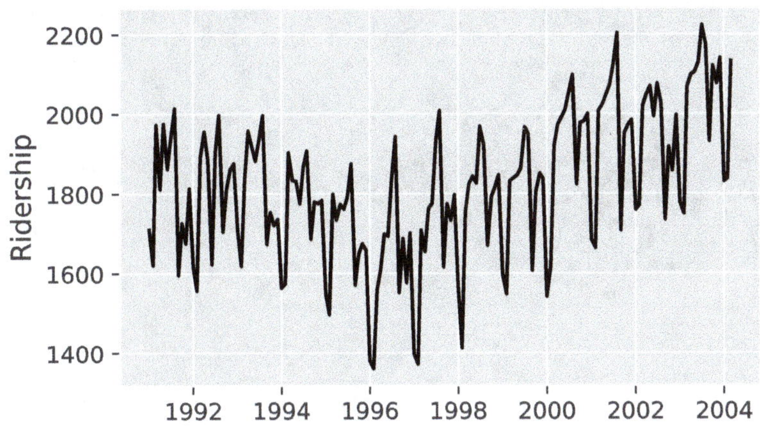

Figure 2.2: Monthly ridership on Amtrak trains (in thousands) from Jan 1991 to March 2004

Code for creating Figure 2.2

See full code at github.com/gshmueli/ptsf-Python

```
ridership = pd.read_csv('Amtrak.csv', parse_dates=['Month'], index_col='Month')
plot_series(ridership)
```

The first statement reads the csv file into a `pandas` *DataFrame* called *ridership*. The arguments specify that the 'Month' column in the csv file is a date, and that 'Month' should be used as the index, or row labels, of the DataFrame. For time series data, the pandas index carries the time structure and this structure may be used by other packages, such as the graphics package `matplotlib`.

The `plot_series` function from the `sktime` package gives us some control over the basic plot features such as axis labels, plotting colors and plot title. Additional features can be specified using functions from `matplotlib`.

Note: It is common practice in Python to abbreviate package names, such as `pd` for `pandas` and `plt` for `matplotlib.pyplot`. To focus on the active commands, the code shown above omits the statements specifying the packages, functions and abbreviations.

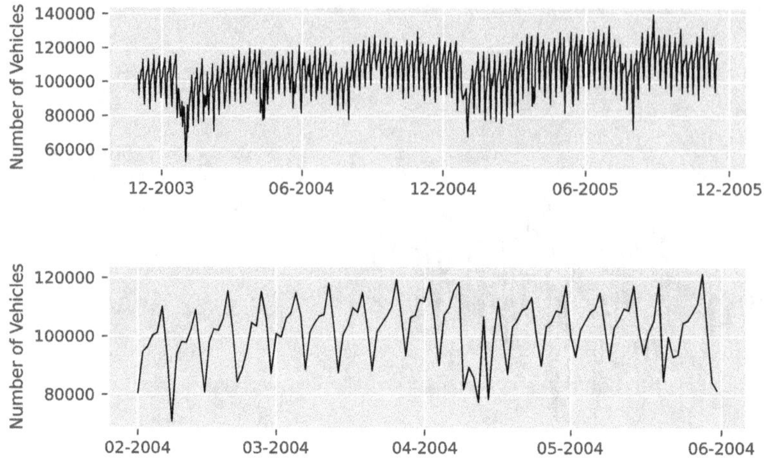

Figure 2.3: Time plots of the daily number of vehicles passing through the Baregg tunnel. The bottom panel zooms in to a 4-month period, revealing a day-of-week pattern.

trend on the new scale appears more linear, then the trend in the original series is closer to an exponential trend.

Adding Trend Lines: Another possibility for better capturing the shape of the trend is to add a trend line. By trying different trend lines, one can see what type of trend (e.g., linear, exponential, quadratic) best approximates the data.

Suppressing Seasonality: It is often easier to see trends in the data when seasonality is suppressed. Suppressing seasonal patterns can be done by plotting the series at a cruder time scale (e.g., aggregating monthly data into years). A second option is to plot separate time plots for each season. A third, popular option is to use moving average plots. We discuss moving average plots in Section 5.2.

Continuing our example of Amtrak ridership, the plots in Figure 2.4 help make the series' components more visible. Some forecasting methods directly model these components by making assumptions about their structure. For example, a popular assumption about a trend is that it is linear or exponential over some, or all, of the given time period. Another common assumption is about the noise structure: many statistical methods

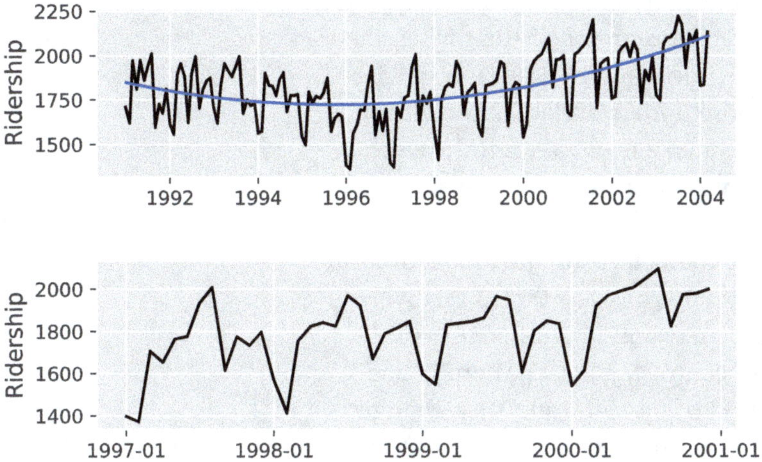

Figure 2.4: Plots that enhance the different components of the time series. Top: overlaid polynomial trend line. Bottom: original series with zoom in to four years of data.

Code for creating Figure 2.4

See full code at github.com/gshmueli/ptsf-Python

```
forecaster = PolynomialTrendForecaster(degree=2)
forecaster.fit(ridership)
fitted_values = forecaster.predict(ridership.index)

ridership_zoom = ridership.loc['1997-01-01':'2000-12-31']

figure, axs = plt.subplots(2, 1, sharex=False, figsize=(6, 4))
axs[0] = plot_series(ridership, fitted_values, ax=axs[0])
axs[1] = plot_series(ridership_zoom, ax=axs[1])
```

In `sktime` each forecasting model is implemented as a derived class of the *BaseForecaster* class, and provides both a `fit()` and a `predict()` method.
Line 1 creates an instance of a quadratic trend model from the *PolynomialTrendForecaster* class and specifies a 2nd degree polynomial. Note that creating a *forecaster* does not involve specifying the data.
Line 2 fits our polynomial forecaster to the *ridership* data, using the `fit()` method.
Line 3 obtains fitted values by applying the fitted model to the same time points that appear in the data (specified in `ridership.index`).
Line 4 zooms in on a subset of *ridership*, using the `pandas loc` indexer and a date range.
The final block of code sets up a 2×1 grid of plots, and then uses `plot_series` on the two different subplots *axs[0]* and *axs[1]*.

assume that the noise follows a normal distribution. The advantage of methods that rely on such assumptions is that when the assumptions are reasonably met, the resulting forecasts will be more robust and the models more understandable. In contrast, data-driven forecasting methods make fewer assumptions about the structure of these components and instead try to estimate them only from the data.

Time plots are also useful for characterizing the global or local nature of the patterns. A global pattern is one that is relatively constant throughout the series. An example is a linear trend throughout the entire series. In contrast, a local pattern is one that occurs only in a short period of the data, and then changes. An example is a trend that is approximately linear within four neighboring time points, but the trend size (slope) changes slowly over time. Operations such as zooming in can help establish more subtle changes in seasonal patterns or trends across periods. Breaking down the series into multiple sub-series and overlaying them in a single plot can also help establish whether a pattern (such as weekly seasonality) changes from season to season.

The Seasonal Plot

When we suspect a series contains seasonality, it is useful to look at a *seasonal plot* to identify patterns and exceptions related to the seasonal pattern. In this plot, the seasons are on the x-axis, and each full cycle of seasons is one line. We can then see if the different lines follow a similar pattern, and when there are exceptions.

Figure 2.5 illustrates a seasonal plot for the monthly Amtrak ridership series. Here, the x-axis is the month-of-year (January, February, . . . , December), and each line is a separate year. We see a pattern of peak ridership in July–August and low ridership in January–February. This pattern is consistent across the years. We also see that, in 1996, ridership was mostly lower than in other years. We can also see exceptions, such as the June 1992 dip (likely due to a nationwide railroad strike).

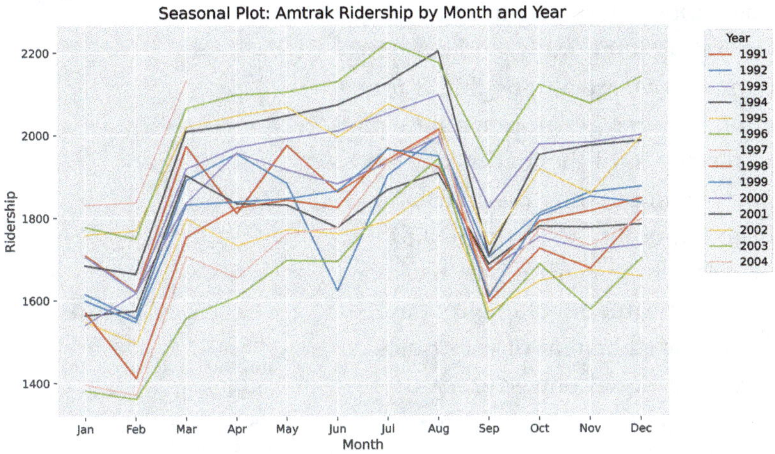

Figure 2.5: Seasonal plot for Amtrak monthly ridership. Each line represents a different year.

Code for creating Figure 2.5

See full code at `github.com/gshmueli/ptsf-Python`

```
import pandas as pd
import matplotlib.pyplot as plt

ridership = pd.read_csv('ptsf-Python/Data/Amtrak.csv', parse_dates=['Month'], index_col='Month')
ridership['Year'] = ridership.index.year
ridership['Mon'] = ridership.index.month

ax = ridership.pivot_table(index='Mon', columns='Year', values='Ridership').plot()

ax.set_xlabel('Month')
ax.set_ylabel('Ridership')
ax.set_title('Seasonal Plot: Amtrak Ridership by Month and Year')
ax.legend(title='Year', bbox_to_anchor=(1.05, 1), loc='upper left')
ax.set_xticks(range(1, 13))
ax.set_xticklabels(['Jan', 'Feb', 'Mar', 'Apr', 'May', 'Jun', 'Jul', 'Aug', 'Sep', 'Oct', 'Nov', 'Dec'])
plt.show()
```

To obtain a seasonal plot, we create a new DataFrame with one row for each month, and one column for each year. This is a special case of creating a *pivot table* from the original DataFrame. To do this, use the `pandas` method `pivot_table()`, based on the new columns 'Year' and 'Mon'.

2.4 *Interactive Visualization*

The various operations described above: zooming in, changing scales, adding trend lines, aggregating temporally, and breaking down the series into multiple time plots, are all possible using Python. However, each operation requires generating a new plot or at least going through several steps until the modified chart is achieved. The time lag between manipulating the chart and viewing the results detracts from our ability to compare and "connect the dots" between the different visualizations. Interactive visualization software[5] offers the same functionality (and usually much more), but with the added benefit of very quick and easy chart manipulation. An additional powerful feature of interactive software is the ability to link multiple plots of the same data. Operations in one plot, such as zooming in, will then automatically also be applied to all the linked plots. A set of such linked charts is often called a "dashboard".

[5] Python packages such as `plotly` allow integrating interactive features into charts, but you must build the logic yourself, which is beyond the scope of this book. Instead, we introduce here dedicated general-purpose interactive visualization software.

Figure 2.6 shows a screenshot of an interactive dashboard built for the daily Baregg tunnel traffic data.[6] The top panel displays an ordinary time plot (like the top panel of Figure 2.3). Just below the date axis is a zoom slider, which can be used to zoom in to specific date ranges. The zoom slider has been set to "global": when applied, all charts in the dashboard are affected.

[6] The dashboard is available at `www.forecastingbook.com/resources/dashboards`. To best appreciate the power of interactivity, access the dashboard from this URL, which allows direct interaction with the visualization.

Recall that aggregating the data by looking at coarser temporal frequencies can help suppress seasonality. The second panel shows the same data, this time aggregated by month. In addition, a quadratic trend line is fitted separately to each year. To break down the months into days, click on the plus sign at the bottom left of the panel (the plus sign appears when you hover over the Monthly Average panel). Note that the daily view will display daily data and fit separate quadratic trends to each month.

Another visualization approach to suppressing seasonality is to look separately at each season. The bottom panel in the dashboard uses separate lines for different days of the week. The filter on the right allows the user to display only lines for certain days and not for others (this filter was set to affect only the bottom panel). It is now clear what the fluctuations in the top

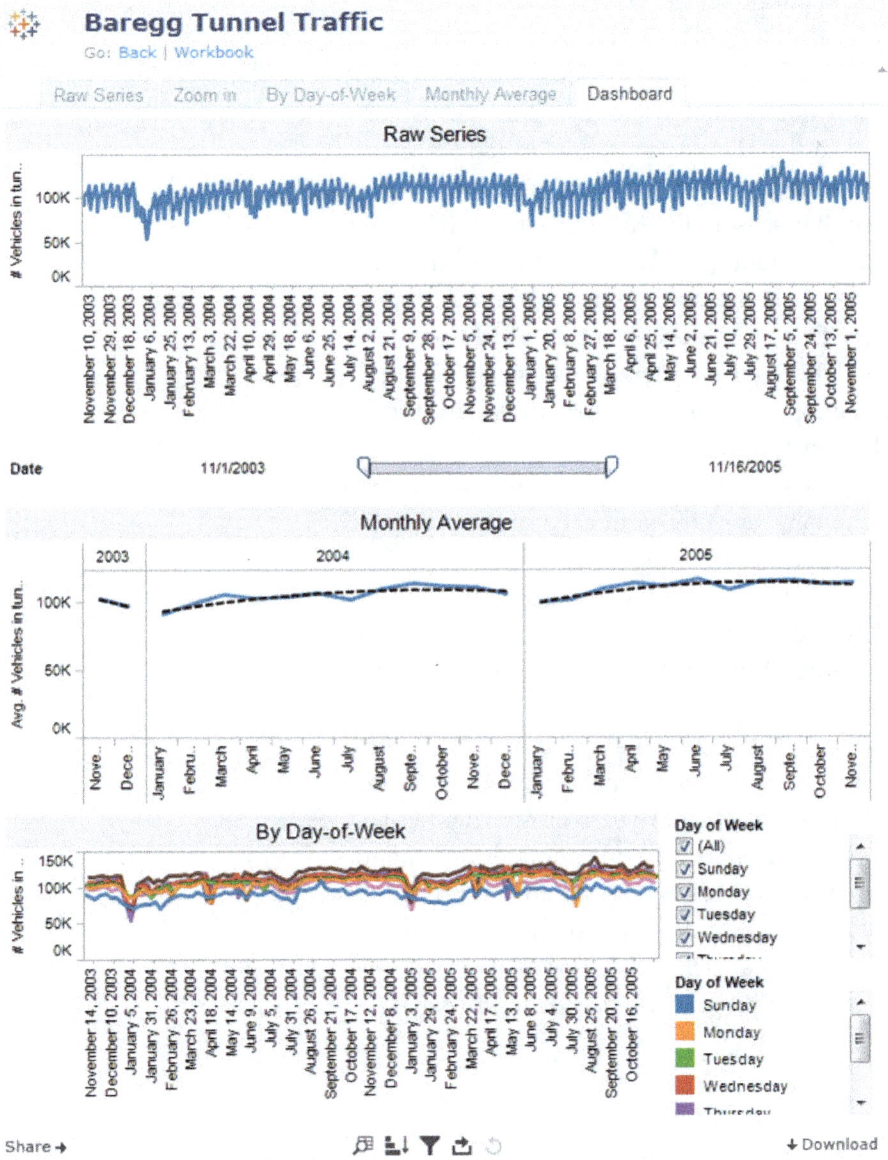

Figure 2.6: Screenshot of an interactive dashboard for visualizing the Baregg tunnel traffic data. The dashboard, created using the free Tableau Public software, is available for interaction at `www.forecastingbook.com`.

panel indicate: tunnel traffic differs quite significantly between different days of week, and especially between Sundays (the lowest line) and other days. This information might lead us to forecast Sunday traffic separately.

Figure 2.7 shows another example of how interactive dashboards are useful for exploring time series data. This dashboard includes time plots for three related series: monthly passenger movement data on air, rail, and vehicles in the United States between 1990–2004. Looking at the three series, aligned horizontally, highlights the similar seasonal pattern that they share. The filters on the right allow zooming in for each series separately. The slider below the x-axis at the bottom allows zooming in to particular date ranges. This will affect all series. Additionally, we can aggregate the data to another temporal level by using the small "Date(Month)" slider at the very bottom. In this example, we can look at yearly, quarterly, and monthly sums. Looking at annual numbers suppresses the monthly seasonal pattern, thereby magnifying the long-term trend in each of the series (ignore 2004, which only has data until April).

The slider to the left of the y-axis allows zooming in to a particular range of values of the series. Note that each series has a different scale on the y-axis, but that the filter still affects all of the series.

The filters and sliders in the right panel of Figure 2.7 can be used for zooming in temporally or in terms of the series values. The "Date" allows looking at particular years or quarters. For instance, we can remove year 2001, which is anomalous (due to the September 11 terror attack). Lastly, we can choose a particular part of a series by clicking and dragging the mouse. The raw data for values and periods that fall in the chosen area will then be displayed in the bottom-right "Details-on-Demand" panel.

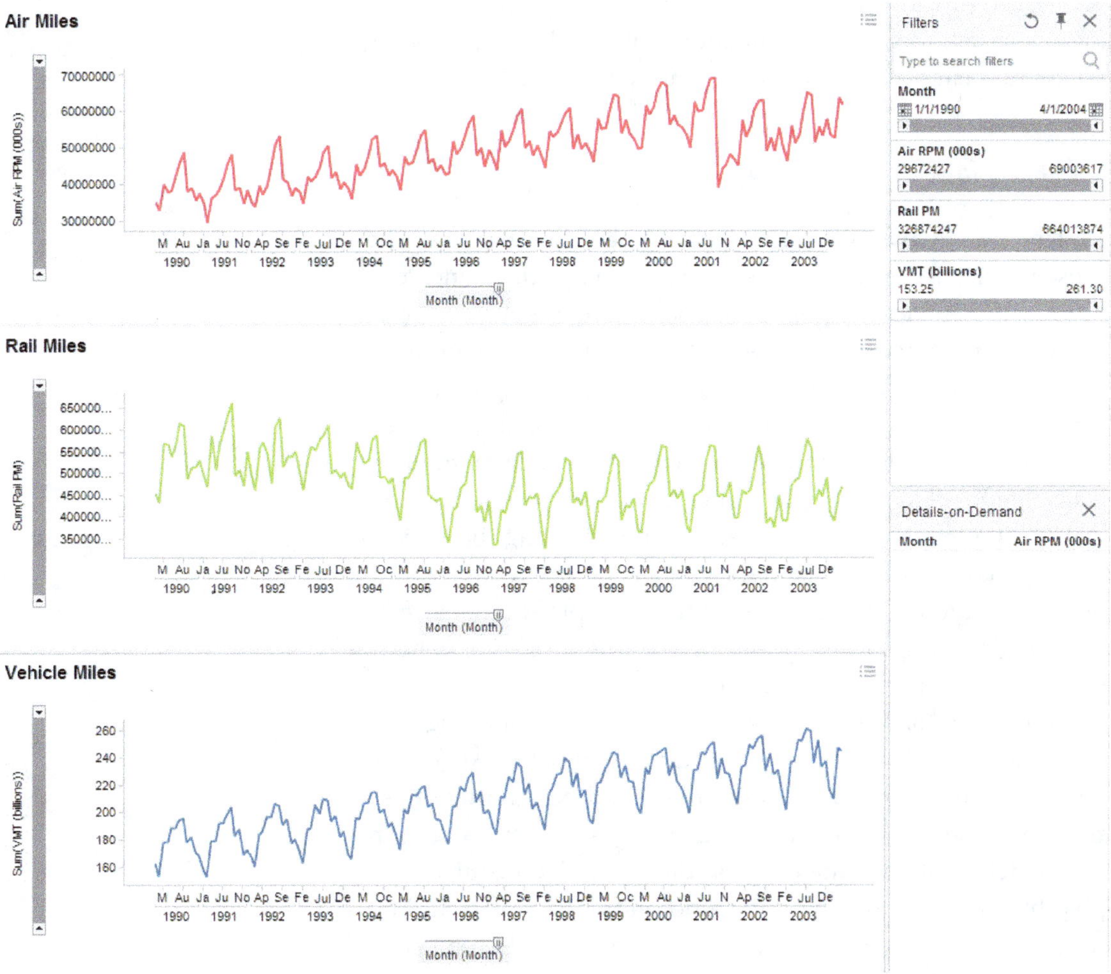

Figure 2.7: Screenshot of an interactive dashboard for visualizing the September 11, 2001 passenger movement data. The dashboard, created using TIBCO Spotfire software, is available for interaction at `www.forecastingbook.com`.

2.5 *Data Pre-Processing*

If done properly, data exploration can help detect problems such as possible data entry errors as well as missing values, unequal spacing and irrelevant periods. In addition to addressing such issues, pre-processing the data also includes a preparation step for enabling performance evaluation, namely data partitioning. We discuss each of these operations in detail next.

Missing Values

Missing values in a time series create "holes" in the series. The presence of missing values has different implications and requires different actions depending on the forecasting method. Forecasting methods such as ARIMA models and smoothing methods (in Chapters 5 and 7) cannot be directly applied to time series with missing values, because the relationship between consecutive periods is modeled directly. With such methods, it is also impossible to forecast values that are beyond a missing value if the missing value is needed for computing the forecast. In such cases, a solution is to impute, or "fill in", the missing values. Imputation approaches range from simple solutions, such as averaging neighboring values, to creating forecasts of missing values using earlier values or external data.

In contrast, forecasting methods such as linear and logistic regression models (Chapters 6, 9) and neural networks (Chapter 8), can be fit to a series with "holes", and no imputation is required. The implication of missing values in such cases is that the model/method is fitted to less data points. Of course, it is possible to impute the missing values in this case as well. The tradeoff between data imputation and ignoring missing values with such methods is the reliance on noisy imputation (values plus imputation error) vs. the loss of data points for fitting the forecasting method. One could, of course, take an ensemble approach where both approaches, one based on imputed data and the other on dropped missing values, are implemented and the two are combined for forecasting.

Missing values can also affect the ability to generate forecasts and to evaluate predictive performance (see Section 3.1).

In short, since some forecasting methods cannot tolerate missing values in a series and others can, it is important to discover any missing values before the modeling stage.

Unequally Spaced Series

Another issue, related to missing values, is unequally spaced data. Equal spacing means that the time interval between two consecutive periods is equal (e.g., daily, monthly, quarterly data). However, some series are naturally unequally spaced. These include series that measure some quantity during events where event occurrences are random (such as bus arrival times), naturally unequally spaced (such as holidays or music concerts), or determined by someone other than the data collector (e.g., bid timings in an online auction).

As with missing values, some forecasting methods can be applied directly to unequally spaced series, while others cannot. Converting an unequally spaced series into an equally spaced series typically involves interpolation using approaches similar to those for handling missing values.

Extreme Values

Extreme values are values that are unusually large or small compared to other values in the series. Extreme values can affect different forecasting methods to various degrees. The decision of whether to remove an extreme value or not must rely on information beyond the data. Is the extreme value the result of a data entry error? Was it due to an unusual event (such as an earthquake) that is unlikely to occur again in the forecast horizon? If there is no grounded justification to remove or replace the extreme value, then the best practice is to generate two sets of forecasts: those based on the series with the extreme values and those based on the series excluding the extreme values.

Choice of Time Span

Another pre-processing operation that is sometimes required is determining how far back into the past we should consider. That is, the time span of the data to be used. While a very short (and recent) series might not contain sufficient information for forecasting purposes, beyond a certain length, additional information will likely be useless at best, and harmful at worst. Considering a very long past of the series might deteriorate the accuracy of future forecasts because of changing context and environment during the data period. For example, in many countries, transportation demand for traditional airlines drastically changed when low-cost airlines entered the market. Using data that spans from both periods to forecast future demand on traditional carriers therefore adds disruptive information. A particular example is first-class ridership on Indian Railways.[7] When low-cost airlines entered the domestic Indian market in the early 2000s, first-class ridership on trains plunged in favor of air travel. A few years later, the first-class rail fares were substantially reduced, and first-class train ridership levels have since increased. Hence, the length of the series for forecasting first-class demand on Indian Railways must extend backwards only to periods where the environment is assumed to be similar to the forecast horizon.

[7] knowindia.net/rail.html

2.6 Problems

1. *Impact of September 11 on Air Travel in the United States:* The Research and Innovative Technology Administration's Bureau of Transportation Statistics (BTS) conducted a study to evaluate the impact of the September 11, 2001, terrorist attack on U.S. transportation. The study report and the data can be found at `www.bts.gov/archive/publications/estimated_impacts_of_9_11_on_us_travel/index`. The goal of the study was stated as follows:

   > The purpose of this study is to provide a greater understanding of the passenger travel behavior patterns of persons making long distance trips before and after September 11.

   The report analyzes monthly passenger movement data between January 1990 and April 2004. Data on three monthly time series are given in the file *Sept11Travel.csv* for this period: (1) actual airline revenue passenger miles (Air), (2) rail passenger miles (Rail), and (3) vehicle miles traveled (Auto).

   In order to assess the impact of September 11, BTS took the following approach: Using data before September 11, it forecasted future data (under the assumption of no terrorist attack). Then, BTS compared the forecasted series with the actual data to assess the impact of the event.

   Plot each of the three pre-event time series (Air, Rail, Car).

   (a) What time series components appear from the plots?

   (b) What type of trend appears? Change the scale of the series, add trend lines, and suppress seasonality to better visualize the trend pattern.

2. *Forecasting Department Store Sales:* The file *DepartmentStore-Sales.csv* contains data on the quarterly sales for a department store over a 6-year period.[8]

   (a) Create a well-formatted time plot of the data.

   (b) Which of the four components (level, trend, seasonality, noise) seem to be present in this series?

[8] Data courtesy of Chris Albright

3. *Shipments of Household Appliances:* The file *ApplianceShip-ments.csv* contains the series of quarterly shipments (in millions of USD) of U.S. household appliances between 1985–1989.[9]

   (a) Create a well-formatted time plot of the data.

   (b) Which of the four components (level, trend, seasonality, noise) seem to be present in this series?

[9] Data courtesy of Ken Black

4. *Canadian Manufacturing Workers Work-Hours:* The time series plot below describes the average annual number of weekly hours spent by Canadian manufacturing workers. The data is available in *CanadianWorkHours.csv*.[10]

   (a) Reproduce the time plot.

   (b) Which of the four components (level, trend, seasonality, noise) appear to be present in this series?

[10] Data courtesy of Ken Black

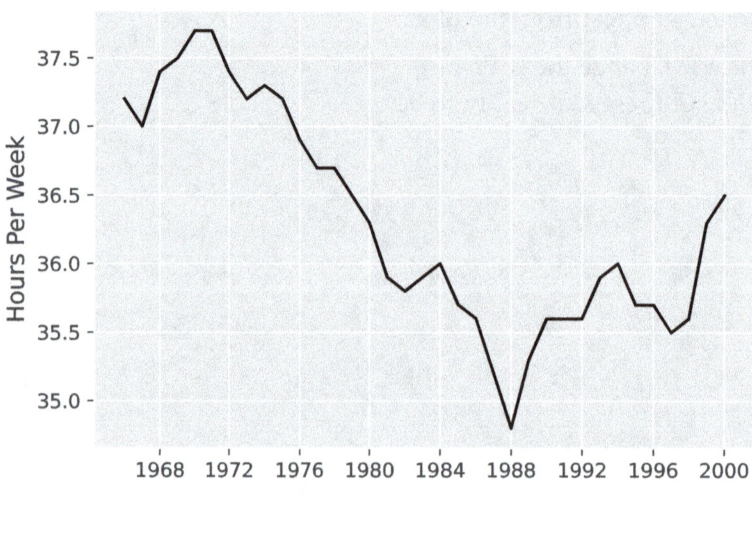

Figure 2.8: Average annual weekly hours spent by Canadian manufacturing workers.

5. *Souvenir Sales:* The file *SouvenirSales.csv* contains monthly sales for a souvenir shop at a beach resort town in Queensland, Australia, between 1995 and 2001.[11]

[11] Source: Hyndman and Yang (2018) tsdl: Time Series Data Library. v0.1.0. github.com/FinYang/tsdl.

Back in 2001, the store wanted to use the data to forecast sales for the next 12 months (year 2002). They hired an analyst to generate forecasts. The analyst first partitioned the data into training and validation periods, with the validation period containing the last 12 months of data (year 2001). She then fit a regression model to sales, using the training period.

(a) Create a well-formatted time plot of the data.

(b) Change the scale of the x-axis, y-axis, or both, to logarithmic scale in order to achieve a linear relationship. Select the time plot that seems most linear.

(c) Comparing the two time plots, what can be said about the type of trend in the data?

6. *Forecasting Shampoo Sales:* The file *ShampooSales.csv* contains data on the monthly sales of a certain shampoo over a three-year period.[12]

[12] Source: Hyndman and Yang (2018) tsdl: Time Series Data Library. v0.1.0. github.com/FinYang/tsdl.

(a) Create a well-formatted time plot of the data.

(b) Which of the four components (level, trend, seasonality, noise) seem to be present in this series?

(c) Do you expect to see seasonality in sales of shampoo? Why?

3
Performance Evaluation

At first glance, we might think it best to choose a model that generates the best forecasts on the data series at hand. However, when we use the same data both to develop the forecasting model and to assess its performance, we introduce bias. This is because when we choose a model among a set of models that works best with the data, this model's superior performance comes from two sources:

1. a superior model
2. chance aspects of the data that happen to match the chosen model better than they match other models

The latter is a particularly serious problem with techniques that do not impose linear or other structure on the data, and thus end up *overfitting* the data. Overfitting means that the model is not only fitting the systematic component of the data, but also the noise. An over-fitted model is therefore likely to perform poorly on new data. To illustrate the notion of overfitting, consider the analogy of a tailor sewing a new suit for a customer. If the suit is tailored to the customer's *exact* measurements, it will likely not be useful beyond immediate use, as small fluctuations in weight and body size over time are normal.

3.1 *Data Partitioning*

To address the problem of overfitting, an important preliminary step before applying any forecasting method is data partitioning, where the series is split into two periods. We develop our forecasting model or method using only one of the periods. After we have a model, we try it out on another period and see how it performs. In particular, we can measure the forecast errors, which are the differences between the predicted values and the actual values, as described in the next section.

Partitioning of Cross-Sectional Data

When building predictive models using cross-sectional data, we typically create two or three data partitions: a *training set*, a *validation set*, and a *test set*. Partitioning the data into training, validation, and test sets is usually done randomly. The training partition, typically the largest partition, contains the data used to build the various models we are examining. The same training partition is generally used to develop multiple models. The validation partition is used to assess the performance of each model so that we can compare models and pick the best one. The test partition (sometimes called the holdout or evaluation partition) is used to assess the performance of the chosen model with new data.

Temporal Partitioning

In time series forecasting, as in the case of cross-sectional data, to avoid overfitting and be able to assess the predictive performance of the model on new data, we first partition the data into a *training period* and a *test period*. However, there is one important difference between data partitioning in cross-sectional and time series data. In cross-sectional data the partitioning is usually done randomly, with a random set of observations designated as training data and the remainder as validation/test data. However, in time series, a random partition creates two problems: Firstly, it does not mimic the temporal uncertainty where we use the past and present to forecast the future. Secondly, it creates two time series with "holes", whereas many standard forecasting methods cannot handle time series with missing values. Therefore, time series partitioning into training and test sets is done differently: The series is trimmed into two periods where the earlier period ($t = 1, 2, \ldots, n$) is designated as the training period and the later period ($t = n + 1, n + 2, \ldots$) as the test period. An illustration is shown in Figure 3.1. Methods are then trained on the earlier training period, and their predictive performance assessed on the later test period. In evaluating and comparing forecasting methods, time plots of the actual and predicted series during both training and test periods can shed light on performance issues and indicate possible improvements.

Note that in time series partitioning there is typically no third *validation period*, which would have comprised of the period between the training and test periods. The reason is that the omission of an even longer recent period from the training period is likely to cause more harm than benefit.

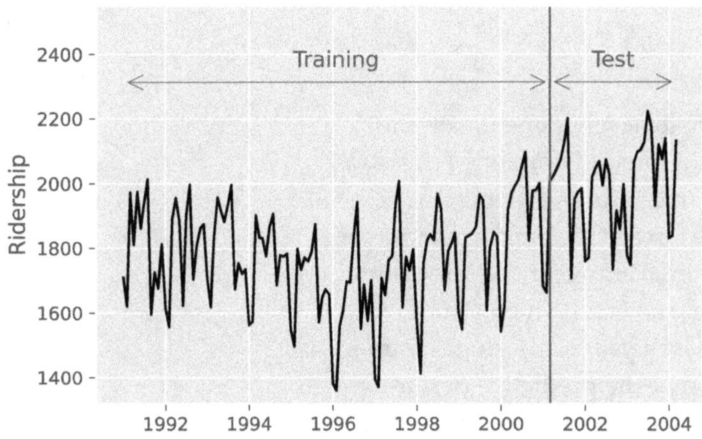

Figure 3.1: Example of temporal partitioning of the monthly ridership data. The training period is Jan 1991 to Mar 2001; the test period is Apr 2001 to March 2004. Forecasts are required for the future period (from April 2004 onward).

Joining Partitions for Forecasting

One last important difference between cross-sectional and time series partitioning occurs when generating the actual forecasts. Before attempting to forecast future values of the series, the training and test periods must be recombined into one long series, and the chosen method/model rerun on the complete data. This final model is then used to forecast future values. The three advantages in recombining are:

1. The test period, which is the most recent period, usually contains the most valuable information in terms of being the closest in time to the forecasted period.

2. With more data (the complete time series compared to only the training period), some models can be estimated more accurately.

3. If only the training period is used to generate forecasts, then it will require forecasting further into the future. For example, if the test set contains four time points, forecasting the next observation will require a five-step-ahead forecast from the training set (F_{n+5}).

Figure 3.2 shows the forecasts in the test period from a quadratic trend model applied to the Amtrak ridership training data (ignore the details of the model itself for now).

Choosing the Test Period

The choice of length of the test period closely depends on the forecasting goal, data frequency, and forecast horizon. The main principle is to choose a test period that mimics the forecast horizon to allow the evaluation of actual predictive performance. For instance, in the Amtrak ridership example, if the forecasting model will be used to produce forecasts for the next year, then the test period should include at least a year. Choosing a shorter test period will not allow evaluation of the predictive performance of longer-term forecasts. Choosing a test period of more than a year, on the other hand, would mean that our training period contains less recent information, and therefore the model will miss out on the most recent information available at the time of prediction.

Note: The presence of missing values in the training period can affect the ability to train a forecasting method, thereby requiring imputation for some forecasting methods (see Section 2.5). As for a test period with missing values, we can still evaluate predictive performance by ignoring the missing points (see Section 3.3 for details).

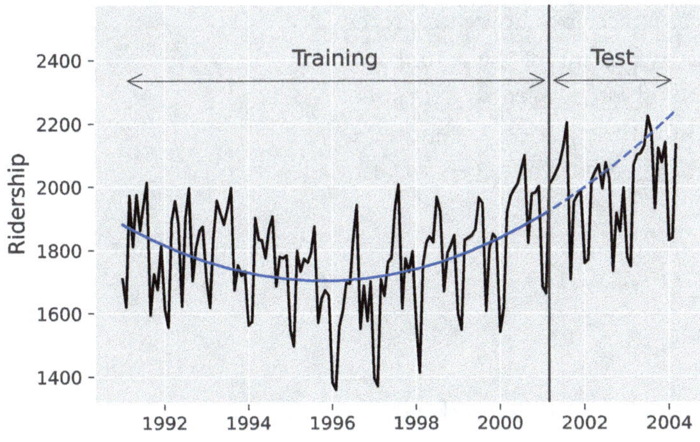

Figure 3.2: Forecasts in the test period from a quadratic trend model estimated from the training period (Amtrak ridership data).

Code for creating Figure 3.2

See full code at `github.com/gshmueli/ptsf-Python`

```
# Partition the series into training and test
test_size = len(ridership.truncate(before='2001-04-01'))
ridership_train, ridership_test = temporal_train_test_split(ridership, test_size=test_size)

# Fit model to training period
forecaster = PolynomialTrendForecaster(degree=2)
forecaster.fit(ridership_train)
fitted_values = forecaster.predict(ridership_train.index)

# Use model to generate forecasts for test period
pred_values = forecaster.predict(ridership_test.index)

fig, ax = plot_series(ridership, fitted_values, pred_values)
```

Block 1 defines the test period to include April 1, 2001 and all later dates. The method `temporal_train_test_split()` creates the training and test sets.
Block 2 sets the forecasting model to be a regression model with polynomial trend of degree 2 (quadratic trend). This forecaster is then fitted to the training set using the `fit()` method. The fitted values for the dates in the training period are obtained using the method `predict()`.
Block 3 uses `predict()` to generate the forecasts for the test period.
Block 4 plots the original series, training period fitted values, and test period forecasts.

3.2 *Measuring Forecast Accuracy*

Forecast accuracy (or *predictive accuracy*) describes how close forecasts are to the actual values. Hence, we compare the actual and forecast values, and also look directly at *forecast errors*. The *forecast error* (sometimes called *residual*) for time period t, denoted e_t, is defined as the difference between the actual value (y_t) and the forecast value (F_t) at time t:

$$e_t = y_t - F_t.$$

Plots

Before getting into metrics, it is extremely useful to start with two visualizations:

1. A time plot of the series along with the model's forecasts.

2. A time plot of the forecast errors.

This pair of plots is useful because they show us not only how well the model is doing, but also *when* it fails. For example, consider the two plots for the Amtrak ridership in Figure 3.3. The top panel shows the ridership series in both the training and test periods, along with the model's forecasts during the training period (called *fitted values*) and during the test period (*forecasts*). The bottom panel shows the forecast errors during the training period (called *residuals*), and during the test period. We see clearly that forecasts in the test period deteriorate into the future and that forecasts are worse for low-ridership months. These patterns are easily visible in the lower panel.

Forecast Accuracy vs. Model Fit

When the purpose of forecasting is to generate accurate forecasts, it is useful to define performance metrics that measure predictive accuracy. Such metrics can tell us how well a particular method performs in general, as well as compared to benchmarks or forecasts from other methods.

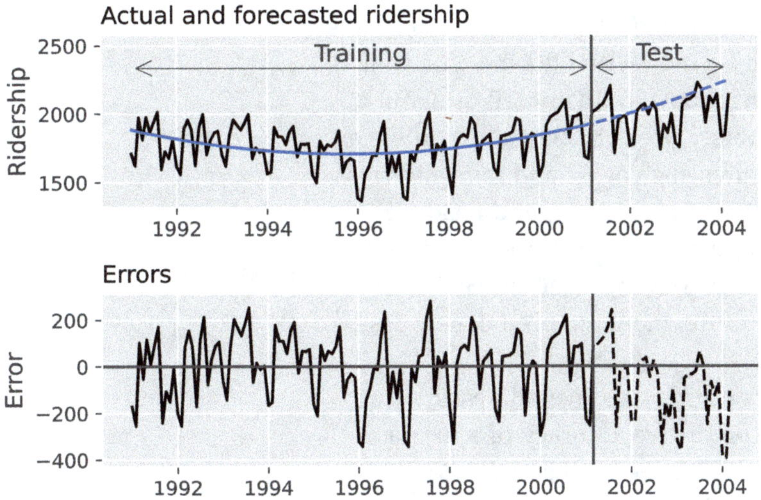

Figure 3.3: Top plot: Amtrak ridership with test period forecasts, based on a quadratic trend model estimated from the training period (the same as in Figure 3.2). Bottom plot: Time plot of forecast errors (training residuals and test errors) from the quadratic trend model.

Code for creating Figure 3.3

See full code at github.com/gshmueli/ptsf-Python

```
# Fit model to training period
forecaster = PolynomialTrendForecaster(degree=2)
forecaster.fit(ridership_train)
fitted_values = forecaster.predict(ridership_train.index)

# Get forecasts for test period
pred_values = forecaster.predict(ridership_test.index)

figure, axs = plt.subplots(2, 1, sharex=False, figsize=(6, 4))

# Plot 1: actuals and forecasts
axs[0] = plot_series(ridership, fitted_values, pred_values, ax=axs[0],
                     title='Actual and forecasted ridership', y_label='Ridership')
ptsf_theme(axs[0], colors=['black','blue','blue'], idx=[0,1,2], lty=['-', '-', '--'])

# Plot 2: errors
axs[1] = plot_series(ridership_train - fitted_values, ridership_test - pred_values, ax=axs[1],
                     title='Errors', y_label='Error')
ptsf_theme(axs[1], colors=['black']*2, idx=[0,1], lty=['-', '--'])
```

Note: The model's *residuals* are the training period errors. In Plot 2 (errors), the first argument in `plot_series()` calculates the residuals. The second argument calculates the forecast errors.

Let us emphasize that *predictive accuracy* (or *forecast accuracy*) is not the same as *goodness of fit* or *strength of fit*. Classical measures of performance that aim to find a model that fits the data well and measure the strength of relationship do not tell us about the ability of a model to accurately predict new values. In linear regression, for example, measures such as R^2 and *standard error of estimate* are popular strength of fit measures, and residual analysis is used to gauge goodness of fit where the goal is to find the best fit for the data. However, these measures do not tell us much about the ability of the model to predict new cases accurately.

For evaluating predictive performance, several measures are commonly used to assess the predictive accuracy of a forecasting method. In all cases, *the measures are based on the test period*, which serves as a more objective basis than the training period to assess predictive accuracy (because records in the test period are not used to select predictors or to estimate model parameters). Measures of accuracy use the prediction error that results from predicting the test period with the model that was trained on the training period.

Common Forecast Accuracy Measures

Consider a test period with v periods. For simplicity, we will use the indexing $t = 1, \ldots, v$ instead of the more accurate but longer notation $t = n+1, \ldots, n+v$. A few popular measures of predictive accuracy are:

MAE or MAD (mean absolute error/deviation) $= \frac{1}{v} \sum_{t=1}^{v} |e_t|$. This gives the magnitude of the average absolute error.

Average error $= \frac{1}{v} \sum_{t=1}^{v} e_t$. This measure is similar to MAD except that it retains the sign of the errors, so that negative errors cancel out positive errors of the same magnitude. It therefore gives an indication of whether the forecasts are on average over- or under-predicting.

MAPE (mean absolute percentage error) $= \frac{1}{v}\sum_{t=1}^{v}\left|\frac{e_t}{y_t}\right| \times 100$. This measure gives a percentage score of how forecasts deviate (on average) from the actual values. It is useful for comparing performance across series of data that have different scales, but it has an inherent flaw: it is systematically biased towards models that under-forecast.[1]

[1] C. Tofallis. A better measure of relative prediction accuracy for model selection and model estimation. *Journal of the Operational Research Society*, 66:1352–1362, 2015

RMSE (root mean squared error) $= \sqrt{\frac{1}{v}\sum_{t=1}^{v} e_t^2}$. This measure has the same units as the data series.

To illustrate the computation of these measures, consider Table 3.1 which shows the test period results of applying a quadratic trend model to the Amtrak ridership data.

Month	Forecast	Actual Value	Forecast Error
Apr 2001	1932.454	2023.792	91.338
May 2001	1939.508	2047.008	107.500
Jun 2001	1946.670	2072.913	126.243
⋮	⋮	⋮	⋮
Mar 2004	2243.161	2132.446	-110.715

Table 3.1: Test period results of applying a quadratic trend model to the Amtrak ridership data.

We use the last column (forecast errors) to compute each of the four predictive measures as follows:

$$\begin{aligned}
MAE &= \frac{1}{36}\left(|91.338| + \cdots + |-110.715|\right) = 133.738 \\
Average\,error &= \frac{1}{36}\left(91.338 + \cdots + (-110.715)\right) = -83.962 \\
MAPE &= \frac{1}{36}\left(\left|\frac{91.338}{2023.792}\right| + \cdots + \left|\frac{-110.715}{2132.446}\right|\right) \times 100 = 7.076\% \\
RMSE &= \sqrt{\frac{1}{36}\left((91.338)^2 + \cdots + (-110.715)^2\right)} = \sqrt{32345.81} = 179.849
\end{aligned}$$

Code for computing predictive measures

See full code at `github.com/gshmueli/ptsf-Python`

```
def accuracy(actual, predicted):
    MAE = mean_absolute_error(actual, predicted)
    ME = np.mean(actual - predicted)
    MAPE = 100 * mean_absolute_percentage_error(actual, predicted)
    RMSE = np.sqrt(mean_squared_error(actual, predicted))
    df = pd.DataFrame({'MAE': MAE, 'ME': ME, 'MAPE': MAPE, 'RMSE': RMSE},
                      index=['Accuracy'])
    return df

print(accuracy(ridership_test['Ridership'], pred_values['Ridership']))
```

For convenience, we define a custom function `accuracy()` that collects the predictive metrics MAE, ME, MAPE and RMSE. The calculations are performed by functions from the `sktime.performance_metrics.forecasting` module. The function takes as its arguments the *actual* and *predicted* values.

Note: Computing these measures using the *training* period does not tell us about predictive accuracy. Instead, it measures how closely the model fits the training period (goodness-of-fit).

Zero counts

When the series contains zero counts, computing MAPE results in an infinite number due to the division by y_t. One solution is to compute MAPE by excluding the zero values, which solves the technical problem but excludes information that might be important. Another solution is to use other measures such as MAE and RMSE (if appropriate). However, the appeal of MAPE as a scale-independent measure has led to the development of the scale-independent *Mean Absolute Scaled Error* (MASE) metric,[2] which can handle zero counts. MASE is a scaled version of MAE, which benchmarks the model's forecast errors against the average naive forecast absolute error by dividing the model MAE by the MAE of the naive forecasts on the training set. The reason for using the *training set* to compute the naive forecast MAE is to avoid a zero value in the denominator, which can

[2] R. J. Hyndman. Another look at forecast-accuracy metrics for intermittent demand. *Foresight: The International Journal of Applied Forecasting*, 4:43–46, 2006

occur due to the fewer observations in the test period.

$$MASE = \frac{\text{test MAE}}{\text{training MAE of naive forecasts}} = \frac{\frac{1}{v}\sum_{t=n+1}^{n+v}|e_t|}{\frac{1}{n-1}\sum_{t=2}^{n}|y_{t-1}-y_t|} \tag{3.1}$$

Because MASE compares the model predictive performance (MAE) to the naive forecast on the training set, values less than 1 indicate that the model has a lower average error than naive forecasts (in the training period). Values greater than 1 indicate poor performance relative to (training period) naive forecasts.

Note that another difference between MAPE and MASE is that MAPE gives a heavier penalty to positive errors (under-forecasts) than negative errors (over-forecasts), while MASE weighs both types of errors equally.

Forecast Accuracy vs. Profitability

The popular measures of MAPE and RMSE are "pessimistic" in the sense that they give more weight to larger errors.[3] In some contexts large deviations are as bad as small deviations.

In many contexts, forecast accuracy is not an adequate performance measure. Instead, it is combined with costs to produce a "profitability" measure. In such cases, it is better to use the profitability measure directly in the performance evaluation step. Costs of forecast errors can be indifferent to the sign of the forecast errors (positive/negative), or they can be more sensitive to one direction than the other. For example, under-estimating demand has different implications than over-estimating demand. Costs of forecast errors can be indifferent to the magnitude of the error beyond some threshold (e.g., if the error is larger than 5% or not), or they can be proportional to the magnitude, where "proportional" can vary from linear to highly non-linear.

While we expect that overall increased predictive accuracy will lead to increased profitability, one case where the two are uncorrelated is when the process being forecasted undergoes stable and extreme periods and when costs are a function of y_t rather than e_t. An example is financial markets, where the forecasted direction of, say, a stock price would lead to a trader's decision to buy or sell at a certain price. The profitability in this

[3] MAPE is based on percentage errors and RMSE on squared errors. Both functions inflate large values relative to small values.

case depends on the difference between the actual price (y_t) and zero, rather than on $y_t - F_t$. In such cases, forecasting methods that perform no better than random during stable periods but better than random during extreme periods will likely have overall positive profitability, although they are likely to show low predictive accuracy. For a discussion and detailed example of this phenomenon, see the article by Batchelor.[4]

An extreme example of a cost function that carries heavy, but different, penalties in each direction is the trial of six Italian scientists and a former government official over the 2009 earthquake in L'Aquilla, Italy. According to BBC News,[5]

> Prosecutors accuse the defendants gave a falsely reassuring statement before the quake after studying hundreds of tremors that had shaken the city ... The defendants face up to 15 years in jail.

Erring in the opposite direction and issuing false alarms also carries a high cost:

> Scientists could warn of a large earthquake every time a potential precursor event is observed, however this would result in huge numbers of false alarms which put a strain on public resources and might ultimately reduce the public's trust in scientists.[6]

Choosing the right profitability measure in this context is therefore dependent on *who* is measuring (the scientists or the government) and how false alerts are measured against disasters that were not forecasted.

[4] R. Batchelor. Accuracy versus profitability. *Foresight: The International Journal of Applied Forecasting*, 21:10–15, 2011

[5] BBC News Europe. Italy scientists on trial over L'aquilla earthquake, 2011. `www.bbc.com/news/world-europe-14981921` Accessed Feb 11, 2024

[6] BBC News Science & Environment. Can we predict when and where quakes will strike?, 2011. `www.bbc.co.uk/news/science-environment-14991654` Accessed Feb 11, 2024

3.3 *Evaluating Forecast Uncertainty*

Distribution of Forecast Errors

Popular forecasting methods such as regression models and smoothing methods produce forecast errors that are not necessarily normally distributed. Forecast errors might not be independent, and not even be symmetrical around zero. While measures such as RMSE and MAPE are favorites in forecasting competitions, in practice it is important to examine not only these aggregates but the entire set of forecast errors.

We examine the forecast errors not so much to test model assumptions (as in linear regression), but more to evaluate forecast uncertainty. Of interest are extremely low or high errors, reflecting extreme over- or under-forecasting. Creating a time plot and histogram of the forecast errors is very useful. For instance, recall the time plot of forecast errors from a quadratic trend model applied to the Amtrak ridership data in Figure 3.3 (bottom), and consider the histogram of these errors in Figure 3.4. From such plots, we can learn about the distribution of forecast errors, and the chances of obtaining forecast errors of different directions and magnitudes. Asymmetries might be useful in some contexts, where, for instance, large under-predictions are extremely costly but large over-predictions are acceptable.

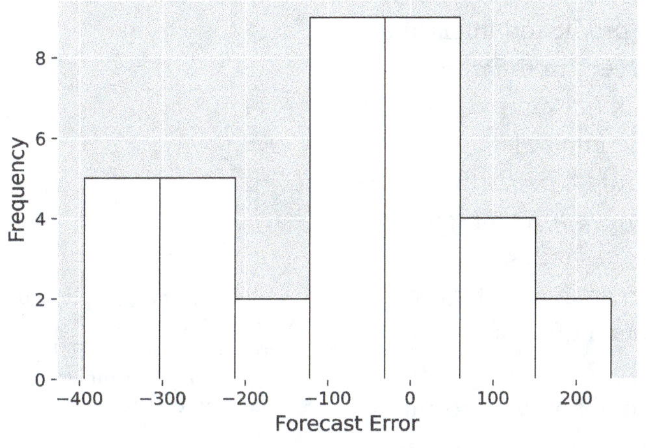

Figure 3.4: Histogram of forecast errors in the test period from a quadratic trend model applied to the Amtrak ridership data.

Code for creating Figure 3.4

See full code at `github.com/gshmueli/ptsf-Python`

```
plt.hist(ridership_test - pred_values, bins=7, color='white', edgecolor='black')
plt.xlabel('Forecast Error')
plt.ylabel('Frequency')
```

Apply the `matplotlib` function `hist()` to the test errors to plot a histogram showing the frequency of forecast errors across seven bins (equal-width bins are automatically generated).

Note: When the test period contains missing values, one can compute performance metrics such as MAE, RMSE and MAPE that exclude the missing periods. Similarly, forecast error plots can be created excluding the missing periods.

Prediction Intervals

A *prediction interval* is a forecast range with an uncertainty level attached to it. A prediction interval is more informative than a single forecast number, called a *point forecast* (F_t), because it tells us about the risk or uncertainty associated with the forecast. For example, to forecast next month's sales, the point forecast $F_t = \$50,000$ does not tell us how far the forecast can go above or below this number. In contrast, a 95% prediction interval of [$40,000,$52,000] tells us that we are 95% certain that the value will fall within this interval. Note that in this example the point forecast $50,000 is not in the middle of the interval.

If forecast errors were normally distributed, prediction intervals would easily be constructed by adding/subtracting a few standard deviations to the point forecast F_t, similar to prediction intervals in cross-sectional regression analysis.[7] Figure 3.5 depicts such 95% prediction intervals from a quadratic model applied to the Amtrak ridership data.

A model's forecast errors, however, are not always normally distributed. For example, we can see from Figure 3.4 that the distribution of forecast errors (from a quadratic trend model applied to the Amtrak ridership data) does not look normal. The left tail of the histogram is longer than the right tail.[8]

When errors are not normally distributed, we can use the forecast errors to construct a prediction interval. We can use the training errors to construct a prediction interval for the test period, or use all errors to construct a prediction interval for the future. For example, a 90% prediction interval can be constructed by using the 5th and 95th percentiles from the sample of forecast errors.[9]

[7] Recall that a 95% prediction interval for normally distributed errors is $F_t \pm 1.96s$, where s is the estimated standard deviation.

[8] Another quick way to check normality is using *normal probability plots*, where the forecast errors, sorted from low to high, are plotted against normal percentiles. To create a normal probability plot in Python, put the forecast error into the function `scipy.stats.probplot()`.

[9] To compute a percentile (also known as a quantile), use the `numpy.percentile()` function.

Prediction Cones

It can be useful to compare sets of prediction intervals from different models. Some forecasting models have different levels of forecast certainty for different future periods, typically with

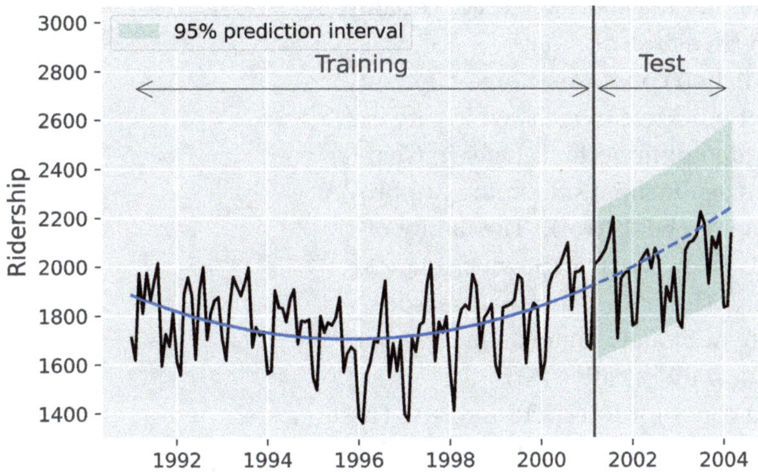

Figure 3.5: Point forecasts and 95% prediction intervals in the test period from a quadratic trend model applied to the Amtrak ridership data.

Code for creating Figure 3.5

See full code at github.com/gshmueli/ptsf-Python

```
pred_interval = forecaster.predict_interval(ridership_test.index, coverage=[0.95])
ax = plot_series(ridership, fitted_values, pred_values, ax=ax, pred_interval=pred_interval)
```

The `plot_series()` function accepts an optional argument *pred_interval* which shows the prediction interval as a shaded region.

Prediction Intervals in `sktime`

Not all `sktime` forecasters provide a method to compute prediction intervals. `sktime` provides utilities to determine which of the hundreds of available machine learning or statistical models ("estimators") have an attribute of interest. For example, the following code outputs all the forecasting models and algorithms ("forecasters") that provide prediction intervals. (There were 56 such forecasters at the time of this writing.)

```
from sktime.registry import all_estimators
fc = all_estimators("forecaster", filter_tags={"capability:pred_int": True})
for item in fc:
    print(item[0])
```

For more information on the *sktime.registry* see www.sktime.net/en/latest/api_reference/auto_generated/sktime.registry.all_estimators.html.

decreasing certainty as we forecast further into the future. When such a model's prediction intervals at a specific level of certainty are contiguous in time, they form a *prediction cone*.

Below we consider the prediction cones from three different models. For now, the details of our three models, which are exponential smoothing models, are not important. Later in Chapter 5, when we formally introduce exponential smoothing, we provide more detail about how these models work. The family of exponential smoothing models is known as ETS, which stands for error, trend, and seasonality. The error, trend, and seasonality components in this family of models can take on different settings, such as additive (A) or multiplicative (M).

Figure 3.6 shows prediction cones for three ETS models. These models were fit to 38 months of data on the number of people worldwide accessing Tumblr's website from April 2010 to May 2013. The prediction intervals used to create the prediction cones are the 20%, 40%, 60%, and 80% prediction intervals at 1-month-ahead, 2-months-ahead,..., up to 115-months-ahead (from June 2013 to December 2022). This data was used in a case study to develop a hypothetical value for Tumblr shortly after its acquisition by Yahoo in 2013 for $1.1 billion.[10]

When the 20% prediction intervals from a model are joined together for all 115 of the step-ahead forecasts, they form the inner shaded prediction cone in each panel. The 80% prediction cone is the outer shaded region. The higher the level of certainty of the prediction interval, the wider the prediction cone. Also, for the same level of certainty, the prediction intervals in a cone typically grow wider over time. To maintain the same level of certainty, we need to make our intervals wider the further ahead in time we forecast. In other words, we are less certain about the distant future than the near future.

For each model in Figure 3.6, the thick line in the middle of the cone represents the model's point forecasts at each step ahead. We see that in this case, the prediction cones differ across models even more than their point forecasts. Such differences can matter a great deal when considering the uncertainty around any point forecast.

[10] The data was originally obtained from Quantcast in July 2013 and appears in the case study "Yahoo's Acquisition of Tumblr" by Kritzer and Lichtendahl from Darden Business Publishing. Data on Tumblr's website traffic is no longer publicly available from Quantcast.

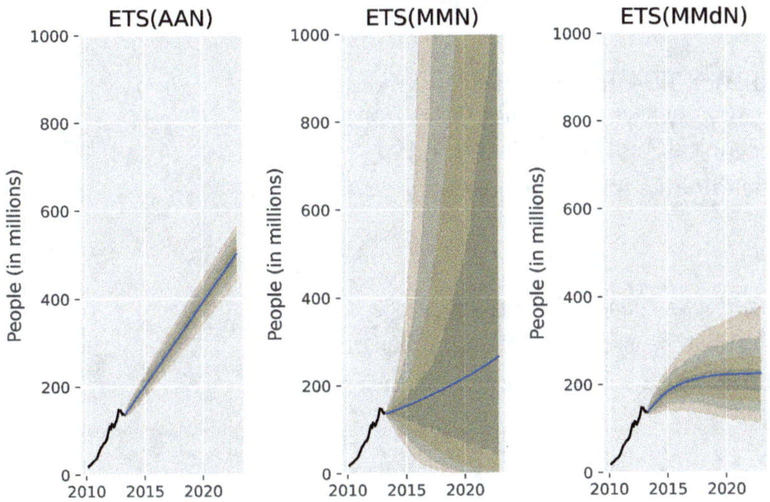

Figure 3.6: Prediction cones from three exponential smoothing models, fit to the Tumblr data.

Code for creating Figure 3.6

See full code at github.com/gshmueli/ptsf-Python

```
tumblr = pd.read_csv('ptsf-Python/Data/Tumblr.csv', parse_dates=True, index_col=0)
tumblr.index = tumblr.index.to_period('M')
views = (tumblr['People Worldwide'] / 1e6).to_frame()

fig, axs = plt.subplots(nrows=1, ncols=3, figsize=(8, 5.2))
plt.subplots_adjust(wspace=0.6)
def customize_plot(ax, title):
    ax.set_title(title)
    ax.set_ylim([0, 1000])
    ax.set_xticks([pd.Period(year, freq='M') for year in ['2010', '2015', '2020']])
    ax.set_xticklabels(['2010', '2015', '2020'])
    ax.get_legend().remove()

fh = ForecastingHorizon(np.arange(1,116), is_relative=True)
models = ["AAN","MMN","MMdN"]
for i, z in enumerate([("add", "add", False), ("mul", "mul", False), ("mul", "mul", True)]):
    forecaster = AutoETS(error=z[0], trend=z[1], damped_trend=z[2]).fit(views)
    pred = forecaster.predict(fh)
    pred_interval = forecaster.predict_interval(fh=fh, coverage=np.array([.8,.6,.4,.2]))
    plot_series(views, pred, ax=axs[i], markers=['',''], colors=['black','blue'],
                pred_interval=pred_interval, y_label="People (in millions)")
    customize_plot(axs[i], f"ETS({models[i]})")
```

Each loop pass (i) specifies a model and fits it to the training data, (ii) calculates the point forecasts, (iii) calculates the prediction intervals, and (iv) plots the results (all in 4 lines of code!). It exemplifies the `sktime` unifying approach: it will work with any `sktime` forecaster supporting the `predict_interval()` method (see the discussion below Figure 3.5).

3.4 Naive Forecasts

Although it is tempting to apply "sophisticated" forecasting methods, one must remember to consider *naive forecasts*. A naive forecast is simply the most recent value of the series. In other words, at time t, the k-step-ahead naive forecast is given by

$$F_{t+k} = y_t \tag{3.2}$$

In the case of a seasonal series, the *seasonal naive forecast* is the value from the most recent identical season (e.g., forecast December using last December's value). For a series with M seasons, we can write the formula

$$\begin{aligned} F_{t+1} &= y_{t-M+1} \\ F_{t+2} &= y_{t-M+2} \\ \vdots &= \\ F_{t+k} &= y_{t-M+k} \end{aligned} \tag{3.3}$$

In Figure 3.7 we generated naive forecasts (orange) and seasonal naive forecasts (cyan) for the test period of the Amtrak ridership series. We see the naive forecasts are identical for each test period, and equal to the value in the last training month. The seasonal naive forecasts "copy" the values in the most recent training year.

The underlying logic behind naive forecasts is that the most recent information is likely to be the most relevant for forecasting the future.[11] Naive forecasts are used for two purposes:

1. As forecasts. Naive forecasts, which are simple to understand and easy to implement, can sometimes achieve sufficiently useful accuracy levels. Following the principle of "the simplest method that does the job", naive forecasts are a serious contender.

2. As a baseline. When evaluating the predictive performance of a certain method, it is important to compare it to some baseline. Naive forecasts should always be considered as a baseline, and the comparative advantage of any other methods considered should be clearly shown.

[11] During the training period, each naive forecast is equal to the value in the previous period. This is because we assume all the training data is available and the most recent period is most informative.

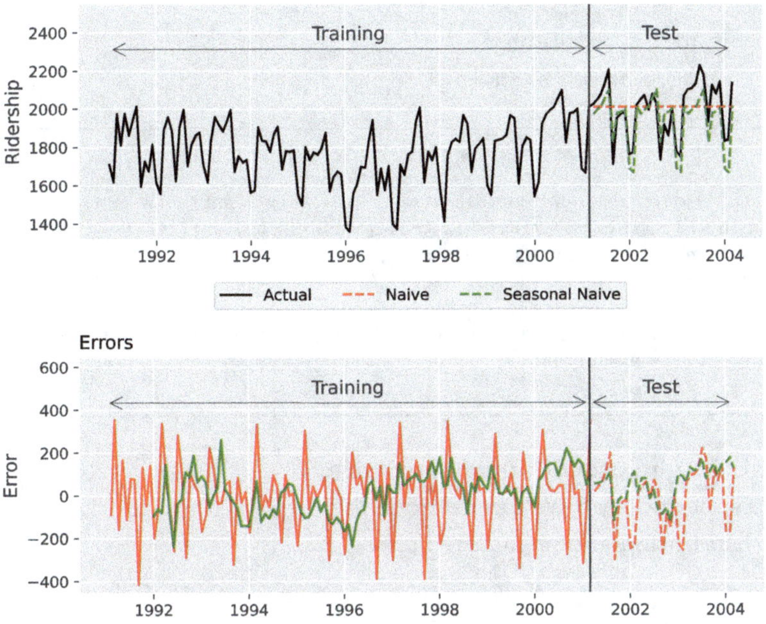

Figure 3.7: Top: Amtrak ridership with naive (red) and seasonal naive (green) forecasts in test period. Bottom: training and test errors for naive and seasonal naive.

Code for creating Figure 3.7

See full code at `github.com/gshmueli/ptsf-Python`

```
from sktime.forecasting.naive import NaiveForecaster

# Fit naive and seasonal naive models to training period
f_naive = NaiveForecaster(strategy='last', sp=1).fit(ridership_train)
f_naive_seas = NaiveForecaster(strategy='last', sp=12).fit(ridership_train)

# Get forecasts for the test period
fh = ForecastingHorizon(ridership_test.index, is_relative=False)
pred_naive = f_naive.predict(fh=fh)
pred_seas = f_naive_seas.predict(fh=fh)

# Plot models
figure, axs = plt.subplots(2, 1, sharex=False, figsize=(8, 7))
axs[0] = plot_series(ridership, pred_naive, pred_seas, ax=axs[0])
```

Naive forecasts are provided by *NaiveForecaster*, setting its *strategy* parameter to 'last'. For Seasonal Naive forecasts set the *seasonal period* (*sp*) parameter appropriately. Set *sp* to 1 to ignore seasonality. The code uses Python chaining to specify the model and fit it in one line. Use the `predict` method to generate the forecasts for the test period (three years). Plot the original series with the two sets of forecasts. And plot the forecast errors (next page).

Code for creating Figure 3.7 - continued
See full code at github.com/gshmueli/ptsf-Python

```
# Plot errors
naive_err_train = ridership_train['Ridership'] - ridership_train['Ridership'].shift(1)
snaive_err_train = ridership_train['Ridership'] - ridership_train['Ridership'].shift(12)
naive_err_test = ridership_test['Ridership'] - pred_naive.iloc[:,0]
snaive_err_test = ridership_test['Ridership'] - pred_seas.iloc[:,0]

axs[1] = plot_series(naive_err_train, snaive_err_train, naive_err_test, snaive_err_test, ax=axs[1],
                    title='Errors', y_label='Error')
```

As with forecasts in general, the forecast performance of naive forecasts is evaluated on the test period, and we can examine the corresponding forecast error distribution and create prediction intervals.

3.5 *Advanced Data Partitioning: Roll-Forward Test*

The method of partitioning the data into fixed training and test periods presented in Section 3.1 (also called *fixed origin*) allows us to evaluate forecast performance in a somewhat limited way: we only see a single one-step-ahead forecast, a single two-step-ahead forecast, etc. For example, if we have monthly data with three years of test data, then we only see performance of a single one-month-ahead forecast, two-months-ahead forecast, three-month-ahead forecast, etc.

An alternative approach that gives us more evaluation data is to use a *roll-forward* test period (also called *rolling origin*). This means creating multiple training-test partitions by moving the partitioning one period at a time. This simulates a deployment scenario where we refresh our forecasts period-by-period. In the monthly ridership example, we can create multiple data partitions by rolling forward one month at a time, as shown in Table 3.2.

The 36 partitions give us 36 one-month-ahead forecasts, 35 two-months-ahead forecasts, 34 three-months-ahead forecasts,

Data Partition	Training Period	Test Period
1	Jan 1991 – Mar 2001	Apr 2001 – Mar 2004
2	Jan 1991 – Apr 2001	May 2001 – Mar 2004
3	Jan 1991 – May 2001	Jun 2001 – Mar 2004
⋮	⋮	⋮
36	Jan 1991 – Feb 2003	Mar 2004

Table 3.2: Roll-forward data partitioning (monthly updating).

etc. Notice that we would only have a single 36-month-ahead forecast. With roll-forward partitions, we therefore have more information about short-term forecasts, and the amount of data decreases as we move further into future forecasting.[12]

The next step, as in fixed partitioning, is to fit a model to the training period and evaluate it on the test period. In the roll-forward scenario this means re-running our model on each of the training sets ("refreshing" the model), and using each of the models for forecasting the corresponding test period.

Finally, we compute performance measures using all the test data, preferably breaking it down by one-step-ahead performance, two-step-ahead performance, etc. To illustrate roll-forward partitioning, consider naive forecasts for the ridership data using either fixed partitioning (as shown in Figure 3.1) or month-by-month roll-forward partitioning (as in Table 3.2).

Figure 3.8 shows naive forecasts for the test period (top) and the resulting forecast errors (bottom), using a fixed 36-month test period vs. one-step-ahead forecasts using a monthly roll-forward test period. The fixed data partitioning produces a constant forecast for all 36 test months (horizontal line), whereas the roll-forward partitioning produces one-month-ahead forecasts that get refreshed every month. We could potentially also draw the roll-forward two-steps-ahead forecasts, three-steps-ahead forecasts, etc.

[12] Roll-forward test that advances one period at a time is analogous to the notion of leave-one-out cross-validation in cross-sectional data (see `robjhyndman.com/hyndsight/crossvalidation`).

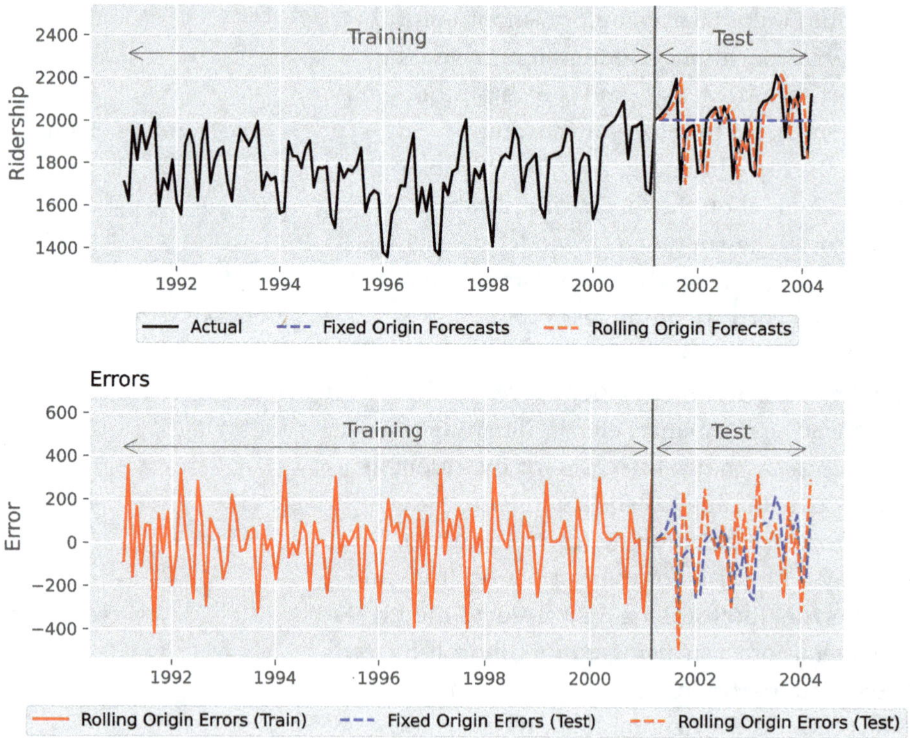

Figure 3.8: Top: Naive forecasts using a fixed test period ("fixed origin") vs. one-step-ahead naive forecasts using a monthly roll-forward test period ("rolling origin") for the Amtrak ridership data. Bottom: Forecast errors from the two methods.

Table 3.3 shows performance measures of the fixed and roll-forward partitioning approaches.

Method	MAE	RMSE	MAPE
Fixed partitioning	115.923	142.755	6.021%
Roll-forward one-month-ahead	119.429	169.173	6.206%
Roll-forward two-months-ahead	159.582	198.104	8.274%
⋮			
Roll-forward 36-month-ahead	124.518	124.518	5.839%
Roll-forward overall	157.760	190.416	7.972%

Table 3.3: Performance of naive forecasts using fixed partitioning vs. roll-forward partitioning, for one-month-ahead to 36-months-ahead forecasts.

Code for performance metrics of roll-forward forecasts in Table 3.3

See full code at github.com/gshmueli/ptsf-Python

```
from sktime.split import ExpandingWindowSplitter
from sktime.forecasting.model_evaluation import evaluate
from sktime.performance_metrics.forecasting import MeanAbsoluteError, mean_absolute_percentage_error

y = ridership.copy() ## shorter name to save space
n_test = 36
y_train, y_test = temporal_train_test_split(y, test_size=n_test)
forecaster = NaiveForecaster(strategy='last')

## Roll-forward calculations
mae, rmse, mape = (lambda: ([], [], []))()
for fh in np.arange(1,n_test + 1):
    cv = ExpandingWindowSplitter(initial_window=len(y_train), step_length=1, fh=[fh])
    res = evaluate(forecaster=forecaster, y=y, cv=cv, return_data=True,
                   scoring=[MeanAbsoluteError(), mean_absolute_percentage_error])
    mae.append(res['test_MeanAbsoluteError'].mean())
    rmse.append(np.sqrt((res['test_MeanAbsoluteError']**2).mean()))
    mape.append(res['test__DynamicForecastingErrorMetric'].mean())

## Mean of roll-forward calculations
mean_values = list(map(lambda x: np.mean(np.array(x)), [mae, rmse, mape]))
```

For each forecasting horizon, use the `sktime` function `ExpandingWindowSplitter` to create the rolling window partitions, stored in the object named *cv* (for cross-validation). Pass the naive forecasting model and the *cv* object to the `evaluate` function, along with the list of metrics in the *scoring* argument.

3.6 *Example: Comparing Two Models*

We introduce the following example to illustrate the notions of data partitioning, naive forecasts, and performance metrics, as well as how they are used in combination to compare models. Using the same Amtrak ridership data, we compare two methods: naive forecasts and seasonal naive forecasts.

Fixed Partitioning

We start with fixed partitioning, where the test period is set to Apr 2001 – Mar 2004. The naive and seasonal naive forecasts for this test period are shown in Table 3.4. We then compute forecast errors and predictive measures based on these forecasts. A comparison is shown in Table 3.5.

Period	Actual	Naive Forecast	Seasonal Naive Forecast
Apr 2001	2023.792	2007.928	1971.493
May 2001	2047.008	2007.928	1992.301
Jun 2001	2072.913	2007.928	2009.763
⋮	⋮	⋮	⋮
Mar 2004	2132.446	2007.928	2007.928

Table 3.4: Naive and seasonal naive forecasts for fixed test period (ridership data).

Method	MAE	RMSE	MAPE
Naive Forecast	115.923	142.755	6.021%
Seasonal Naive Forecast	84.094	95.62433	4.248%

Table 3.5: Performance of naive vs. seasonal naive forecasts on test, using fixed partitioning.

Roll-Forward Partitioning

We now repeat the comparison of the two models (naive and seasonal naive), this time using the advanced partitioning method of roll-forward test. We use the 36 data partitions shown in Table 3.2. For each partition, we use the naive and seasonal naive on the training period and generate one-step-ahead forecasts for the corresponding test period. We have already seen the performance measures for the naive method in the first row of Table

3.3. Table 3.6 compares these measures to the seasonal naive forecast measures. We see that the seasonal naive forecasts outperform the naive forecasts on one-step-ahead forecasting. To compare the k-steps-ahead performance of these two models, we can adapt the Python code that accompanies Table 3.6 by changing the `1` in `fh=[1]` to the required value k.

Method	MAE	RMSE	MAPE
Naive Forecast	119.429	169.173	6.206%
Seasonal Naive Forecast	78.473	98.205	3.906%

Table 3.6: Performance of naive vs. seasonal naive one-step-ahead forecasts using roll-forward partitioning.

Code for Naive and Seasonal Naive Forecasts and Predictive Metrics

See full code at `github.com/gshmueli/ptsf-Python`

```
# fixed test period forecasts
f_naive = NaiveForecaster(strategy='last', sp=1).fit(y_train)
f_naive_seas = NaiveForecaster(strategy='last', sp=12).fit(y_train)

pred_naive = f_naive.predict(fh=np.arange(n_test)+1).squeeze()
pred_seas = f_naive_seas.predict(fh=np.arange(n_test)+1).squeeze()

# fixed test period accuracy
def accuracy_df(method, y, y_pred):
    mae = mean_absolute_error(y, y_pred)
    rmse = np.sqrt(mean_squared_error(y, y_pred))
    mape = mean_absolute_percentage_error(y, y_pred)
    df = pd.DataFrame({'MAE': mae, 'RMSE': rmse, 'MAPE': mape}, index=[method])
    return df

df2 = pd.concat([accuracy_df("Naive Forecast", y_test, pred_naive), \
            accuracy_df("Seasonal Naive Forecast", y_test, pred_seas)])
```

Use *NaiveForecaster* with *sp* set to 1 to ignore seasonality in the forecasts, or 12 to include monthly seasonality. (See Table 3.4 for the comparison.) Define a convenience function `accuracy_df` to compute the predictive measures (shown in Table 3.5).

3.7 *Problems*

1. *Souvenir Sales:* The file *SouvenirSales.csv* contains monthly sales for a souvenir shop at a beach resort town in Queensland, Australia, between 1995 and 2001.[13]

   Back in 2001, the store wanted to use the data to forecast sales for the next 12 months (year 2002). They hired an analyst to generate forecasts. The analyst first partitioned the data into training and test periods, with the test period containing the last 12 months of data (year 2001). She then fit a forecasting model to sales, using the training period.

   Partition the data into the training and test periods as explained above.

   (a) Why was the data partitioned?

   (b) Why did the analyst choose a 12-month test period?

   (c) What is the naive forecast for the test period? (Assume that you must provide forecasts for 12 months ahead.)

   (d) Compute the RMSE and MAPE for the naive forecasts.

   (e) Plot a histogram of the forecast errors that result from the naive forecasts (for the test period). Plot also a time plot for the naive forecasts and the actual sales numbers in the test period. What can you say about the behavior of the naive forecasts?

   (f) The analyst found a forecasting model that gives satisfactory performance on the test set. What must she do to use the forecasting model to generate forecasts for year 2002?

[13] Source: Hyndman and Yang (2018) tsdl: Time Series Data Library. v0.1.0. `github.com/FinYang/tsdl`.

2. *Forecasting Shampoo Sales:* The file *ShampooSales.csv* contains data on the monthly sales of a certain shampoo over a three-year period.[14]

   If the goal is forecasting sales in future months, which of the following steps should be taken? (choose one or more)

   - Partition the data into training and test periods.
   - examine time plots of the series and of model forecasts only for the training period.

[14] Source: Hyndman and Yang (2018) tsdl: Time Series Data Library. v0.1.0. `github.com/FinYang/tsdl`.

- Look at MAPE and RMSE values for the training period.
- Look at MAPE and RMSE values for the test period.
- Compute naive forecasts.

3. *Performance on Training and Test Data:* Two different models were fit to the same time series. The first 100 time periods were used for the training period and the last 12 periods were treated as a test period. Assume that both models make sense practically and fit the data reasonably well. Below are the RMSE values for each of the models:

	Training Period	Test Period
Model A	543	690
Model B	669	675

   (a) Which model appears more useful for retrospectively describing the different components of this time series? Why?

   (b) Which model appears to be more useful for forecasting purposes? Why?

4 Forecasting Methods: Overview

Why is there such a variety of forecasting methods for time series? The answer is that different methods perform differently depending on the nature of the data and the forecasting requirements. Recall that an important benchmark to consider is naive forecasts (see Section 3.4). This simple approach is often powerful and should always be considered as a baseline for performance comparison of more sophisticated forecasting methods.

Before going into the details of particular forecasting methods, let us examine some of the differences underlying the major forecasting methods.

4.1 Model-Based vs. Data-Driven Methods

Forecasting methods can be roughly divided into model-based methods and data-driven methods.

Model-based methods use a statistical, mathematical, or other scientific model to approximate a data series. The training data is used to estimate the parameters of the model, and then the model with estimated parameters is used to generate forecasts. In Chapters 6 and 7 we describe model-based forecasting models such as multiple linear regression and autoregressive models, where the user specifies a certain linear model and then estimates it from the time series. Logistic regression models, as described in Chapter 9, are also model-based. Model-based methods are especially advantageous when the series at hand is very short. With an assumed underlying model, few data points are needed for estimating the model parameters.

Chapter 5 covers the data-driven approach of smoothing, where algorithms "learn" patterns from the data. Data-driven methods are advantageous when model assumptions are likely to be violated, or when the structure of the time series changes over time. Naive forecasts are also data-driven, in that they simply use the last data point in the series for generating a forecast. Another advantage of many data-driven forecasting methods is that they require less user input, and are therefore more "user proof" as well as more easily automated. The lower user input, however, means that more data (that is, a longer series) is required for adequate learning. We also note that data mining methods such as neural networks (see Chapter 8), regression trees and other algorithms for predicting cross-sectional data are sometimes used for time series forecasting, especially for incorporating external information into the forecasts.[1]

[1] For an example of using regression trees and random forests for time series forecasting, see the presentation by the winners of the Kaggle "RTA Freeway Travel Time Prediction Challenge" at `web.archive.org/web/20161205060935/blog.kaggle.com/wp-content/uploads/2011/03/team_irazu_screencast.pdf`.

Another difference between model-based and data-driven approaches relates to global vs. local patterns in the series. Model-based methods are generally preferable for forecasting series with global patterns that extend throughout the data period, as they use all the data to estimate the global pattern. For a local pattern, a model would require specifying how and when the patterns change, which is usually impractical and often unknown. Therefore, data-driven methods are preferable for forecasting series with local patterns. Such methods "learn" patterns from the data, and their memory length can be set to best adapt to the rate of change in the series. Patterns that change quickly warrant a "short memory", whereas patterns that change slowly warrant a "long memory".

4.2 *Extrapolation Methods, Econometric Models, and External Information*

The methods presented in this book create forecasts for a time series based on its history. Such methods are termed *extrapolation methods*. Naive forecasts are an example of extrapolation. In some applications, multiple related time series must be forecasted simultaneously (e.g., the monthly sales of multiple products), and it is expected that the values of one series are correlated with those of other series. Even in such cases, the most popular forecasting practice is to forecast each series using only its own historical values. The advantage of this practice is simplicity. The disadvantage is that forecasts do not take into account possible relationships between the series.

Econometric models approach cross-correlation between series from a causal standpoint, and often include information from one or more series as inputs into another series. Such models are based on assumptions of causality that are derived from theoretical models. An alternative approach is to capture the *associations* between the series of interest and model them directly into the forecasting method. The statistics literature contains models for *multivariate time series* that directly model the cross-correlations between a set of series. Such methods tend to make restrictive assumptions about the data and the cross-series structure, and they also require statistical expertise for estimation and maintenance.

A third alternative to both causal econometric models and multivariate time series models, when the purpose is forecasting, is to capture external information that correlates with a series more heuristically. An example is using the sales of lipstick to forecast some measure of the economy, based on the observation by Leonard Lauder, past chairman of Estée Lauder Companies Inc., that lipstick sales tend to increase before tough economic times (a phenomenon called the "leading lipstick indicator"). The most important factor to keep in mind is that whatever external information we integrate into the forecasting method must be available at the time of prediction. For example, consider a model for forecasting the average weekly airfare on a certain route. The model uses weekly gas prices and past weekly airfare rates as inputs. Should we include only gas prices from past weeks or also from the week to be forecasted? The airfare forecast will obviously be more accurate if it is based on gas prices during the same week. However, that information is unavailable at the time of prediction! We could try and forecast gas prices, and include the forecast in the airfare model. However, it is obviously very difficult (and maybe impossible) to accurately forecast gas prices. In fact, if you are able to forecast gas prices accurately, you might no longer be interested in forecasting airfare... The moral is: *forecasting methods must only use values (or estimates) that are available at the time of prediction.*

In Chapters 6–8 we focus on extrapolation methods. While smoothing methods are strictly extrapolation methods, regression models and neural networks can be adapted to capture external information. Section 7.4 in Chapter 7 discusses the inclusion of external information in regression models. The same considerations apply to neural networks.

4.3 *Manual vs. Automated Forecasting*

The level of required automation was briefly discussed in Chapter 1. In particular, the level of automation depends on the nature of the forecasting task and on how forecasts will be used in practice. More automation is usually required when many series are to be forecasted on a continuous basis, and not much forecasting expertise can be allocated to the process (recall the example of forecasting Point of Sale (POS) data for purposes of inventory control across many stores).

In terms of forecasting methods, some methods are easier to automate than others. Typically, data-driven methods are easier to automate, because they "learn" patterns from the data. Note, however, that even data-driven methods can perform poorly if the characteristics of the series (seasonality, trend) are not correctly specified, or if there is insufficient data.

Model-based methods also range in their fitness for automation. Models that are based on many assumptions for producing adequate forecasts are less likely to be useful for automation, as they require constantly evaluating whether the assumptions are met. Similarly, models that fit global patterns can be automated only if they are evaluated periodically to check whether the patterns changed or if they are fitted to a moving window of time.

Data-driven methods such as smoothing methods (Chapter 5) are preferable for automated forecasting, because they require less tweaking, are suitable for a range of trends and seasonal patterns, are computationally fast, require very little data storage, and adjust when the behavior of a series changes over time. Neural networks (Chapter 8) are similarly useful for automation, although they are computationally more demanding and require a lot of past data. One serious danger with data-driven methods is overfitting the training period. Hence, performance should be carefully evaluated and constantly monitored to avoid this pitfall.

Even with an automated system in place, it is advisable to monitor the forecasts and forecast errors produced by an automated system and occasionally re-examine their suitability and update the system accordingly.

Finally, combined forecasts are usually good candidates for automated forecasting, because they are more robust to sensitivities of a single forecasting method. We discuss combined forecasts in the next section.

4.4 *Combining Methods and Ensembles*

While it might appear that we should choose one method for forecasting among the various options, it turns out that *combining* multiple forecasting methods can lead to improved predictive performance. Combining methods can be done via two-level (or multilevel) methods, where the first method uses the original time series to generate forecasts of future values, and the second method uses the forecast errors from the first layer to generate forecasts of future forecast errors, thereby "correcting" the first level forecasts. We describe two-level forecasting in Section 7.1.

Another combination approach is via *ensembles*, where multiple methods are applied to the time series, each generating separate forecasts. The resulting forecasts are then averaged in some way to produce the final forecast. Combining methods can take advantage of the capability of different forecasting methods to capture different aspects of the time series. For the same reason, ensembles are useful for predicting in cross-sectional settings. Averaging across multiple methods can lead to forecasts that are more robust and are of higher precision. We can even use different methods for forecasting different horizons or periods—for example, when one method performs better for one-step-ahead forecasting and another method for two or more periods ahead, or when one method is better at forecasting weekends and another weekdays. Chapter 11 describes an ensemble approach used by the winner of a tourism forecasting competition.

Ensembles of predictions from multiple methods are also commonly used for predicting cross-sectional data. Ensembles played a major role in the million-dollar Netflix Prize[2] contest, where teams competed to create the most accurate predictions of movie preferences by users of the Netflix DVD rental service. Different teams ended up joining forces to create ensemble predictions, which proved more accurate than the individual predictions. The winning team, called "BellKor's Pragmatic Chaos" combined results from the "BellKor" and "Big Chaos" teams alongside additional members. In a 2010 article in *Chance* magazine, the Netflix Prize winners described the power of their ensemble approach:

[2] `en.wikipedia.org/wiki/Netflix_Prize`

> An early lesson of the competition was the value of combining sets of predictions from multiple models or algorithms. If two prediction sets achieved similar RMSEs, it was quicker and more effective to simply average the two sets than to try to develop a new model that incorporated the best of each method. Even if the RMSE for one set was much worse than the other, there was almost certainly a linear combination that improved on the better set.[3]

[3] R. M. Bell, Y. Koren, and C. Volinsky. All together now: A perspective on the Netflix Prize. *Chance*, 23:24–29, 2010

The principle of improving forecast precision (that is, reducing the variance of forecast errors) via ensembles is the same principle underlying the advantage of portfolios and diversification in financial investment. Improvement is greatest when the forecast errors are negatively correlated, or at least uncorrelated.

Finally, another combination approach is to use different series measuring the phenomenon of interest (e.g., temperature) and take an average of the multiple resulting forecasts. For example, when a series of interest is available from multiple sources, each with slightly different numbers or precision (e.g., from manual and electronic collection systems or from different departments or measuring devices), we can create ensembles of forecasts, each based on a different series. In the Amtrak rid-

Figure 4.1: The 2009 Netflix Prize ensemble of winners. (Image courtesy of AT&T)

ership example, we might have daily passenger data collected manually from ticket collectors. Monthly ridership forecasts based on this data can be combined with forecasts from the monthly series collected by the electronic system. Of course, the performance of such an ensemble should be evaluated by comparing the ensemble forecasts against the actual values from the goal-defined series. In the Amtrak example, if forecast accuracy will eventually be measured against the official monthly ridership numbers reported to the Bureau of Transportation Statistics, then the ensemble forecasts should be evaluated relative to the same official ridership series (rather than relative to the manual ticket collector data).

The website `www.forecastingprinciples.com`, that was run and supported by forecasting experts, had a detailed Q&A page on combining forecasts.[4] The authors explained how and why ensembles improve forecast accuracy. To the question: "What are the disadvantages of combined forecasts?" they responded:

a) Increased costs

b) Need analysts who are familiar with a number of methods

c) Need to ensure that a pre-determined rule for combining is agreed upon. Otherwise, people can find a forecast to suit their biases.

[4] At the time of writing, the website is no longer available.

They also addressed the question "Why isn't it common to use combined forecasts?" as follows:

a) It is counter-intuitive. People think you only get an average forecast and they believe that if they can pick a method, they will do better. (This explanation has been supported by experiments.)

b) This solution is too simple. People like complex approaches.

4.5 Problems

1. A large medical clinic would like to forecast daily patient visits for staffing purposes.

   (a) If data is available only for the last month, how does this affect the choice of model-based vs. data-driven methods?

   (b) The clinic has access to the admissions data of a nearby hospital. Under what conditions will including the hospital information be potentially useful for forecasting the clinic's daily visits?

   (c) Thus far, the clinic administrator takes a heuristic approach, using the visit numbers from the same day of the previous week as a forecast. What is the advantage of this approach? What is the disadvantage?

   (d) What level of automation appears to be required for this task? Explain.

   (e) Describe two approaches for improving the current heuristic (naive) forecasting approach using ensembles.

2. The ability to scale up renewable energy, and in particular wind power and speed, is dependent on the ability to forecast its short-term availability. Soman et al. (2010) describe different methods for wind power forecasting (the quote is slightly edited for brevity):[5]

   Persistence Method: This method is also known as 'Naive Predictor'. It is assumed that the wind speed at time $t + \delta t$ will be the same as it was at time t. Unbelievably, it is more accurate than most of the physical and statistical methods for very-short to short term forecasts...

   Physical Approach: Physical systems use parameterizations based on a detailed physical description of the atmosphere...

   Statistical Approach: The statistical approach is based on training with measurement data and uses difference between the predicted and the actual wind speeds in immediate past to tune model parameters. It is easy to model, inexpensive, and provides timely predictions. It is not based on any predefined mathematical model and rather it is based on patterns...

[5] S. S. Soman, H. Zareipour, O. Malik, and P. Mandal. A review of wind power and wind speed forecasting methods with different time horizons. In *Proceedings of the 42nd North American Power Symposium (NAPS), Arlington, Texas, USA*, 2010

Hybrid Approach: In general, the combination of different approaches such as mixing physical and statistical approaches or combining short term and medium-term models, etc., is referred to as a hybrid approach.

(a) For each of the four types of methods, describe whether it is model-based, data-driven, or a combination.

(b) For each of the four types of methods, describe whether it is based on extrapolation, causal modeling, correlation modeling or a combination.

(c) Describe the advantages and disadvantages of the hybrid approach.

5
Smoothing Methods

In this chapter we describe popular flexible methods for forecasting time series that rely on smoothing. Smoothing is based on averaging values over multiple periods in order to reduce the noise. We start with two simple smoothers, the moving average and simple exponential smoothing, which are suitable for forecasting series that contain no trend and no seasonality. In both cases forecasts are averages of previous values of the series. The length of the series' history used and the weights used in the averaging differ between the methods. We also show how a moving average can be used, with a slight adaptation, for data visualization. We then proceed to describe smoothing methods that are suitable for forecasting series with a trend and/or seasonality. Smoothing methods are data-driven and are able to adapt to changes in the series' patterns over time. Although highly automated, the user must specify smoothing constants, which determine how fast the method adapts to new data. We discuss the choice of such constants and their meaning. The different methods are illustrated using the Amtrak ridership series.

5.1 Introduction

Smoothing methods are a family of forecasting methods that are data-driven in the sense that they estimate time series components directly from the data without a predetermined structure. Data-driven methods are especially useful in series where components change over time. Here we consider a type of data-driven methods called "smoothing methods." Such methods "smooth" out the noise in a series in an attempt to uncover the patterns. Smoothing is done by averaging values over multiple time periods, where different smoothers differ by the number of values averaged, how the average is computed, how many times averaging is performed, etc.

5.2 *Moving Average*

The moving average is a simple smoother; it consists of averaging values across a window of consecutive periods, thereby generating a series of averages. A moving average with window width w means averaging across each set of w consecutive values, where w is determined by the user. In general, there are two types of moving averages: a *centered moving average* and a *trailing moving average.* Centered moving averages are powerful for visualizing trends because the averaging operation can suppress seasonality and noise, thereby making the trend more visible. Trailing moving averages are useful for forecasting. The difference between the two is the placement of the averaging window over the time series.

Centered Moving Average for Visualization

In a centered moving average, the value of the moving average at time t (MA_t) is computed by centering the window around time t and averaging across the w values within the window:

$$MA_t = \left(y_{t-(w-1)/2} + \cdots + y_{t-1} + y_t + y_{t+1} + \cdots + y_{t+(w-1)/2} \right) / w. \tag{5.1}$$

For example, with a window of width $w = 5$, the moving average at time point $t = 3$ means averaging the values of the series at time points 1, 2, 3, 4, 5; at time point $t = 4$ the moving average is the average of the values at time points 2, 3, 4, 5, 6, and so on.[1] This is illustrated in the top panel of Figure 5.1.

Choosing the window width in a seasonal series is straightforward: because the goal is to suppress seasonality to better visualize the trend, the default choice should be the length of a

[1] Equation (5.1) is for a window width that is an odd number. See footnote 2 when the width w is an even number.

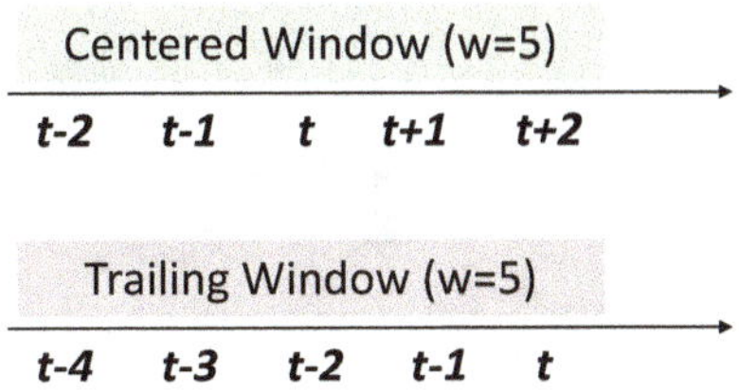

Figure 5.1: Schematic of centered moving average (top) and trailing moving average (bottom), both with window width $w = 5$.

seasonal cycle. Returning to the Amtrak ridership data, the annual seasonality indicates a choice of $w = 12$. Figure 5.2 shows a centered moving average line overlaid on the original series.[2] We can see a global U-shape, but the moving average shows some deviation from this shape, such as a slight dip during the last year.

[2] In Python, to plot a centered moving average, apply the `rolling` method to a Pandas *DataFrame* or *Series* object (rolling windows). For a centered moving average set `center=True` and take a mean. For a window of even width $2n$, this method uses a slightly lopsided window, with n values to the left and n-1 values to the right of the current period. (Other software packages may use different conventions for a centered moving average of a window of even length).

Trailing Moving Average for Forecasting

Centered moving averages are computed by averaging across data both in the past and future of a given time point. In that sense they cannot be used for forecasting because at the time of forecasting, the future is typically unknown. Hence, for purposes of forecasting, we use trailing moving averages, where the window of width w is placed over the most recent available w values of the series. The k-step-ahead forecast F_{t+k} ($k = 1, 2, 3, \ldots$) is then the average of these w values (see red line in Figure 5.1):

$$F_{t+k} = \left(y_t + y_{t-1} + \cdots + y_{t-w+1}\right) / w. \tag{5.2}$$

For example, in the Amtrak ridership series, to forecast ridership in February 1992 or later months given information until January 1992 and using a moving average with window width w=12, we would take the average ridership during the most recent 12 months (February 1991 to January 1992).

Next we illustrate a 12-month moving average forecaster for the Amtrak ridership. We partition the Amtrak ridership time series, leaving the last 36 months as the test period. Applying a moving average forecaster[3] with window $w = 12$, we obtained the output shown in Figure 5.3.

[3] In Python, to obtain a trailing moving average forecaster with $w = 12$, create a `NaiveForecaster` object with `window_length=12`.

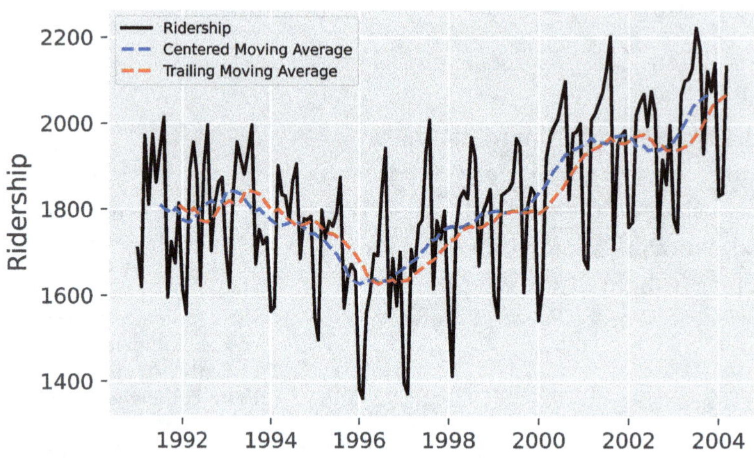

Figure 5.2: Centered moving average and trailing moving average with window width $w = 12$, overlaid on Amtrak ridership series

Code for creating Figure 5.2

See full code at `github.com/gshmueli/ptsf-Python`

```
a = ridership.copy() ## use shorter name
WIDTH = 12
a['Centered'] = a['Ridership'].rolling(window=WIDTH, min_periods=WIDTH, center=True).mean()
a['Trailing'] = a['Ridership'].rolling(window=WIDTH, min_periods=WIDTH, center=False).mean()

fig, ax = plt.subplots(figsize=(5.5,3.5))
ax = plot_series(a['Ridership'], a['Centered'], a['Trailing'], markers=['']*3,
                 labels=['Ridership', 'Centered Moving Average', 'Trailing Moving Average'],
                 x_label="", y_label="Ridership", ax=ax)
ptsf_theme(ax, colors=['black','blue','red'], idx=[0,1,2], lty=['-','--','--'])
plt.legend(loc='upper left', fontsize=7)
```

The first block of code creates the centered and trailing moving average series.

The second block of code plots the ridership and two moving average series.

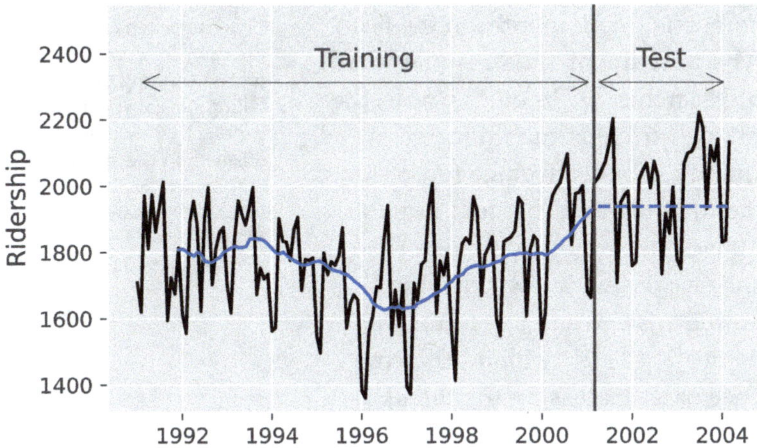

Figure 5.3: Trailing moving average forecaster with $w = 12$ applied to Amtrak ridership series.

Code for creating Figure 5.3

See full code at `github.com/gshmueli/ptsf-Python`

```
y = ridership.copy() ## use a shorter name
y_train = y.truncate(after='2001-03-31')
y_test = y.truncate(before='2001-04-01')

ma_trailing = NaiveForecaster(strategy='mean', window_length=12)
ma_trailing.fit(y_train)
fitted = ma_trailing.predict(y_train.index[12:])
pred = ma_trailing.predict(y_test.index)

fig, ax = plt.subplots(figsize=(5.5,3.5))
ax = plot_series(y, fitted, pred, markers=['']*3, x_label="", y_label="Ridership", ax=ax)
ptsf_theme(ax, colors=['black','blue','blue'], idx=[0,1,2], lty=['-','-','--'])
```

The first block partitions the data into training and test periods.

In the second block, we create a *NaiveForecaster* object whose forecasts are the trailing 12-month moving averages. The usual `fit` and `predict` methods are then used to determine the fitted values for the training period and forecasts for the test period.

The final block plots the three series: actual, forecasts for the training period (lagged trailing moving average), and (constant) forecasts for the test period.

Note that for the first 12 records of the training period, there is no forecast because there are fewer than 12 past values to average.[4] Also, note that the forecasts for all months in the test period are identical (1938.481) because the method assumes that information is known only until March 2001. In other words, the test period forecasts are *not* roll-forward next-month forecasts.

[4] We can potentially create forecasts for some of the first 12 training periods by taking partial windows. This is done by reducing the offset 12 in the statement that computes the fitted values. For example `fitted = ma_trailing.predict(y_train.index[6:])`.

In this example, it is clear that the moving average forecaster is inadequate for generating monthly forecasts because it does not capture the seasonality in the data. Seasons with high ridership are under-forecasted, and seasons with low ridership are over-forecasted. A similar issue arises when forecasting a series with a trend: the moving average "lags behind", thereby under-forecasting in the presence of an increasing trend and over-forecasting in the presence of a decreasing trend. This "lagging behind" of the trailing moving average can also be seen in Figure 5.2.

In general, the moving average can be used for forecasting only in series that lack seasonality and trend. Such a limitation might seem impractical. However, there are a few popular methods for removing trends (*de-trending*) and removing seasonality (*deseasonalizing*) from a series, such as regression models (Chapter 6), advanced exponential smoothing methods (Section 5.5), and the operation of *differencing* (Section 5.3). The moving average can then be used to forecast such de-trended and deseasonalized series, and then the trend and seasonality can be added back to the forecast.

Choosing Window Width (w)

With moving average forecasting or visualization, the only choice that the user must make is the width of the window (w). As with other data-driven methods, the choice of the smoothing parameter is a balance between under-smoothing and over-smoothing. For visualization (using a centered window), wider windows will expose more global trends, while narrow windows will reveal local trend. Hence, examining several window widths is useful for exploring trends of different local/global nature. For forecasting (using a trailing window), the choice should incorporate some domain knowledge in terms of relevance of past observations and how fast the series changes. Empirical predictive evaluation can also be done by experimenting with different values of w and comparing performance. However, care should be taken not to overfit the training and/or test series.

Note: A trailing moving average with $w = 1$ generates naive forecasts, while $w = n$ (the length of the training period) means using the average of the series over the entire training period.

5.3 *Differencing*

A simple and popular method for removing a trend and/or a seasonal pattern from a series is by the operation of *differencing*. Differencing means taking the difference between two values. A lag-1 difference (also called first difference) means taking the difference between every two consecutive values in the series ($y_t - y_{t-1}$). Differencing at lag-k means subtracting the value from k periods back ($y_t - y_{t-k}$). For example, for a daily series, lag-7 differencing means subtracting from each value (y_t) the value on the same day in the previous week (y_{t-7}).

To remove trends and seasonal patterns we can difference the original time series and obtain a differenced series that lacks trend and seasonality. Lag-1 differencing results in a differenced series that measures the changes from one period to the next.

Removing Trend (De-trending)

Lag-1 differencing is useful for removing a trend. An example of the Amtrak lag-1 differenced series[5] is shown in the bottom left panel of Figure 5.4. Compared to the original series (top left panel), which exhibits a U-shaped trend, the lag-1 differenced series contains no visible trend. One advantage of differencing over other methods (e.g., a regression with a trend — see Chapter 6) is that differencing does not assume that the trend is global, that is, that the trend shape is fixed throughout the entire period.

For quadratic and exponential trends, often another round of lag-1 differencing must be applied in order to remove the trend. This means taking lag-1 differences of the differenced series.

[5] In Python, a lag-1 difference of the Amtrak ridership is created by running `ridership['Ridership'].diff(1)`.

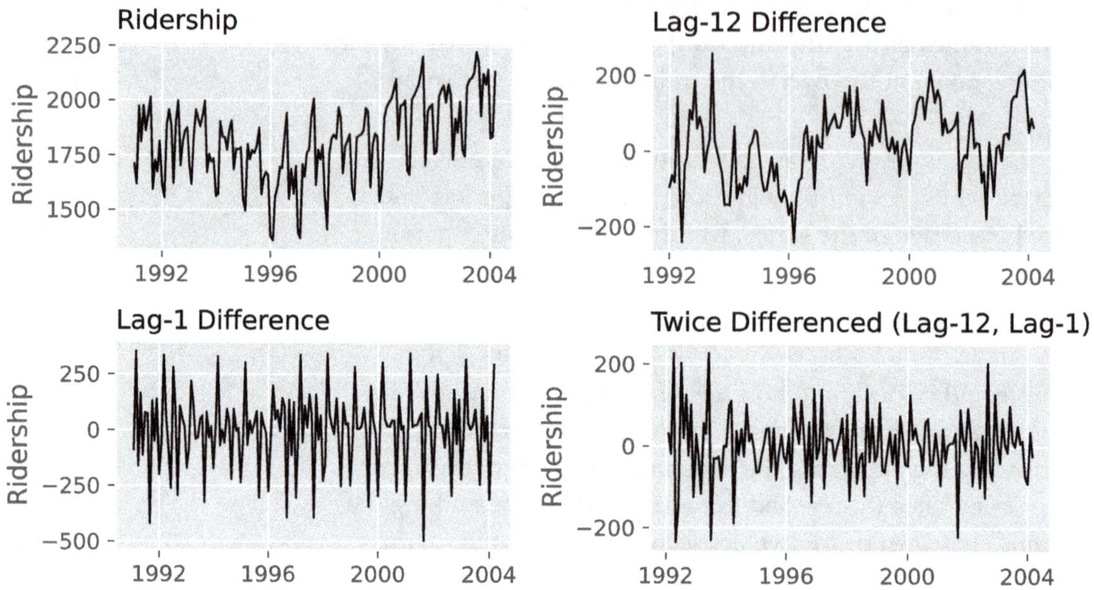

Figure 5.4: Differencing the Amtrak ridership series. Top left: original series with trend and seasonality. Bottom left: lag-1 differenced series. Top right: lag-12 differenced series. Bottom right: twice differenced series (lag-12 then lag-1).

Removing Seasonality (Seasonal Adjustment, Deseasonalizing)

For removing a seasonal pattern with M seasons, we difference at lag M. For example, to remove a day-of-week pattern in daily data, we can take lag-7 differences. Figure 5.4 (top right panel) illustrates a lag-12 differenced series of the Amtrak monthly data.[6] The monthly pattern no longer appears in this differenced series.

[6] In Python, a lag-12 difference of the Amtrak ridership is created by running `ridership['Ridership'].diff(12)`.

Removing Trend and Seasonality

When both trend and seasonality exist, we can apply differencing twice to the series in order to de-trend and deseasonalize it. We performed double differencing on the Amtrak series, which contains both trend and seasonality. The bottom right panel of Figure 5.4 shows the result after first differencing at lag-12, and then applying a lag-1 difference to the differenced series.[7] The result is a series with no trend and no monthly seasonality.

[7] In Python, this twice differencing is created by running `ridership['Ridership'].diff(12).diff(1)`.

Note: Differencing is often used as a pre-processing step before applying a forecasting model to a series. However, when the forecasting method is a data-driven artificial intelligence algorithm such as neural networks (see Chapter 4), differencing appears to produce inferior results as compared to including lag variables as predictors.[8]

[8] N. K. Ahmed, A. F. Atiya, N. El Gayar, and H. El-Shishiny. An empirical comparison of machine learning models for time series forecasting. *Econometric Reviews*, 29:594–621, 2010

5.4 *Simple Exponential Smoothing*

A popular forecasting method in business is exponential smoothing. Its popularity derives from its flexibility, ease of automation, cheap computation, and good performance. Simple exponential smoothing is similar to forecasting with a moving average, except that instead of taking a simple average over the w most recent values, we take a *weighted average* of *all* past values, so that the weights decrease exponentially into the past. The idea is to give more weight to recent information, yet not to completely ignore older information. Like the moving average, simple exponential smoothing should only be used for *forecasting series that have no trend or seasonality*. As mentioned earlier, such series can be obtained by removing trend and/or seasonality from raw series, and then applying exponential smoothing to the series of residuals (which are assumed to contain no trend or seasonality).

The exponential smoother generates a forecast at time $t+1$ (F_{t+1}) as follows:

$$F_{t+1} = \alpha y_t + \alpha(1-\alpha)y_{t-1} + \alpha(1-\alpha)^2 y_{t-2} + \cdots \tag{5.3}$$

where α is a constant between 0 and 1 called the *smoothing constant*. The above formulation displays the exponential smoother as a weighted average of all past observations, with exponentially decaying weights.

We can also write the exponential forecaster in another way, which is very useful in practice:

$$F_{t+1} = F_t + \alpha e_t, \tag{5.4}$$

where e_t is the forecast error at time t. This formulation presents the exponential forecaster as an "active learner". It looks at the previous forecast (F_t) and at its distance from the actual value (e_t), and then corrects the next forecast based on that information. If the forecast was too high in the last period, the subsequent period is adjusted down. The amount of correction depends on the value of the smoothing constant α. The formulation in equation (5.4) is also advantageous in terms of data storage and computation time: we need to store and use only the forecast and forecast error from the previous period, rather than the entire series. In applications where real-time forecasting is done, or many series are being forecasted in parallel and continuously, such savings are critical.

Note that forecasting further into the future yields the same forecasts as a one-step-ahead forecast. Because the series is assumed to lack trend and seasonality, forecasts into the future rely only on information that is available at the time of prediction. Hence, the k-step-ahead forecast is given by $F_{t+k} = F_{t+1}$.

Choosing Smoothing Constant α

The smoothing constant α, which is set by the user, determines the rate of learning. A value close to 1 indicates fast learning (that is, only the most recent values influence the forecasts), whereas a value close to 0 indicates slow learning (past observations have a large influence on forecasts). This can be seen by plugging 0 or 1 into the two equations (5.3) and (5.4). Hence, the choice of α depends on the required amount of smoothing, and on how relevant the history is for generating forecasts. Default values that have been shown to work well are in the range 0.1–0.2. Trial and error can also help in the choice of α. Examine the time plot of the actual and predicted series, as well as the predictive accuracy (e.g., MAPE or RMSE of the test period).

The α value that optimizes one-step-ahead predictive accuracy over the training period can be used to determine the degree of local versus global nature of the level. However, beware of choosing the "best α" for forecasting, as this can lead to model overfitting and low predictive accuracy over the test period and/or future.

In Python, forecasting using simple exponential smoothing can be done via the *ExponentialSmoothing* forecaster in `sktime.forecasting.exp_smoothing`. Applying this function to a time series will yield forecasts and forecast errors (residuals) for both the training and test periods. You can use *ExponentialSmoothing* with a default value of `alpha` = 0.2 ($\alpha = 0.2$), set `alpha` to another value or, alternatively, use *AutoETS* to find the optimal α in terms of minimizing RMSE over the training period.[9]

Next we compare the performance of the simple exponential smoothing model with α=0.2 to the one with an optimally chosen α. Table 5.1 provides a summary of the optimal model, followed by a comparison of its performance to the model with α=0.2. In the case of the twice-differenced Amtrak ridership data, the optimally chosen α is essentially zero ($\alpha = 0.0001$, the smallest possible value of the *AutoETS* function for α). This choice means that the level is global. The global level (also the initial level `l` according to the *AutoETS* forecaster) is 1.6593. Because this level is global, it is the model's forecast for each month in the test period. Compared to the model with α=0.2, the optimal model has a lower RMSE in both the training set and the test set.

We leave it to the reader to investigate the other items provided in the reports from the *AutoETS* and `accuracy` functions.[10]

[9] The *AutoETS* forecaster chooses the optimal α and initial level value by maximizing something called the *likelihood* over the training period. In the case of simple exponential smoothing model, maximizing the *likelihood* is equivalent to minimizing the RMSE in the training period (the RMSE in the training period is equal to σ, the standard deviation of the training residuals).

[10] See the online textbook *Forecasting: Principles and Practice* by Hyndman and Athanasopoulos at `www.otexts.org/fpp`.

Link Between Moving Average and Simple Exponential Smoothing

In both the moving average and simple exponential smoothing methods, the user must specify a single parameter: in moving averages, the window width (w); and in exponential smoothing, the smoothing constant (α). In both cases, the parameter determines the importance of fresh information over older information. In fact, the two smoothers are approximately equal if the window width of the moving average is equal to $w = \frac{2}{\alpha} - 1$.

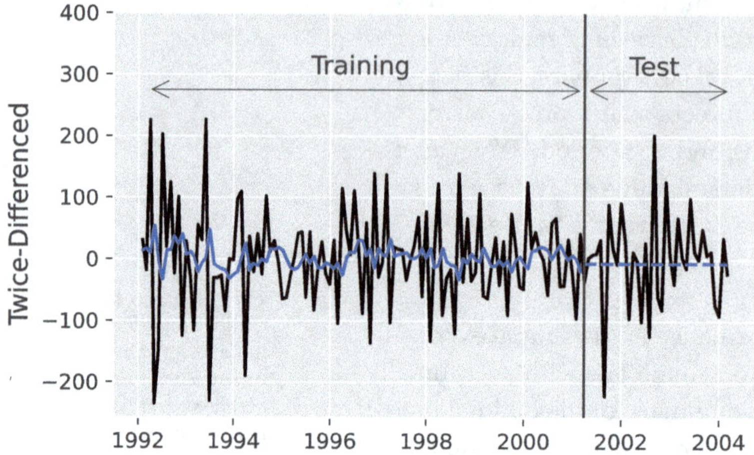

Figure 5.5: Forecasts from a simple exponential smoothing forecaster with α=0.2, applied to the twice-differenced Amtrak ridership data (which lack trend and seasonality).

Code for creating Figure 5.5

See full code at github.com/gshmueli/ptsf-Python

```
from sktime.forecasting.exp_smoothing import ExponentialSmoothing
from sktime.forecasting.model_selection import temporal_train_test_split

diff_twice = ridership.diff(12).diff(1).dropna().copy()
diff_twice.index = diff_twice.index.to_period('M')
N_TEST = 36
diff_twice_train, diff_twice_test = \
    temporal_train_test_split(diff_twice, test_size=N_TEST)

ses = ExponentialSmoothing(smoothing_level=0.2) ## trend=seasonal=None
ses.fit(diff_twice_train)
ses_fitted = ses.predict(diff_twice_train.index)
ses_pred = ses.predict(diff_twice_test.index)

fig, ax = plt.subplots(figsize=(5.5,3.5))
ax = plot_series(diff_twice, ses_fitted, ses_pred, markers=['']*3,
            x_label="", y_label="Twice-Differenced", ax=ax)
ptsf_theme(ax, colors=['black','blue','blue'], idx=[0,1,2], lty=['-','-','--'])
```

The first block of code creates training and test sets with fixed partitioning using the function `temporal_train_test_split`.

The second block creates an SES model with the *ExponentialSmoothing* forecaster. To specify $\alpha = 0.2$ we pass the argument `smoothing_level=0.2`. By default, trend and seasonality are not modeled. The model is fitted to the training data and forecasts are produced for the test period.

The third block plots the three series: actual, fitted, and forecasts.

Model	Series	RMSE	MAE	MAPE	MASE
α=0.2	Training	90.8	68.0	225	0.658
α=0.2	test	76.0	54.9	178	0.531
Opt. α	Training	82.8	62.9	106	0.609
Opt. α	test	75.8	53.0	112	0.513

Table 5.1: Comparison of performance of two simple exponential smoothing models (α = 0.2 and optimal α), fit to the twice-differenced Amtrak ridership data.

Code for creating Table 5.1

See full code at github.com/gshmueli/ptsf-Python

```
from sktime.performance_metrics.forecasting import mean_absolute_error, mean_squared_error, \
        mean_absolute_percentage_error, mean_absolute_scaled_error

def accuracy_df(method, y, y_pred, y_train):
    metrics = {'RMSE': np.sqrt(mean_squared_error(y, y_pred)), 'MAE': mean_absolute_error(y, y_pred),
        'MAPE': mean_absolute_percentage_error(y, y_pred),
        'MASE': mean_absolute_scaled_error(y_true=y, y_pred=y_pred, y_train=y_train) }
    return pd.DataFrame(metrics, index=[method])

ses = ExponentialSmoothing(smoothing_level=0.2) ## trend=seasonal=None
ses.fit(diff_twice_train)
ses_fitted = ses.predict(diff_twice_train.index)
ses_pred = ses.predict(diff_twice_test.index)

ses_opt = AutoETS(auto=False, trend=None, seasonal=None, return_params=False, n_jobs=-1)
ses_opt.fit(diff_twice_train)
ses_opt_fitted = ses_opt.predict(diff_twice_train.index)
ses_opt_pred = ses_opt.predict(diff_twice_test.index)

pd.concat([accuracy_df("Training", diff_twice_train, ses_fitted, diff_twice_train), \
           accuracy_df("Test", diff_twice_test, ses_pred, diff_twice_train), \
           accuracy_df("Training", diff_twice_train, ses_opt_fitted, diff_twice_train), \
           accuracy_df("Test", diff_twice_test, ses_opt_pred, diff_twice_train)])
```

The first block of code creates a custom function `accuracy_df` to compute the performance metrics: RMSE, MAE, MAPE and MASE. It returns a one-row DataFrame.
The second block creates and fits a simple exponential smoothing model with $\alpha = 0.2$ and computes the fitted and forecast values.
The third block creates and fits the optimal simple exponential smoothing model.
The final block assembles the metrics in a table to allow for comparison between the training and test periods and between the two models.

5.5 *Advanced Exponential Smoothing*

As mentioned earlier, both moving average and simple exponential smoothing should only be used for forecasting series with no trend or seasonality; that is, for series that have only a level and noise. One solution for forecasting series with trend and/or seasonality is first to remove those components (e.g., via differencing). Another solution is to use a more sophisticated version of exponential smoothing, which can capture trend and/or seasonality.

Series with an Additive Trend

For series that contain a trend, we can use *double exponential smoothing*, also called Holt's linear trend model. The trend in this model is not assumed to be global, but rather it can change over time.[11] In double exponential smoothing, the local trend is estimated from the data and is updated as more data becomes available. Similar to simple exponential smoothing, the level of the series is also estimated from the data, and is updated as more data becomes available. The k-step-ahead forecast is given by combining the level estimate at time t (L_t) and the trend estimate (which is assumed additive) at time t (T_t):

$$F_{t+k} = L_t + kT_t. \tag{5.5}$$

Note that in the presence of a trend, one-, two-, three-step-ahead (etc.) forecasts are no longer identical. The level and trend are updated through a pair of updating equations:

$$L_t = \alpha y_t + (1-\alpha)(L_{t-1} + T_{t-1}), \tag{5.6}$$
$$T_t = \beta(L_t - L_{t-1}) + (1-\beta)T_{t-1}. \tag{5.7}$$

The first equation means that the level at time t is a weighted average of the actual value at time t and the level in the previous period, adjusted for trend (in the presence of a trend, moving from one period to the next requires factoring in the trend). The second equation means that the trend at time t is a weighted average of the trend in the previous period and the more recent information on the change in level.[12]-1in]There are various ways

[11] This is in contrast to linear regression — see Chapter 6.

[12] [

to estimate the initial values L_0 and T_0, but the difference between estimates usually disappears after a few periods. `sktime`'s *AutoETS* forecaster uses the term `smoothing_level` for α, `smoothing_trend` for β, `initial_level` for L_0 and `initial_trend` for T_0. (See the `summary` method of *AutoETS*). Two smoothing constants, α and β, determine the rate of learning. As in simple exponential smoothing, they are both constants between 0 and 1, set by the user, with higher values giving faster learning (more weight to most recent information).

Before moving on to discuss another type of trend, we introduce the two types of errors an exponential smoothing model can capture. The first type is an additive error. It means that y_t consists not only of level+trend but also an additional error:

$$y_t = L_t + T_t + e_t. \tag{5.8}$$

In the additive error case, the errors are assumed to have a fixed magnitude, irrespective of the current level+trend of the series. If, however, it is more reasonable that the size of the error grows as the level of the series increases, then we will want to use a multiplicative error:

$$y_t = (L_t + T_t) \times (1 + e_t). \tag{5.9}$$

Here the error acts as a percentage increase in the current level-plus-trend. In `sktime`'s *AutoETS*, we can choose to include either an additive error or a multiplicative error in an additive trend model (without seasonality). To do so, we include either the option `error="add"` or `error="mul"` when we specify the model using *AutoETS* . For example, for a model with additive error, additive trend, and no seasonality, we use the following statement: `AutoETS(auto=False, error="add", trend="add")`.

Series with a Multiplicative Trend

The additive trend model assumes that the level changes from one period to the next by a fixed amount. Hence, the forecasting equation (5.5) adds k trend estimates. In contrast, a multiplicative trend model assumes that the level changes from one period to the next by a factor. Exponential smoothing with a multiplicative trend therefore produces k-step-ahead forecasts using the formula

$$F_{t+k} = L_t \times T_t^k. \tag{5.10}$$

and the updating equations for the level and trend are

$$L_t = \alpha y_t + (1-\alpha)(L_{t-1} \times T_{t-1}), \tag{5.11}$$
$$T_t = \beta(L_t/L_{t-1}) + (1-\beta)T_{t-1}. \tag{5.12}$$

As with the additive trend model, we can include either an additive or multiplicative error in the multiplicative trend model. The additive error takes the form

$$y_t = L_t \times T_t + e_t, \tag{5.13}$$

while the multiplicative error takes the form

$$y_t = (L_t \times T_t) \times (1 + e_t). \tag{5.14}$$

With the *AutoETS* forecaster in `sktime`, we can use the multiplicative trend model by specifying the argument `trend="mul"`. For example, to estimate an ETS model with additive error, multiplicative trend, and no seasonality, we use the following model specification: `AutoETS(auto=False, error="add", trend="mul")` (for multiplicative error, use `error="mul"`).

Series with a Trend and Seasonality

For series that contain both trend and seasonality, the *Holt-Winters exponential smoothing* method can be used. This is a further extension of double exponential smoothing, where the k-step-ahead forecast also takes into account the season at period $t + k$. Just like for trend, there exist formulations for additive and multiplicative seasonality. In *multiplicative seasonality*, values on different seasons differ by percentage amounts, whereas in *additive seasonality*, they differ by a fixed amount.

Assuming seasonality with M seasons (e.g., for daily series with weekly seasonality $M = 7$), the forecast for an additive trend and multiplicative seasonality is given by:

$$F_{t+k} = (L_t + kT_t)S_{t+k-M}. \tag{5.15}$$

Note that in order to produce forecasts using this formula, the series must have included at least one full cycle of seasons by the forecasting time t, i.e., $t > M$.

Being an adaptive method, Holt-Winters exponential smoothing allows the level, trend, and seasonality patterns to change over time. The three components are estimated and updated as new information arrives. The updating equations for this additive trend and multiplicative seasonality version are given by:

$$L_t = \alpha y_t / S_{t-M} + (1-\alpha)(L_{t-1} + T_{t-1}) \quad (5.16)$$
$$T_t = \beta(L_t - L_{t-1}) + (1-\beta)T_{t-1} \quad (5.17)$$
$$S_t = \gamma\,(y_t / L_t) + (1-\gamma)S_{t-M}. \quad (5.18)$$

The first equation is similar to that in double exponential smoothing, except that it uses the seasonally adjusted value at time t rather than the raw value. This is done by dividing y_t by its seasonal index, as estimated in the last cycle. The second equation is identical to double exponential smoothing. The third equation means that the seasonal index is updated by taking a weighted average of the seasonal index from the previous cycle and the current trend-adjusted value.

The *additive seasonality* version of Holt-Winters exponential smoothing, where seasons differ by a constant amount, can be constructed from the multiplicative version by replacing multiplication/division signs by addition/subtraction signs for the seasonal component:

$$F_{t+k} = L_t + kT_t + S_{t+k-M} \quad (5.19)$$
$$L_t = \alpha\,(y_t - S_{t-M}) + (1-\alpha)(L_{t-1} + T_{t-1}) \quad (5.20)$$
$$T_t = \beta(L_t - L_{t-1}) + (1-\beta)T_{t-1} \quad (5.21)$$
$$S_t = \gamma\,(y_t - L_t) + (1-\gamma)S_{t-M}. \quad (5.22)$$

To illustrate forecasting a series with an additive trend and additive seasonality using the Holt-Winters method, consider the raw Amtrak ridership data. As we observed earlier, the data contains both a trend and monthly seasonality. Figure 5.6 depicts the fitted and forecasted values from the *AutoETS* function in `sktime`. We chose to include a multiplicative error in the model.

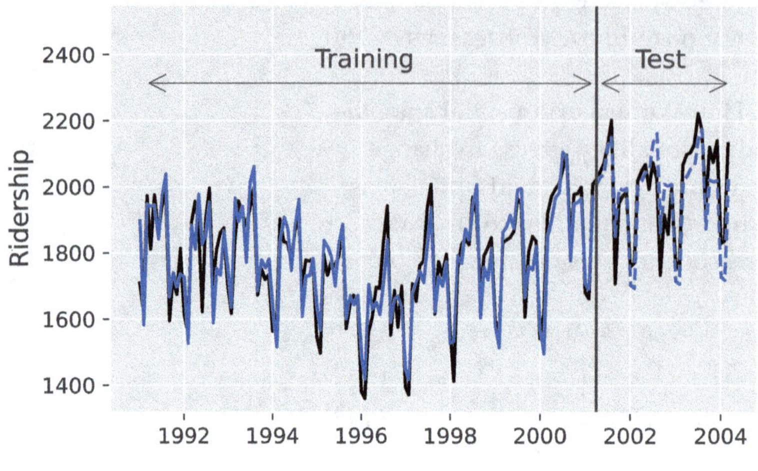

Figure 5.6: Forecasts from the Holt-Winters exponential smoothing model applied to the Amtrak ridership series.

Code for creating Figure 5.6 and Table 5.2

See full code at github.com/gshmueli/ptsf-Python

```
y = ridership.copy() ## shorter name
y.index = y.index.to_period('M')
n_test = 36
y_train, y_test = temporal_train_test_split(y, test_size=n_test)

hwin = AutoETS(auto=False, error="mul", trend="add", seasonal="add", sp=12, n_jobs=-1)
hwin.fit(y_train)
hwin_fitted = hwin.predict(y_train.index)
hwin_pred = hwin.predict(y_test.index)

fig, ax = plt.subplots(figsize=(5.5,3.5))
ax = plot_series(y, hwin_fitted, hwin_pred, markers=['']*3,
            x_label="", y_label="Ridership", ax=ax)
ptsf_theme(ax, colors=['black','blue','blue'], idx=[0,1,2], lty=['-','-','--'])

hwin = AutoETS(auto=False, error="mul", trend="add", seasonal="add", sp=12, n_jobs=-1)
hwin.fit(y_train)
print(hwin.summary())
```

The first block creates the training and test sets.
The second block creates an "MAA" Holt-Winters model, i.e. with multiplicative error, additive trend and additive seasonality. The argument `sp=12` specifies that the seasonal period is 12 months. As we have seen previously, we use the methods `fit` and `predict` to do the fitting and forecasting, respectively.
The third block plots the three series: actual, fitted, and forecasts.
The final block generates the output in Table 5.2.

Table 5.2 presents a summary of the model in Figure 5.6. The middle table shows the three smoothing parameters and the initial states of the level, trend, and seasonal components. Because α (`smoothing_level`) is far from zero, we conclude that the level adapts locally, while the trend and seasonality are global (β - `smoothing_trend` and γ - `smoothing_seasonality` are both near zero). The initial seasonal indexes (in the middle table) are in the following order from the beginning of the training set: `initial_seasonal.11` for January 1991, `initial_seasonal.10` for Feb 1991, ..., and `initial_seasonal.0` for Dec 1991. The states for the final 12 months of the training period are shown in the bottom table (the corresponding month is in the left column).[13] A comparison of the initial and final states indicates that the seasonality indices have changed very little from their initial estimates. In addition to identifying a global seasonal pattern, we notice that the trough and peak seasons are February and August, respectively. February (initial_seasonal.10) has 43.81 thousand riders less than January (the reference month), while August (initial_seasonal.4) has 414.19 thousand more riders than January.

[13] The seasonal indexes, as computed by `AutoETS`, are interpreted as the season's difference from a reference category. Here, January (`initial_seasonal.11`) is the reference category (as can be seen by its 0 index).

5.6 *Summary of Exponential Smoothing Using* AutoETS

For the additive seasonality and multiplicative seasonality versions of the exponential smoothing model introduced above, we can include either an additive or multiplicative error. We can also specify an additive trend, a multiplicative trend, or no trend at all. This flexibility of the *AutoETS* class in Python gives us 18 model choices: 2 error types × 3 trend types × 3 seasonality types.

There is another trend type that the *AutoETS* class allows: the additive damped trend (`Ad`). This trend type applies to time series whose trends will eventually dampen to a flat line in the distant future.[14] With this additional trend type, the number of possible models the *AutoETS* class can fit increases to 24. These models are summarized in Table 5.3 where the error (`Z`) can be either set to additive (`A`) or multiplicative (`M`).

[14] For more information on this trend type, see Section 8/2 of the online textbook *Forecasting: Principles and Practice* by Hyndman and Athanasopoulos at `www.otexts.com/fpp3/holt.html`.

Some comments regarding the *AutoETS* forecaster are in place. *AutoETS* by default restricts the use of some models in Ta-

```
                                 ETS Results
==============================================================================
Dep. Variable:                      y   No. Observations:                  123
Model:                        ETS(MAA)  Log Likelihood                -668.907
Date:                 Wed, 30 Apr 2025  AIC                           1373.815
Time:                         21:39:42  BIC                           1424.434
Sample:                     01-31-1991  HQIC                          1394.376
                          - 03-31-2001  Scale                            0.001
Covariance Type:                approx
=========================================================================================
                            coef    std err          z      P>|z|      [0.025      0.975]
-----------------------------------------------------------------------------------------
smoothing_level           0.5635      0.095      5.945      0.000       0.378       0.749
smoothing_trend        5.635e-05        nan        nan        nan         nan         nan
smoothing_seasonal     4.365e-05        nan        nan        nan         nan         nan
initial_level          1681.8735   6.78e+04      0.025      0.980   -1.31e+05    1.35e+05
initial_trend             0.9025      2.845      0.317      0.751      -4.673       6.478
initial_seasonal.0      241.7333   6.78e+04      0.004      0.997   -1.33e+05    1.33e+05
initial_seasonal.1      203.9839   6.78e+04      0.003      0.998   -1.33e+05    1.33e+05
initial_seasonal.2      214.2249   6.78e+04      0.003      0.997   -1.33e+05    1.33e+05
initial_seasonal.3       92.4909   6.78e+04      0.001      0.999   -1.33e+05    1.33e+05
initial_seasonal.4      414.1855   6.78e+04      0.006      0.995   -1.32e+05    1.33e+05
initial_seasonal.5      362.5427   6.78e+04      0.005      0.996   -1.32e+05    1.33e+05
initial_seasonal.6      251.3476   6.78e+04      0.004      0.997   -1.33e+05    1.33e+05
initial_seasonal.7      291.8162   6.78e+04      0.004      0.997   -1.33e+05    1.33e+05
initial_seasonal.8      257.8401   6.78e+04      0.004      0.997   -1.33e+05    1.33e+05
initial_seasonal.9      256.5485   6.78e+04      0.004      0.997   -1.33e+05    1.33e+05
initial_seasonal.10     -43.8074   6.78e+04     -0.001      0.999   -1.33e+05    1.33e+05
initial_seasonal.11            0   6.78e+04          0      1.000   -1.33e+05    1.33e+05
==========================================================================================

Final states:
=============
               level     trend    seasonal
Month
2000-04  1684.079401  0.892802  257.839663
2000-05  1693.713786  0.893676  291.815275
2000-06  1730.563554  0.897272  251.344940
2000-07  1708.918058  0.895017  362.541398
2000-08  1694.865889  0.893523  414.184414
2000-09  1715.738294  0.895521   92.490442
2000-10  1742.631441  0.898120  214.225688
2000-11  1762.628073  0.900030  203.984671
2000-12  1760.649580  0.899742  241.733358
2001-01  1717.371713  0.895325   -0.000153
2001-02  1712.037410  0.894702  -43.807434
2001-03  1734.595832  0.896868  256.549692
```

Table 5.2: Summary of a Holt-Winters exponential smoothing model applied to the Amtrak ridership data. Included are the initial and final states.

Trend	Seasonality None	Additive	Multiplicative
None	ZNN	ZNA	ZNM
Additive	ZAN	ZAA	ZAM
Multiplicative	ZMN	ZMA	ZMM
Additive damped	ZAdN	ZAdA	ZAdM

Table 5.3: Possible exponential smoothing models in *AutoETS* where `Z` can be set to `A` or `M`, corresponding to additive or multiplicative error, respectively.

ble 5.3. It does so because some combinations of error, trend, and seasonality can cause numerical difficulties when fit to some time series ("models of infinite variance"). For instance, the *AutoETS* class will not consider `AAM`, `AMA`, `AMM`, or `MMA` models unless we turn the restriction off by passing the argument `restrict = False`. When fitting a restricted model, check that the results seem plausible. The forecaster will also not consider multiplicative trend models unless you set `allow_multiplicative_trend = True`.

Automated Model Selection in AutoETS

If you do not know which model to choose, you can request the *AutoETS* forecaster to do automated model selection. By setting the argument `auto = True`, the forecaster will fit several models and choose the "best" one. As mentioned earlier, some models are restricted by default and to include them in the search requires the overriding of the defaults.

How does *AutoETS* define "best" for choosing between models with different numbers of parameters? It uses a criterion called Akaike's Information Criterion (AIC),[15] which combines fit to the training data with a penalty for the number of smoothing parameters and initial values (L_0, T_0, etc.) included in a model. The AIC criterion penalizes a model for having a poor fit to the training period and for being more complicated. Recall that simpler models (those with few smoothing parameters/initial states) can help avoid overfitting a model to the training period and hence can improve predictions in the test period or the future.

[15] AIC is defined as:

$$AIC = -log(likelihood) + 2p$$

where *likelihood* is a measure of fit to the training period and p is the number of smoothing parameters and initial states in the model. The concept is similar to adjusted-R^2 used in regression models, which combines the model's fit with a penalty on the number of parameters.

The output from applying automated model selection to the Amtrak ridership data is shown in Table 5.4. The selected `MNA` model has multiplicative error, no trend, and additive seasonality. Its AIC is 1369.9, which is 3.9 lower than the `MAA` model fit using the Python code for creating Figure 5.6.

As a rule of thumb, an AIC difference between 0 and 2 does not favor one model or the other. Here, an AIC difference of 3.9 weakly favors the `MNA` model. A more careful study of the output in Table 5.2 indicates it it is essentially equivalent to an `MNA` model, specified as an `MAA` model. The `initial_trend` is 0.9, which is less than 0.0006 of the average level and the confidence interval for the initial trend includes 0. The value of β (`smoothing_trend`) for the `MAA` model is close to 0, indicating the trend's initial value does not change. Together, these observations indicate a series with no trend, that is, an `MNA` model.[16] The best comparison would be between the test performance of the two models.

Finally, a word of caution about automated model selection is in order. Although it can be tempting to automate the hard work of model selection,[17] our practical experience suggests that it is better to compare the performance of several models on the test set (using either fixed or roll-forward partitioning) whenever possible. On the basis of these out-of-sample predictions, you might choose the best model (or an average of the better models) for forecasting the future. Indeed, we see from Table 5.5 that the manually selected `MAA` model outperforms the automatically selected `MNA` model when comparing their RMSEs in the test set.

[16] Theoretically, the AIC for an `MAA` model applied to data with no trend should differ from the AIC for the corresponding `MNA` model by 4, equivalent to 2 × (2 extra parameters). Hence the 3.9 value that we see.

[17] Automation is inevitable in applications that require forecasting many series.

Table 5.4: Automated model selection applied to the Amtrak ridership data.

```
                                 ETS Results
==============================================================================
Dep. Variable:                      y   No. Observations:                  123
Model:                       ETS(MNA)   Log Likelihood                -668.937
Date:                Wed, 30 Apr 2025   AIC                           1369.874
Time:                        22:00:20   BIC                           1414.869
Sample:                    01-31-1991   HQIC                          1388.151
                         - 03-31-2001   Scale                            0.001
Covariance Type:               approx
=======================================================================================
                          coef    std err          z      P>|z|      [0.025      0.975]
---------------------------------------------------------------------------------------
smoothing_level         0.5645      0.099      5.718      0.000       0.371       0.758
smoothing_seasonal   4.355e-05        nan        nan        nan         nan         nan
initial_level        1686.3377   8.85e+04      0.019      0.985   -1.72e+05    1.75e+05
initial_seasonal.0    242.3147   8.85e+04      0.003      0.998   -1.73e+05    1.74e+05
initial_seasonal.1    204.5743   8.85e+04      0.002      0.998   -1.73e+05    1.74e+05
initial_seasonal.2    215.0409   8.85e+04      0.002      0.998   -1.73e+05    1.74e+05
initial_seasonal.3     93.8395   8.85e+04      0.001      0.999   -1.73e+05    1.74e+05
initial_seasonal.4    415.1497   8.85e+04      0.005      0.996   -1.73e+05    1.74e+05
initial_seasonal.5    364.9590   8.85e+04      0.004      0.997   -1.73e+05    1.74e+05
initial_seasonal.6    253.8604   8.85e+04      0.003      0.998   -1.73e+05    1.74e+05
initial_seasonal.7    294.0880   8.85e+04      0.003      0.997   -1.73e+05    1.74e+05
initial_seasonal.8    259.6486   8.85e+04      0.003      0.998   -1.73e+05    1.74e+05
initial_seasonal.9    257.9031   8.85e+04      0.003      0.998   -1.73e+05    1.74e+05
initial_seasonal.10   -42.3007   8.85e+04     -0.000      1.000   -1.74e+05    1.73e+05
initial_seasonal.11          0   8.85e+04          0      1.000   -1.74e+05    1.74e+05
==================================================================================
```

Code for creating Table 5.4

See full code at github.com/gshmueli/ptsf-Python

```
hwin_auto = AutoETS(auto=True, sp=12)
hwin_auto.fit(y_train)
print(hwin_auto._fitted_forecaster.summary())
```

Model	Data	RMSE	MAE	MAPE	MASE
Manual	Training	55.9	44.2	2.52	0.353
Manual	Test	76.7	62.4	3.14	0.498
Optimal	Training	55.9	44.3	2.52	0.353
Optimal	Test	87.8	73.1	3.67	0.583

Table 5.5: Comparison of manual and automated model selection, applied to the Amtrak ridership data.

5.7 *Extensions of Exponential Smoothing*

Multiple Seasonal Cycles

In some applications, the resulting time series contain multiple seasonal cycles such as both daily and monthly seasonality, or hourly and daily seasonality. One example is electricity demand, which often exhibits a day-of-week cycle as well as a within-day cycle. Other examples include call center arrivals where operating hours differ on weekdays and weekends,[18] hospital admissions, and transportation and internet traffic.

We can generate forecasts for series with multiple seasonal cycles by combining exponential smoothing (function `ETS`) or ARIMA (see Chapter 7) with the STL method (function `STL`). The STL method decomposes a time series into seasonal, trend, and error components using Loess.[19] Once the time series is decomposed, the seasonal component is subtracted from the time series to obtain a deseasonalized series. We can then use exponential smoothing or ARIMA to generate forecasts for the deseasonalized series. Finally, the resulting forecasted values are re-seasonalized by adding a seasonal naive forecast using the seasonal component.

We apply this method to a popular dataset on hourly Bike Sharing.[20] This data was downloaded from UCI's Machine Learning Repository.[21] The file `BikeSharingHourly.csv` has hourly counts of bike rentals from Capital Bikeshare in Washington, D.C. between 2011 and 2012. For illustration, we focus on hourly rentals during the month of July 2012. We start by looking at time plots of the series. Figure 5.7 displays the three-week training period (top) and a zoomed-in plot of four days.

From these plots, we see that the bike rentals series has two seasonal cycles: weekly (day-of-week) and daily (hour-of-day). With the information about the two cycles (weekly and daily), we now train the model on the first 21 days of hourly rentals (504 hours), and then forecast the next 10 days of hourly rentals (240 hours). The result is shown in Figure 5.8.

[18] J. W. Taylor and R. D. Snyder. Forecasting intraday time series with multiple seasonal cycles using parsimonious seasonal exponential smoothing. *Omega*, 40(6):748–757, 2012

[19] Loess is a non-linear regression technique.

[20] H. Fanaee-T and J. Gama. Event labeling combining ensemble detectors and background knowledge. *Progress in Artificial Intelligence*, pages 1–15, 2013

[21] `archive.ics.uci.edu/ml/datasets/Bike+Sharing+Dataset`

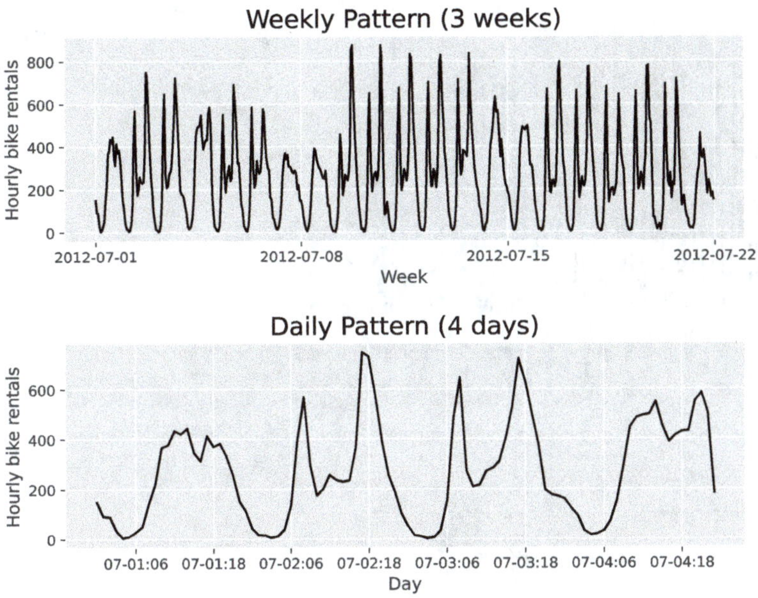

Figure 5.7: Hourly counts of bike rentals. Top: three weeks of data. Bottom: zoom-in to four days. The plots show a weekly weekend trough (top) and a daily trough/peak/peak of 4am/8am/6pm (bottom).

Code for creating Figure 5.7

See full code at github.com/gshmueli/ptsf-Python

```
bike_df = pd.read_csv('ptsf-Python/Data/BikeSharingHourly.csv',parse_dates=True,index_col=1)
rides = bike_df['cnt'].to_frame()
rides = rides.truncate(before='2012-07-01').truncate(after='2012-07-31')
date_range = pd.date_range(start=rides.index.min(),
            end=rides.index.min()+pd.Timedelta(hours=24*31-1), freq='H')
rides.index = date_range
rides_train = rides.iloc[:(21*24),:] # 3 weeks
rides_zoom = rides.iloc[:(4*24)] # 4 days

# create a figure with two plots stacked vertically
fig, ax = plt.subplots(nrows=2, ncols=1, figsize=(8.5,6.5))

ax[0] = plot_series(rides_train, markers=[''], x_label='Week', y_label="Hourly bike rentals",
                title='Weekly Pattern (3 weeks)', colors=['black'], ax=ax[0])

ax[1] = plot_series(rides_zoom, markers=[''], x_label='Day', y_label="Hourly bike rentals",
                title='Daily Pattern (4 days)', colors=['black'], ax=ax[1])
```

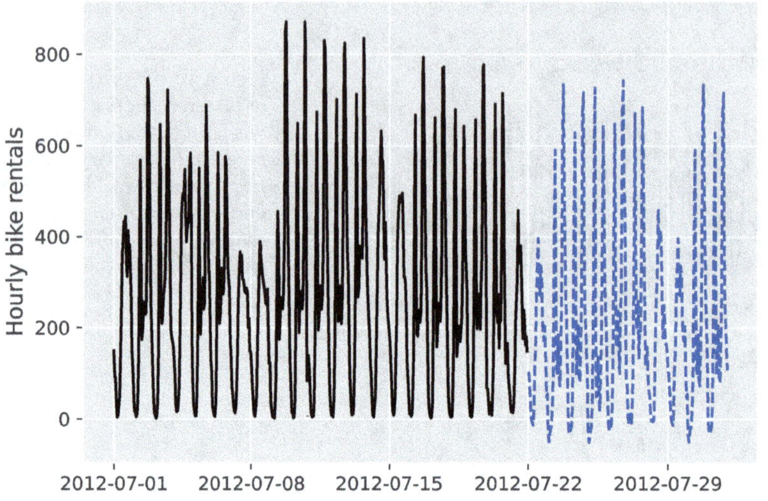

Figure 5.8: Forecasts from the STL decomposition + exponential smoothing applied to the bike sharing series. Dashed blue line indicates forecasts.

Code for creating Figure 5.8

See full code at github.com/gshmueli/ptsf-Python

```
from sktime.transformations.series.detrend.mstl import MSTL
mstl = MSTL(periods=np.array([24, 7*24]), return_components=False)
deseas = mstl.fit(rides_train).transform(rides_train)

fh = ForecastingHorizon(np.arange(1,241,1), is_relative=True) ## 10 days = 240 hourly forecasts
deseas_pred = AutoETS(auto=False, seasonal=None, n_jobs=-1).fit(deseas).predict(fh)

daily_pred = NaiveForecaster(strategy="last",sp=24).fit(mstl.seasonal_['seasonal_24']).predict(fh)
weekly_pred = NaiveForecaster(strategy="last",sp=7*24).fit(mstl.seasonal_['seasonal_168']).predict(fh)

pred = deseas_pred['cnt'].add(daily_pred).add(weekly_pred)

plot_series(rides_train, pred, markers=['',''], y_label="Hourly bike rentals", ax=ax)
```

The first code block creates an STL object with daily and weekly periods and fits it to the training data. It then extracts the deseasonalized series.
The second block fits a double exponential model (i.e. without seasonality) to the deseasonalized series, and computes forecasts for the next 10 days (240 hourly forecasts).
The third block uses Seasonal Naive forecasters with daily and weekly seasonality to compute the corresponding seasonal adjustments for the next 10 days.
The fourth block adds the seasonal adjustments to the deseasonalized forecasts.
The final block plots the training data and the subsequent 10-day forecasts.

Adaptive Smoothing Constants

The smoothing constants (α, β, γ) in exponential smoothing are fixed (hence the term "constants"), so that their value does not change over time. There have been several attempts to incorporate time-varying smoothing constants, to further increase the flexibility of the exponential smoothing algorithm in adapting to changes in the time series characteristics over time.

One example is the "smooth transition exponential smoothing" (STES) approach by Taylor (2004)[22] where the smoothing constant for simple exponential smoothing is given by the logit function (which is restricted to the range 0–1):

[22] J. W. Taylor. Smooth transition exponential smoothing. *Journal of Forecasting*, 23:385–394, 2004

$$\alpha_t = \frac{1}{1 + exp\{a + bV_t\}}, \qquad (5.23)$$

where V_t is a user-specified transition variable, which "is of crucial importance to the success of the method" (Taylor suggests using the square or the absolute value of the forecast error from the most recent period). The parameters a, b are estimated from the training period.

Reported empirical performance of the various proposed methods shows mixed and sometimes contradictory results: forecast accuracy improves in some cases but drops dramatically in others. For more information, see Gardner (2006).[23]

[23] E. J. Gardner. Exponential smoothing: The state of the art - Part II. *International Journal of Forecasting*, 22:637–666, 2006

5.8 Problems

1. *Impact of September 11 on Air Travel in the United States:* The Research and Innovative Technology Administration's Bureau of Transportation Statistics (BTS) conducted a study to evaluate the impact of the September 11, 2001, terrorist attack on U.S. transportation. The study report and the data can be found at `www.bts.gov/archive/publications/estimated_impacts_of_9_11_on_us_travel/index`. The goal of the study was stated as follows:

   > The purpose of this study is to provide a greater understanding of the passenger travel behavior patterns of persons making long distance trips before and after September 11.

   The report analyzes monthly passenger movement data between January 1990 and April 2004. Data on three monthly time series are given in the file *Sept11Travel.csv* for this period: (1) actual airline revenue passenger miles (Air), (2) rail passenger miles (Rail), and (3) vehicle miles traveled (Auto).

   In order to assess the impact of September 11, BTS took the following approach: Using data before September 11, it forecasted future data (under the assumption of no terrorist attack). Then, BTS compared the forecasted series with the actual data to assess the impact of the event. Our first step, therefore, is to split each of the time series into two parts: pre- and post-September 11. We now concentrate only on the earlier time series.

   (a) Create a time plot for the pre-event Air time series. What time series components appear from the plot?

   (b) Figure 5.9 is a time plot of the seasonally adjusted pre-September-11 Air series. Which of the following smoothing methods would be adequate for forecasting this series?

   - Naive forecasts
   - Moving average (with what window width?)
   - Simple exponential smoothing
   - Double exponential smoothing
   - Holt-Winters exponential smoothing

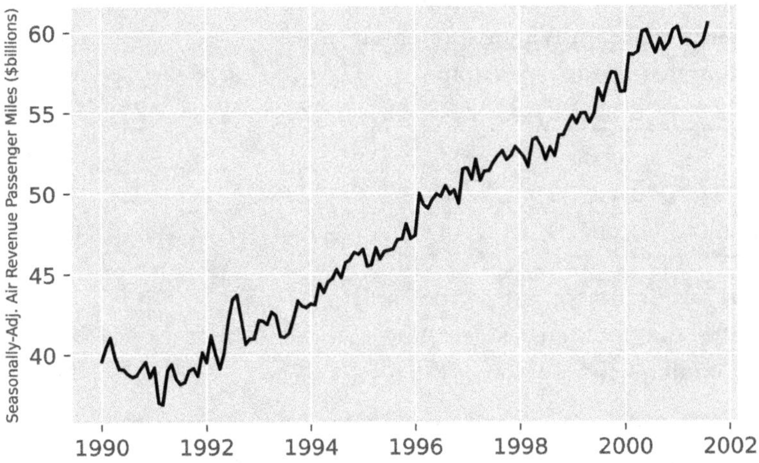

Figure 5.9: Seasonally adjusted pre-September-11 air series.

2. *Relationship between Moving Average and Exponential Smoothing:* Assume that we apply a moving average to a series, using a very short window span. If we wanted to achieve an equivalent result using simple exponential smoothing, what value should the smoothing constant take?

3. *Forecasting with a Moving Average:* For a given time series of sales, the training period consists of 50 months. The first 5 months of data are shown below:

Month	Sales
Sept 98	27
Oct 98	31
Nov 98	58
Dec 98	63
Jan 99	59

   (a) Compute the sales forecast for January 1999 based on a moving average model with span $w = 4$.

   (b) Compute the forecast error for the above forecast.

4. *Optimizing Exponential Smoothing:* The table below shows the optimal smoothing constants from applying exponential smoothing to data, using automated model selection:

Level	1.000
Trend	0.000
Seasonality	0.246

   (a) Using a series partitioned into training/test periods and the *AutoETS* class in `sktime`, the optimized smoothing constants are those that maximize (choose one of the following):
   - The likelihood over the training period
   - The likelihood over the test period
   - The likelihood over the training period with a penalty on the number of parameters
   - The likelihood over the test period with a penalty on the number of parameters

   (b) The value of zero that is obtained for the trend smoothing constant means that (choose one of the following):
   - There is no trend
   - The trend is estimated only from the first two points
   - The trend is updated throughout the data
   - The trend is statistically insignificant

   (c) What is the danger of using the optimal smoothing constant values?

5. *Forecasting Department Store Sales:* The file *DepartmentStore-Sales.csv* contains data on the quarterly sales for a department store over a 6-year period.[24]

   The time plot of the data is shown in Figure 5.10.

[24] Data courtesy of Chris Albright

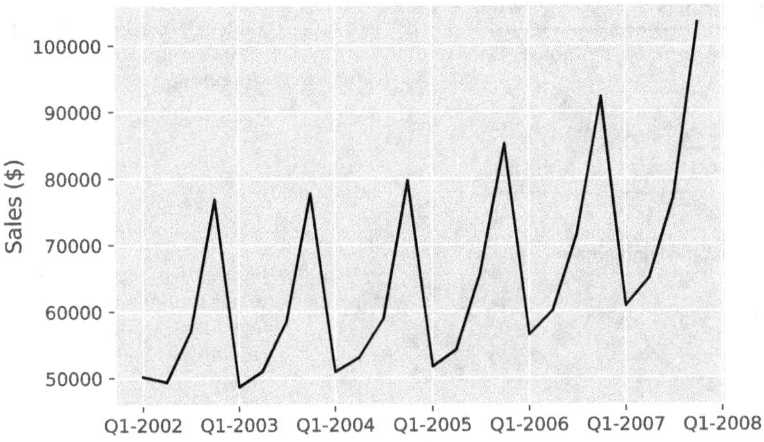

Figure 5.10: Department store quarterly sales series.

(a) Which of the following methods would not be suitable for forecasting this series?

- Moving average of raw series
- Moving average of deseasonalized series
- Simple exponential smoothing of the raw series
- Double exponential smoothing of the raw series
- Holt-Winters exponential smoothing of the raw series

(b) A forecaster was tasked to generate forecasts for four quarters ahead. She therefore partitioned the data so that the last four quarters were designated as the test period. The forecaster approached the forecasting task by using multiplicative Holt-Winters exponential smoothing (`MAA`). The smoothing constants used were $\alpha = 0.2, \beta = 0.15, \gamma = 0.05$.

i. Run this method on the data. Request the forecasts on the test period.

ii. The Holt-Winters forecasts for the test set are given in Table 5.6. Compute the MAPE values for the forecasts of quarters Q1 2007 and Q2 2007.

(c) The fit and residuals are displayed in Figure 5.11. Using all the information from (b) and Figure 5.11, is this model suitable for forecasting quarters Q1 2007 and Q2 2007?

Quarter	Actual	Forecast	Error
2007 Q1	60800	64755.83	-3955.83
2007 Q2	64900	68279.84	-3379.84
2007 Q3	76997	78474.96	-1477.96
2007 Q4	103337	99352.75	3984.25

Table 5.6: Forecasts for test series using exponential smoothing.

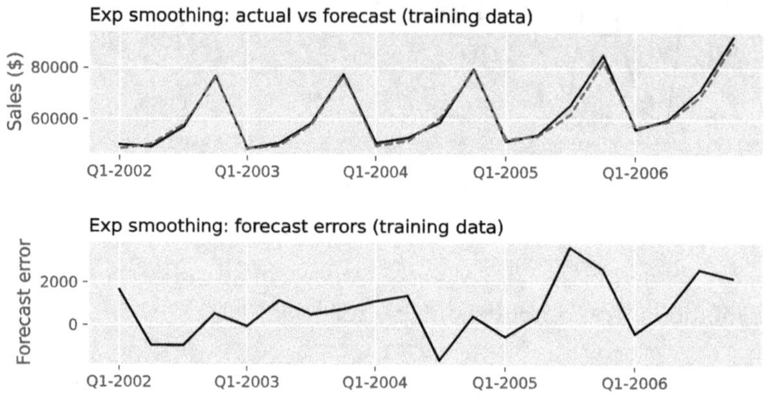

Figure 5.11: Top: Forecasts (dashed line) and actuals (solid line) using exponential smoothing. Bottom: forecast errors.

(d) Another analyst decided to take a much simpler approach, and used differencing instead of exponential smoothing. Use differencing to remove the trend and seasonal pattern. Which order works better: first removing trend and then seasonality, or the opposite order? Show a time plot of your final series.

(e) Forecast quarters Q1 2007 and Q2 2007 using the average of the double-differenced series from (d). Remember to use only the training period (until quarter 20), and to adjust back for the trend and seasonal pattern.[25]

(f) Compare the forecasts from (e) to the exponential smoothing forecasts in the table in (b). Which of the two forecasting methods would you choose? Explain.

(g) What is an even simpler approach that should be compared as a baseline?

[25] *Hint:* to adjust the forecast for trend and seasonality (re-trend and re-seasonalize): If you first differenced to remove trend (D1 series) and then differenced again to remove seasonality (D2 series), then add to your forecast the value in D1 from four quarters ago (re-seasonalize) and the original sales from last quarter (re-trend). Alternatively, if you first differenced to remove seasonality (D1 series) followed by removing trend (D2 series), then add to your forecast the previous value in D1 (re-trend) and the original sales from 4 quarters ago (re-seasonalize).

6. *Shipments of Household Appliances:* The file *ApplianceShipments.csv* contains the series of quarterly shipments (in millions of USD) of U.S. household appliances between 1985 and 1989.[26] A time plot of the data is shown in Figure 5.12.

[26] Data courtesy of Ken Black

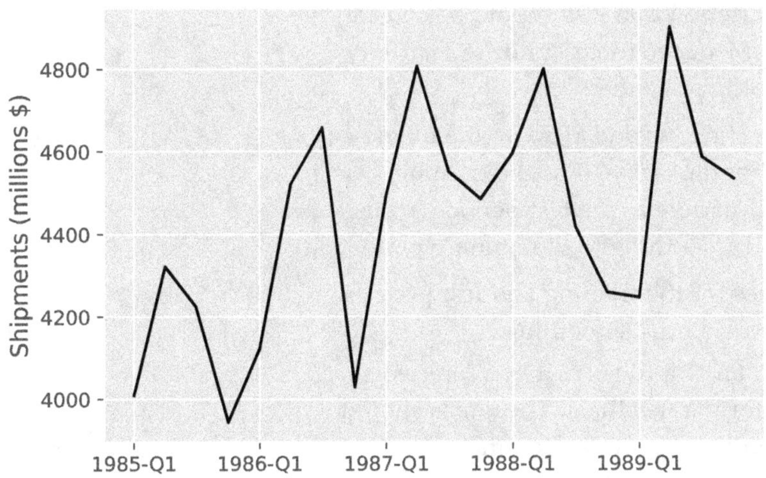

Figure 5.12: Quarterly shipments of U.S. household appliances over five years.

(a) Which of the following methods would be suitable for forecasting this series if applied to the raw data?

- Naive forecasts
- Moving average
- Simple exponential smoothing
- Double exponential smoothing
- Holt-Winters exponential smoothing

(b) Apply a moving average with window span $w = 4$ to the data. Use all but that last year as the training period. Create a time plot of the moving average series.

i. What does the MA(4) chart reveal?

ii. Use the MA(4) model to forecast appliance sales in Q1-1990.

iii. Use the MA(4) model to forecast appliance sales in Q1-1991.

iv. Is the Q1-1990 forecast most likely to underestimate, overestimate, or accurately estimate the actual sales on Q1-1990? Explain.

v. Management feels most comfortable with moving averages. The analyst therefore plans to use this method for forecasting future quarters. What else should be considered before using the MA(4) to forecast future quarterly shipments of household appliances?

(c) We now focus on forecasting beyond 1989. In the following, continue to use all but the last year as the training period and the last four quarters as the test period. Apply Holt-Winters exponential smoothing to the training period.

i. Compute MAPE values for the training and test periods using Holt-Winters exponential smoothing.

ii. Draw two time plots: one for the actual and forecasted values and the other for the residuals. The x-axis should include the training and test periods. Comment on the model fit in the training and test periods.

7. *Forecasting Shampoo Sales:* The time series plot in Figure 5.13 below describes monthly sales of a certain shampoo over a three-year period. Data available in *ShampooSales.csv*.[27]

[27] Source: Hyndman and Yang (2018) tsdl: Time Series Data Library. v0.1.0. `github.com/FinYang/tsdl`.

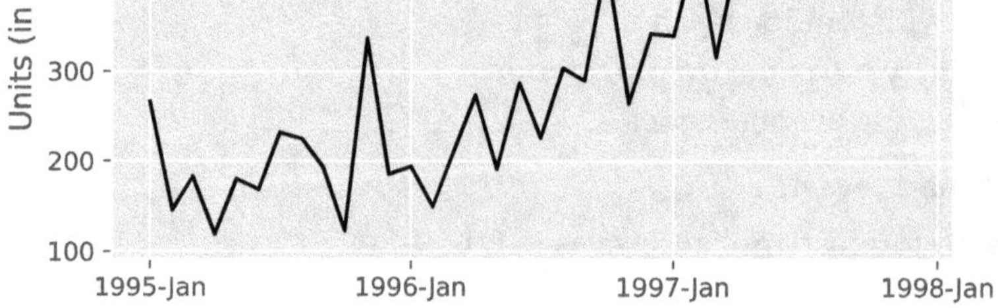

Figure 5.13: Monthly sales of shampoo over three years.

Which of the following methods would be suitable for forecasting this series if applied to the raw data?

- Moving average
- Simple exponential smoothing
- Double exponential smoothing
- Holt-Winters exponential smoothing

8. *Forecasting Australian Wine Sales:* Figure 5.14 shows time plots of monthly sales of six types of Australian wines (red, rose, sweet white, dry white, sparkling, and fortified) for 1980-1994. Data available in *AustralianWines.csv*.[28] The units are thousands of liters. You are hired to obtain short-term forecasts (2–3 months ahead) for each of the six series, and this task will be repeated every few months.

   (a) Which smoothing method would you choose if you had to choose the same method for forecasting all series? Why?

   (b) Fortified wine has the largest market share of the six types of wine. You are asked to focus on fortified wine sales alone and produce as accurate a forecast as possible for the next two months.

   - Start by partitioning the data using the period until Dec-1993 as the training period.
   - Apply Holt-Winters exponential smoothing (with multiplicative seasonality) to sales.

   (c) Create two time plots based on the Holt-Winter's exponential smoothing results: (1) sales and forecasts and (2) forecast errors. The plots should include both training and test periods.

   i. Based on these plots, which of the following statements are reasonable?

   - Decembers are not captured well by the model.
   - There is a strong correlation between sales on the same calendar month.
   - The model does not capture the seasonality well.
   - We should first deseasonalize the data and then apply Holt-Winters exponential smoothing.

   ii. How can you handle the above effect while still using exponential smoothing?

[28] Source: Hyndman and Yang (2018) tsdl: Time Series Data Library. v0.1.0. `github.com/FinYang/tsdl`.

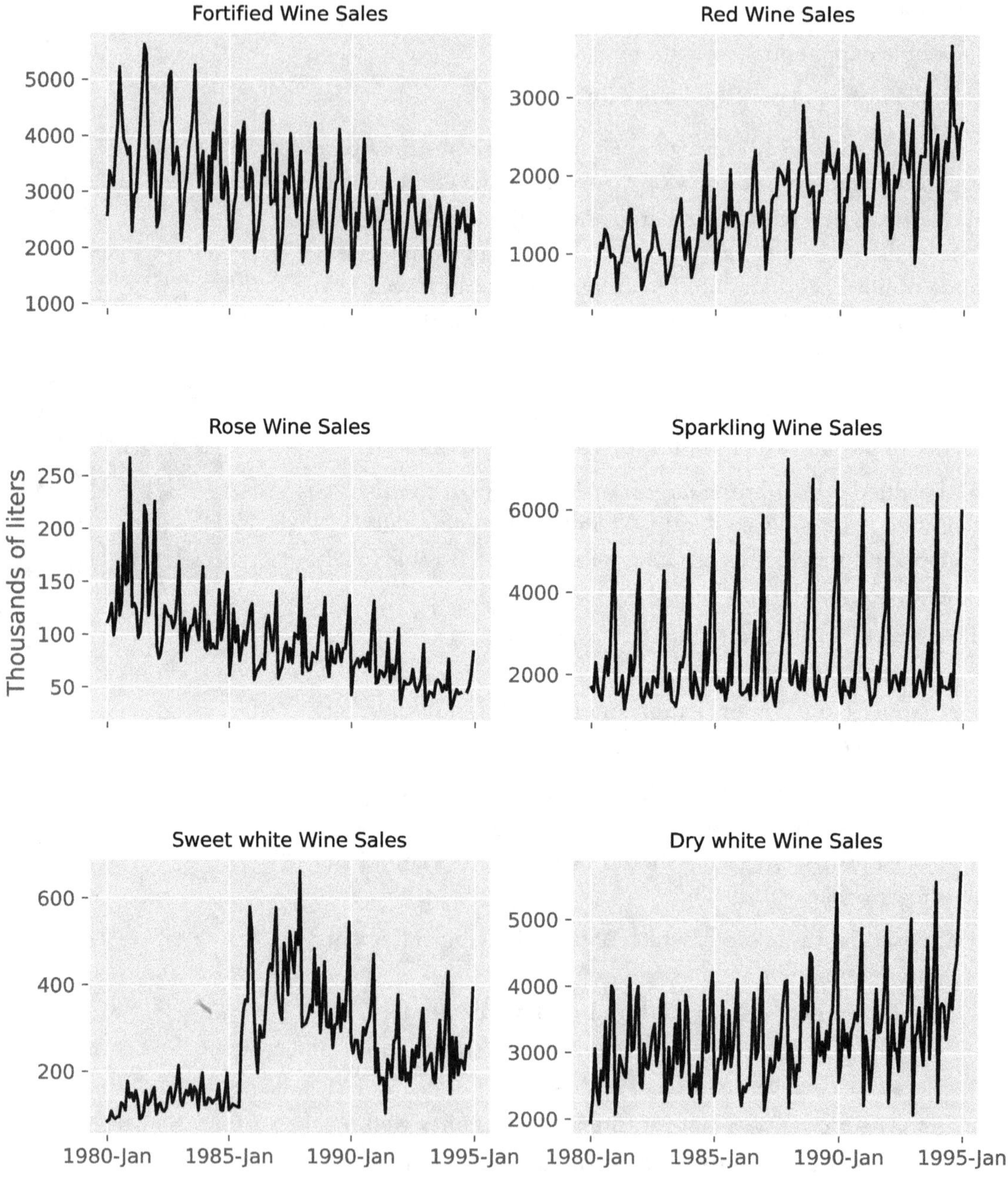

Figure 5.14: Monthly sales of six types of Australian wines between 1980–1994.

9. *Natural Gas Sales:* Figure 5.15 shows a time plot of quarterly natural gas sales (in billions of BTU's) of a certain company, over a period of four years.[29] The company's analyst is asked to use a moving average model to forecast sales in Winter 2005.

[29] Data courtesy of George McCabe

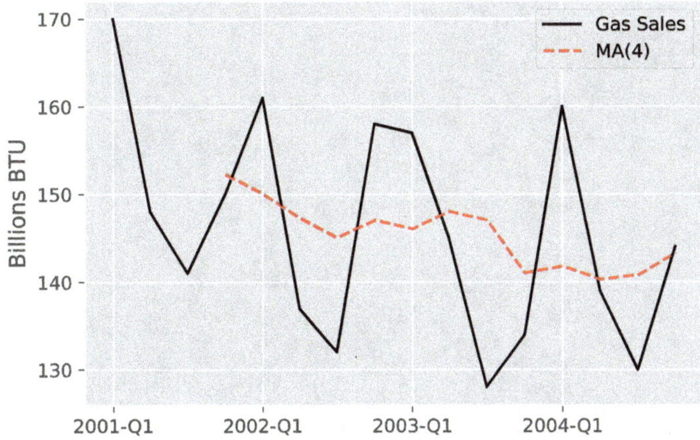

Figure 5.15: Quarterly sales of natural gas over four years.

(a) Reproduce the time plot with the overlaying MA(4) line.

(b) What can we learn about the series from the MA line?

(c) Run a moving average forecaster with adequate season length. Are forecasts generated by this method expected to over-forecast, under-forecast, or accurately forecast actual sales? Why?

6 Regression-Based Models: Capturing Trend and Seasonality

A popular forecasting method is based on *linear regression* models, using suitable predictors to capture trend and/or seasonality as well as other patterns. In this chapter, we show how a linear regression model can be set up to capture a time series with a trend, seasonality, autocorrelation, and external information. The model, which is estimated from the training period, can then produce forecasts for future periods by inserting the relevant predictor information into the estimated regression equation. We describe different types of common trends (linear, exponential, polynomial, etc.), and seasonality (additive, multiplicative, and smoothly transitioning seasons). The various steps of fitting linear regression models, using them to generate forecasts, and assessing their predictive accuracy are illustrated using the Amtrak ridership series.

6.1 Model with Trend

Linear regression can be used to fit a global trend that applies to the entire series and will apply in the forecasting period. A linear trend means that the values of the series increase or decrease linearly in time, whereas an exponential trend captures an exponential increase or decrease. We can also use more flexible functions, such as quadratic functions or higher order polynomials, to capture more complex trend shapes. This section discusses each of several common trend types and how to set up the linear regression accordingly.

Linear Trend

To create a linear regression model that captures a time series with a global linear trend, the output variable (y) is set as the time series measurement or some function of it, and the predictor (x) is set as a time index. Let us consider a simple example: fitting a linear trend to the Amtrak ridership data. The first step is to create a new column that is a time index $t = 1, 2, 3, \ldots$. This will serve as our predictor. A snapshot of the two corresponding columns (y and t) in Excel is shown in Figure 6.1.

Month	Ridership	t
Jan-91	1709	1
Feb-91	1621	2
Mar-91	1973	3
Apr-91	1812	4
May-91	1975	5
Jun-91	1862	6
Jul-91	1940	7
Aug-91	2013	8
Sep-91	1596	9
Oct-91	1725	10
Nov-91	1676	11
Dec-91	1814	12
Jan-92	1615	13
Feb-92	1557	14

Figure 6.1: Output variable (*Ridership*) and predictor variable (t) used to fit a linear trend.

Before fitting the linear regression, we partition the ridership time series into training and test periods, so that the last three years of data (Apr 2001 to March 2004) is the test period. Reasons for keeping at least 12 months in the test set are (1) if the purpose is to provide monthly forecasts for a year ahead, and (2) to allow evaluating forecasting performance in different months of the year.

A linear trend fitted to the training period is shown in Figure 6.2. From the time plot it is obvious that the global trend of the series is not linear. However, we use this example to illustrate how a linear trend is fit, and later we consider other models for this series.

To fit a linear relationship between *Ridership* and *Time*, we set the output variable y as the Amtrak ridership and the predictor as the time index t in the regression model:

$$y_t = \beta_0 + \beta_1 t + \epsilon \qquad (6.1)$$

where y_t is the Ridership at time point t and ϵ is the standard noise term in a linear regression. Thus, we are modeling three of the four time series components: level (β_0), trend (β_1), and noise (ϵ). Seasonality is not modeled.

The next step is to use the linear trend model (also a linear regression model) to make forecasts in the test period. Figure 6.3 depicts the linear model and its predictions in the test period. Table 6.1 presents the model's summary output.

Note: Beware of examining only the coefficients and their statistical significance for making decisions about the trend, as this can

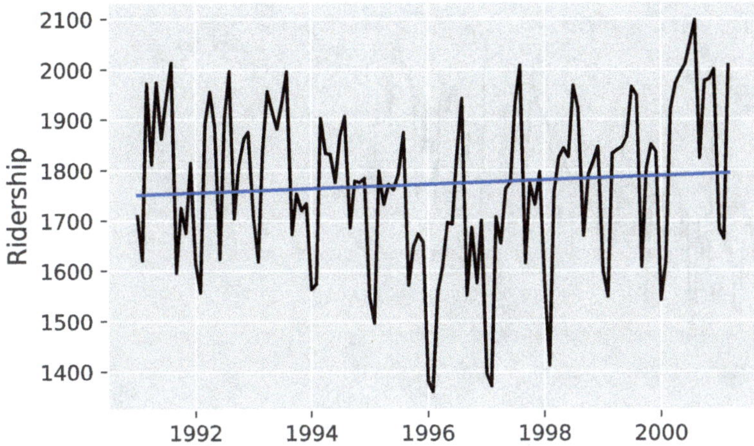

Figure 6.2: Linear trend fitted to the Amtrak ridership data.

Code for creating Figure 6.2

See full code at github.com/gshmueli/ptsf-Python

```
from sktime.forecasting.ardl import ARDL
ridership.index = ridership.index.to_period('M')
test_size = len(ridership.truncate(before='2001-04-01'))
ridership_train, ridership_test = temporal_train_test_split(ridership, test_size=test_size)

lm = ARDL(lags=0, trend='ct', seasonal=False, auto_ardl=False)
lm.fit(ridership_train, X=None)
fitted = lm.predict(ridership_train.index)

fig, ax = plt.subplots(figsize=(5.5,3.5))
ax = plot_series(ridership_train, fitted, markers=['',''],
                 labels=None, x_label="", y_label="Ridership", ax=ax)
ptsf_theme(ax, colors=['black','blue'], idx=[0,1], lty=['-']*2)
```

The first code block splits the data into training and test periods.

The second code block creates a linear regression model via the *ARDL* class. Setting `trend='ct'` fits a model with both an intercept (constant) and a trend. The `predict` method computes the fitted values.

The final block plots the training series and the regression fitted values.

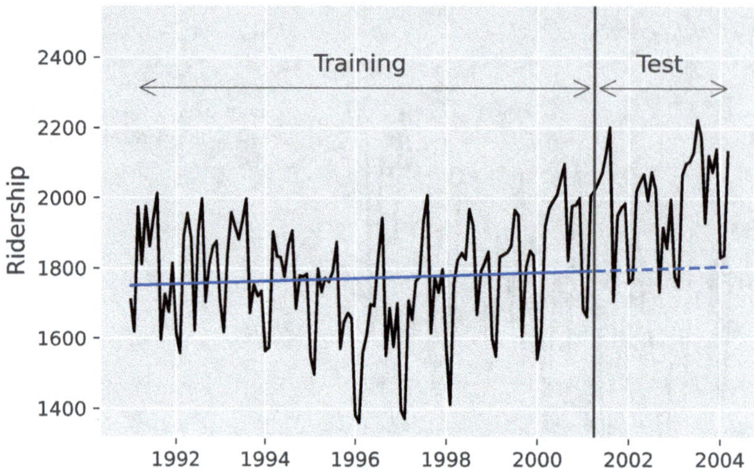

Figure 6.3: Linear trend fitted to the Amtrak ridership training data and used to generate forecasts for the test period.

Code for creating Figure 6.3 and Table 6.1

See full code at github.com/gshmueli/ptsf-Python

```
pred = lm.predict(ridership_test.index)

fig, ax = plt.subplots(figsize=(6,4))
ax = plot_series(ridership, fitted_values, pred, markers=['']*3,
            labels=None, x_label="", y_label="Ridership", ax=ax)
ptsf_theme(ax, colors=['black','blue','blue'], idx=[0,1,2], lty=['-','-','--'])

print(lm.summary())
```

be misleading. A significant coefficient for trend does not mean that a linear fit is adequate. An insignificant coefficient does not mean that there is no trend in the data. In our example, the slope coefficient (0.3514) is insignificant (p-value = 0.39), yet there may be a trend in the data (often once we control for seasonality). For instance, when we run a linear regression on the deasonalized Amtrak ridership data in the top right panel of Figure 5.4, we find the trend coefficient (0.8294) is statistically significant (p-value < 0.001). To determine the suitability of any trend shape, look at the time plot of the (deseasonalized) time series with the trend overlaid, examine the residual time plot, and look at performance measures on the test period.

```
                              ARDL Model Results
==============================================================================
ep. Variable:                       y   No. Observations:                  123
Model:                       ARDL(0,)   Log Likelihood                -797.948
Method:               Conditional MLE   S.D. of innovations            158.927
Date:                Thu, 24 Oct 2024   AIC                           1601.896
Time:                        17:05:30   BIC                           1610.333
Sample:                    01-01-1991   HQIC                          1605.323
                         - 03-01-2001
==============================================================================
                 coef    std err          z      P>|z|      [0.025      0.975]
------------------------------------------------------------------------------
const       1750.3595     29.073     60.206      0.000    1692.802    1807.917
trend          0.3514      0.407      0.864      0.390      -0.454       1.157
==============================================================================
```

Table 6.1: Summary of output from a linear regression model applied to the Amtrak ridership training data.

Exponential Trend

Several alternative trend shapes are useful and easy to fit via a linear regression model. Recall the use of trend lines and other plots that help assess the type of trend in the data. One such shape is an exponential trend. An exponential trend implies a multiplicative increase/decrease of the series over time ($y_t = ce^{\beta_1 t+\epsilon}$).

To fit an exponential trend, simply replace the output variable y with $\log(y)$ and fit a linear regression:[1]

$$\log(y_t) = \beta_0 + \beta_1 t + \epsilon \qquad (6.2)$$

[1] We use "log" to denote the natural logarithm (base e). In Python, use either the function `math.log` or `numpy.log` .

In the Amtrak example, for instance, we would fit a linear regression of *log(Ridership)* on the index variable t. Exponential trends are popular in sales data, where they reflect percentage growth.

An exponential trend reflects percentage increase/decrease.

Note: As in the general case of linear regression, when comparing the predictive accuracy of models that have a different output variable, such as comparing a linear trend model (with y) and an exponential trend model (with $\log(y)$), it is essential to compare forecasts or forecast errors on the same scale. An exponential trend model will produce forecasts in logarithmic scale, and the forecast errors reported by many software packages[2] will therefore be of the form $\log(y_t) - F_t$.

[2] In `sktime` we can automate the process of obtaining forecasts in the original scale by using the `pipeline` methodology of `sklearn`. See footnote 3 and Fig. 6.4.

Polynomial Trend

Another nonlinear trend shape that is easy to fit via linear regression is a polynomial trend, and in particular, a quadratic relationship of the form

$$y_t = \beta_0 + \beta_1 t + \beta_2 t^2 + \epsilon. \quad (6.3)$$

This is done by creating an additional predictor t^2 (the square of t) and fitting a multiple linear regression with the two predictors t and t^2. For the Amtrak ridership data, we have already seen a U-shaped trend in the data. We therefore fit a quadratic model to the training period. See the output in Table 6.2.

From the plot of the quadratic fit (Figure 3.2 in Chapter 3), we can see that this shape captures the pattern in the trend in the training period. The residuals (shown in Figure 3.3) now exhibit only seasonality. In general, any type of trend shape can be fit as long as it has a mathematical representation. However, the underlying assumption is that this shape is applicable throughout the period of data that we currently have as well as during the test period and future. Do not choose an overly complex shape, because although it will fit the training period well, it will likely be overfitting the data. To avoid overfitting, always examine performance on the test period and refrain from choosing overly complex trend patterns.

6.2 *Trend Models in Python*

Several forecasters in `sktime` can be used for fitting a linear regression model. We chose the *ARDL* class because it can fit a range of patterns, including different trend and seasonality types, exogenous variables, and more. It also conveniently has a `summary` method for displaying the estimated model.

Figure 6.4 illustrates the use of *ARDL* for fitting linear, quadratic, and exponential[3] trends to the Amtrak series. In *ARDL*, time stamps can be unevenly spaced. Periods with missing values can be handled using `dropna` with the `fit` method. For example, the second line could be `lm.fit(ridership_train.dropna())`.

[3] To obtain forecasts in the original scale, we use the `pipeline` methodology of `sklearn` that chains building blocks in creating models. In `sktime`, the building block components are either `transformers` or `forecasters`. See third code block in Figure 6.4.

```
                              ARDL Model Results
==============================================================================
Dep. Variable:                      y   No. Observations:                  123
Model:                       ARDL(0,)   Log Likelihood                -788.335
Method:               Conditional MLE   S.D. of innovations            146.979
Date:                Sun, 30 Mar 2025   AIC                           1584.669
Time:                        19:29:02   BIC                           1595.918
Sample:                    01-31-1991   HQIC                          1589.239
                         - 03-31-2001
=================================================================================
                    coef    std err          z      P>|z|      [0.025      0.975]
---------------------------------------------------------------------------------
const          1888.8840     40.915     46.166      0.000    1807.875    1969.893
trend            -6.2978      1.523     -4.134      0.000      -9.314      -3.282
trend_squared     0.0536      0.012      4.506      0.000       0.030       0.077
=================================================================================
```

Code for creating Table 6.2

See full code at github.com/gshmueli/ptsf-Python

```
ridership.index = ridership.index.to_period('M')

qm = ARDL(lags=0, trend='ctt', seasonal=False, auto_ardl=False)
qm.fit(train)

print(qm.summary())
```

The first block sets the series index to be of type PeriodIndex with monthly frequency.

The second block creates a quadratic trend model and fits it to the training period data.

The final block prints the statistical summary of the fit. The quadratic equation fitted is $1888.8840 - 6.2978t + 0.0536t^2$ where t (or trend) runs from 1 to 123 in the training period and from 124 to 159 in the test period.

Table 6.2: Summary of output from fitting a quadratic trend to the Amtrak ridership training data.

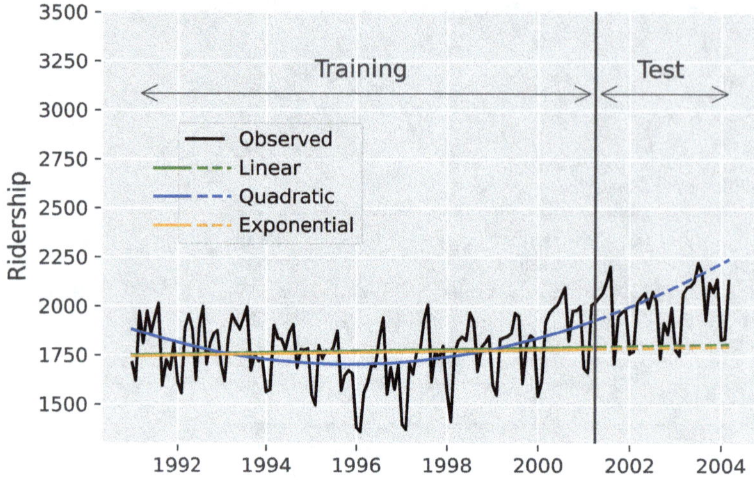

Figure 6.4: Exponential (and linear) trend fitted to the Amtrak ridership data in the training period and forecasted in the test period.

Code for creating Figure 6.4

See full code at `github.com/gshmueli/ptsf-Python`

```
lm = ARDL(lags=0, trend='ct', seasonal=False, auto_ardl=False)
lm.fit(ridership_train)
lm_fitted = lm.predict(ridership_train.index)
lm_pred = lm.predict(ridership_test.index)

qm = ARDL(lags=0, trend='ctt', seasonal=False, auto_ardl=False)
qm.fit(ridership_train)
qm_fitted = qm.predict(ridership_train.index)
qm_pred = qm.predict(ridership_test.index)

exp_lm = LogTransformer() * ARDL(lags=0, trend='ct', seasonal=False, auto_ardl=False)
exp_lm.fit(ridership_train)
exp_lm_fitted = exp_lm.predict(ridership_train.index)
exp_lm_pred = exp_lm.predict(ridership_test.index)
```

The first code block uses *ARDL* to create a linear trend model.

The second block uses *ARDL* to create a quadratic trend model.

The third block models and fits an exponential trend. The first line uses a convenient `sktime` shorthand to create a forecaster that transforms its input via `log()` and then performs a linear regression on the transformed series. Forecasts are automatically converted back to the original units.*

The linear and exponential trend models produce almost identical results for this data.

*The exponential trend model produces the median forecast. For code to compute the mean forecast see `github.com/gshmueli/ptsf-Python`

6.3 *Model with Seasonality*

A seasonal pattern in a time series means that observations that fall in some seasons have consistently higher or lower values than those that fall in other seasons. Examples are day-of-week patterns, monthly patterns, and quarterly patterns. The Amtrak ridership time series, as can be seen in the time plot, exhibits strong monthly seasonality (with highest traffic during summer months).

The most common way to capture seasonality in a regression model is by creating a new categorical variable that denotes the season for each observation. This categorical variable is then turned into dummy variables, which in turn are included as predictors in the regression model. To illustrate this, we created a new Month column for the Amtrak ridership data, as shown in Figure 6.5.

Month	Ridership	Season
Jan-91	1709	Jan
Feb-91	1621	Feb
Mar-91	1973	Mar
Apr-91	1812	Apr
May-91	1975	May
Jun-91	1862	Jun
Jul-91	1940	Jul
Aug-91	2013	Aug
Sep-91	1596	Sep
Oct-91	1725	Oct
Nov-91	1676	Nov
Dec-91	1814	Dec
Jan-92	1615	Jan
Feb-92	1557	Feb
Mar-92	1891	Mar
Apr-92	1956	Apr
May-92	1885	May

Figure 6.5: New categorical variable "Season" (right) to be used (via dummy variables) as predictor(s) in a linear regression model.

In order to include the season categorical variable as a predictor in a regression model for y (e.g., Ridership), we turn it into dummy variables. For m seasons we create m-1 dummy variables, which are binary variables that take on the value 1 if the record falls in that particular season, and 0 otherwise. The mth season does not require a dummy, since it is identified when all the m-1 dummies take on zero values.

Table 6.3 shows the output of a linear regression fit to Ridership (y) on 11-month dummy variables (using the training period). The fitted series and the residuals from this model are shown in Figure 6.6. The model appears to capture the seasonality in the data. However, since we have not included a trend component in the model (as shown in Section 6.1), the fitted values do not capture the existing trend, as evident by the three months with "dips" in the middle of the series and the months with peaks at the end of the series. Therefore, the residuals, which are the difference between the actual and fitted values, clearly display the remaining U-shaped trend. During the middle period, the series is over-predicted, while the start and end of the series are under-predicted.

When seasonality is added as described above (create a categorical seasonal variable, then create dummy variables from it,

```
                              ARDL Model Results
==============================================================================
Dep. Variable:                      y   No. Observations:                  123
Model:                 Seas. ARDL(0,)   Log Likelihood                -736.380
Method:               Conditional MLE   S.D. of innovations             96.340
Date:                Mon, 31 Mar 2025   AIC                           1498.759
Time:                        09:17:53   BIC                           1535.318
Sample:                    01-01-1991   HQIC                          1513.609
                         - 03-01-2001
==============================================================================
                 coef    std err          z      P>|z|      [0.025      0.975]
------------------------------------------------------------------------------
const       1573.9722     30.578     51.475      0.000    1513.381    1634.564
s(2,12)      -42.9302     43.243     -0.993      0.323    -128.620      42.759
s(3,12)      260.7677     43.243      6.030      0.000     175.078     346.457
s(4,12)      245.0919     44.311      5.531      0.000     157.286     332.897
s(5,12)      278.2222     44.311      6.279      0.000     190.417     366.028
s(6,12)      233.4598     44.311      5.269      0.000     145.654     321.265
s(7,12)      345.3265     44.311      7.793      0.000     257.521     433.132
s(8,12)      396.6595     44.311      8.952      0.000     308.854     484.465
s(9,12)       75.7615     44.311      1.710      0.090     -12.044     163.567
s(10,12)     200.6076     44.311      4.527      0.000     112.802     288.413
s(11,12)     192.3552     44.311      4.341      0.000     104.550     280.161
s(12,12)     230.4151     44.311      5.200      0.000     142.610     318.221
==============================================================================
```

Code for creating Table 6.3

See full code at `github.com/gshmueli/ptsf-Python`

```
seas = ARDL(lags=0, order=0, trend='c', seasonal=True, auto_ardl=False)
seas.fit(train, X=None)
print(seas.summary())
```

We set the `seasonal` argument to `True` when creating the *ARDL* forecaster object. This tells the model to include a set of 11 dummy variables, one for each season – except for the first season, January. The naming of the coefficients is as follows: `s(2,12)` stands for February, `s(3,12)` stands for March, etc.

Table 6.3: Summary of output from fitting additive seasonality to the Amtrak ridership data in the training period.

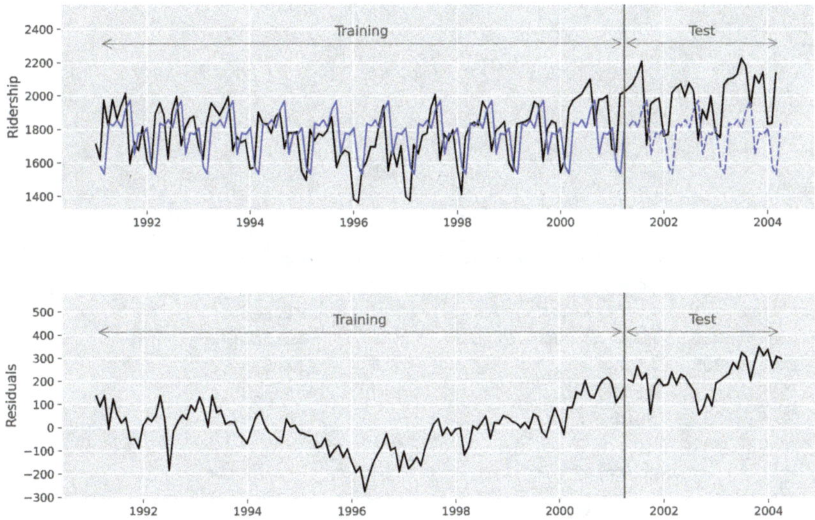

Figure 6.6: Regression model with additive seasonality fitted to the Amtrak ridership data in the top panel (model is blue line in training and dashed line in test). The model's residuals are in the bottom panel.

and then regress on y), it captures *additive seasonality*. This means that the average value of y in a certain season is higher or lower by a fixed amount compared to another season. For example, in the Amtrak ridership, the coefficient for August (396.66) indicates that the average number of passengers in August is higher by 396,660 passengers than the average in January (the reference category). Using regression models, we can also capture *multiplicative seasonality*, where average values on a certain season are higher or lower by a fixed percentage compared to another season. To fit multiplicative seasonality, we use the same model as above, except that we use $\log(y)$ as the output variable.

6.4 *Model with Trend and Seasonality*

We can create models that capture both trend and seasonality by including predictors of both types. Our exploration of the Amtrak ridership data indicates that the series has a quadratic trend and monthly seasonality. We therefore fit a model with 13 predictors: 11 dummy variables for month, and t and t^2 for trend. The output for this final model is in Table 6.4. The model's fit and residuals are depicted in Figure 6.7.

```
                              ARDL Model Results
==============================================================================
Dep. Variable:                      y   No. Observations:                  123
Model:                 Seas. ARDL(0,)   Log Likelihood                -691.268
Method:               Conditional MLE   S.D. of innovations             66.761
Date:                Mon, 31 Mar 2025   AIC                           1412.536
Time:                        09:55:04   BIC                           1454.719
Sample:                    01-01-1991   HQIC                          1429.670
                         - 03-01-2001
=================================================================================
                    coef    std err          z      P>|z|      [0.025      0.975]
---------------------------------------------------------------------------------
const          1696.9794     27.675     61.318      0.000    1642.128    1751.831
trend            -7.1559      0.729     -9.812      0.000      -8.601      -5.710
trend_squared     0.0607      0.006     10.660      0.000       0.049       0.072
s(2,12)         -43.2458     30.241     -1.430      0.156    -103.182      16.690
s(3,12)         260.0149     30.242      8.598      0.000     200.076     319.954
s(4,12)         260.6175     31.021      8.401      0.000     199.135     322.100
s(5,12)         293.7966     31.020      9.471      0.000     232.316     355.278
s(6,12)         248.9615     31.020      8.026      0.000     187.481     310.442
s(7,12)         360.6340     31.020     11.626      0.000     299.153     422.115
s(8,12)         411.6513     31.021     13.270      0.000     350.169     473.134
s(9,12)          90.3162     31.022      2.911      0.004      28.831     151.801
s(10,12)        214.6037     31.024      6.917      0.000     153.115     276.092
s(11,12)        205.6711     31.026      6.629      0.000     144.178     267.165
s(12,12)        242.9294     31.029      7.829      0.000     181.430     304.429
=================================================================================
```

Code for creating Table 6.4

See full code at `github.com/gshmueli/ptsf-Python`

```
quad_seas = ARDL(lags=0, order=0, trend='ctt', seasonal=True, auto_ardl=False)
quad_seas.fit(train)
print(quad_seas.summary())
```

Table 6.4: Summary of output from fitting a regression model with quadratic trend and additive seasonality to the Amtrak ridership training data.

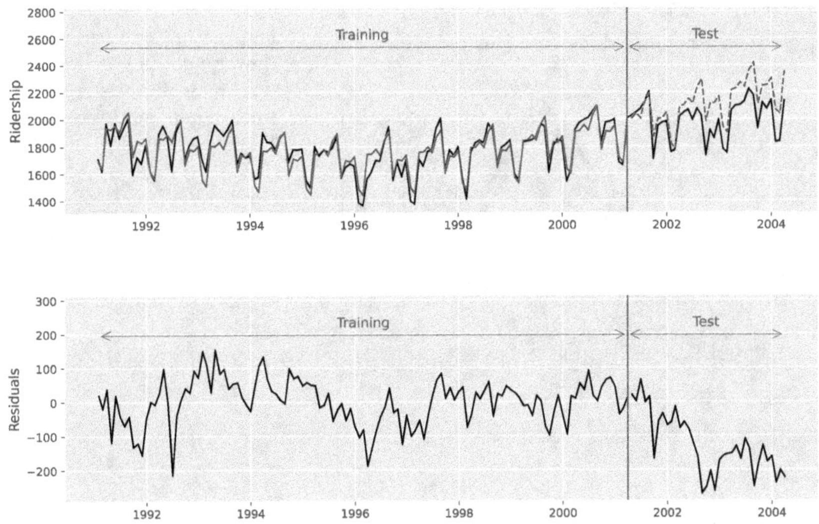

Figure 6.7: Regression model with quadratic trend and additive seasonality fitted to the Amtrak ridership data in the top panel. The model's residuals are in the bottom panel.

Smooth Seasonal Patterns

When the seasonal pattern transitions smoothly from one season to the next, we can use continuous mathematical functions to approximate the seasonal pattern, such as including sinusoidal functions as predictors in the regression model. For example, the Centers for Disease Control and Prevention in the United States use a regression model for modeling the percent of weekly deaths attributed to pneumonia and influenza in 122 cities. The model includes a quadratic trend as well as sine and cosine functions for capturing the smooth seasonality pattern.[4] In particular, they use the following regression model:

$$y_t = \beta_0 + \beta_1 t + \beta_2 t^2 + \beta_3 \sin(2\pi t/52.18) + \beta_4 \cos(2\pi t/52.18) + \epsilon \tag{6.4}$$

The trend terms t and t^2 accommodate long-term linear and curvilinear changes in the background proportion of pneumonia and influenza deaths arising from factors such as population growth or improved disease prevention or treatment. The sine and cosine terms capture the yearly periodicity of weekly data (with 52.18 weeks per year).[5] This regression model is then fitted to five years of data to create a "baseline" against which new weekly mortality is compared, called the 'Serfling method' (see

[4] See www.cdc.gov/mmwr/preview/mmwrhtml/mm5914a3.htm.

[5] To capture the same type of pattern with daily data, one can use $\sin(2\pi t/365.25)$ and $\cos(2\pi t/365.25)$.

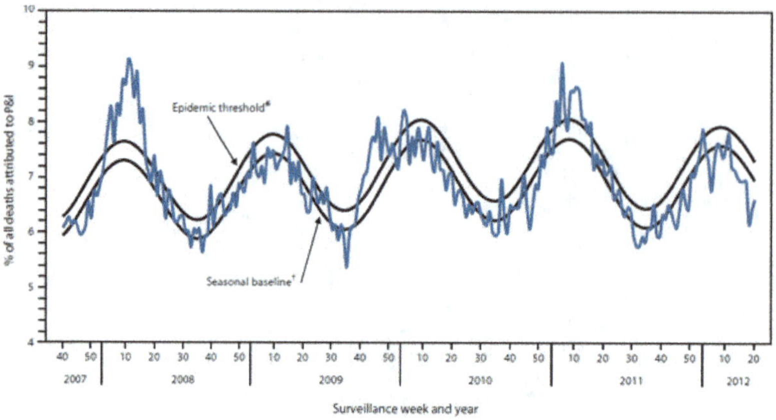

Figure 6.8: Regression model (lower smooth line) for weekly deaths attributed to pneumonia and influenza. From `www.cdc.gov`.

Figure 6.8). For more on the use of forecasting in early disease detection, see the article by Burkom et al. (2007).[6]

Including sinusoidal functions in `sktime` can be done easily with *FourierFeatures*. For example, to fit a model to the Amtrak ridership series with quadratic trend and sine and cosine terms, we add the sine and cosine predictors to the quadratic trend model as follows:

[6] H. S. Burkom, S. P. Murphy, and G. Shmueli. Automated time series forecasting for biosurveillance. *Statistics in Medicine*, 26:4202–4218, 2007

```
from sktime.transformations.series.fourier import FourierFeatures

transformer = FourierFeatures(sp_list=[12], fourier_terms_list=[1])
X = transformer.fit_transform(ridership)
quad = ARDL(lags=0, order=0, trend='ctt', seasonal=False, auto_ardl=False)
quad.fit(train, X=X.iloc[:len(train),:])
```

To capture the monthly seasonality in our series, we add one pair of predictors of the form $\sin(2\pi t/12)$ and $\cos(2\pi t/12)$.[7] This is achieved via the argument *fourier_terms_list=[1]*.

[7] For more on using sine and cosine (Fourier terms) as predictors in time series, see `otexts.com/fpp3/useful-predictors.html`.

6.5 *Creating Forecasts from the Chosen Model*

After exploring different regression models and choosing the model to be used for forecasting, we refit the chosen regression model to the recombined training and test periods. Then, the model can be used to generate k-step-ahead forecasts, denoted F_{t+k} (see Section 1.4).

6.6 Problems

1. *Impact of September 11 on Air Travel in the United States:* The Research and Innovative Technology Administration's Bureau of Transportation Statistics (BTS) conducted a study to evaluate the impact of the September 11, 2001, terrorist attack on U.S. transportation. The study report and the data can be found at `www.bts.gov/archive/publications/estimated_impacts_of_9_11_on_us_travel/index`. The goal of the study was stated as follows:

   > The purpose of this study is to provide a greater understanding of the passenger travel behavior patterns of persons making long distance trips before and after September 11.

   The report analyzes monthly passenger movement data between January 1990 and April 2004. Data on three monthly time series are given in the file *Sept11Travel.csv* for this period: (1) actual airline revenue passenger miles (Air), (2) rail passenger miles (Rail), and (3) vehicle miles traveled (Auto).

   In order to assess the impact of September 11, BTS took the following approach: Using data before September 11, it forecasted future data (under the assumption of no terrorist attack). Then, BTS compared the forecasted series with the actual data to assess the impact of the event. Our first step, therefore, is to split each of the time series into two parts: pre- and post-September 11. We now concentrate only on the earlier time series.

   (a) Plot the pre-event Air time series. Which time series components appear from the plot?

   (b) Figure 6.9 shows a time plot of the *seasonally adjusted* pre-September-11 Air series. Which of the following methods would be adequate for forecasting this series?

   - Linear regression model with dummy variables
   - Linear regression model with trend
   - Linear regression model with dummy variables and trend

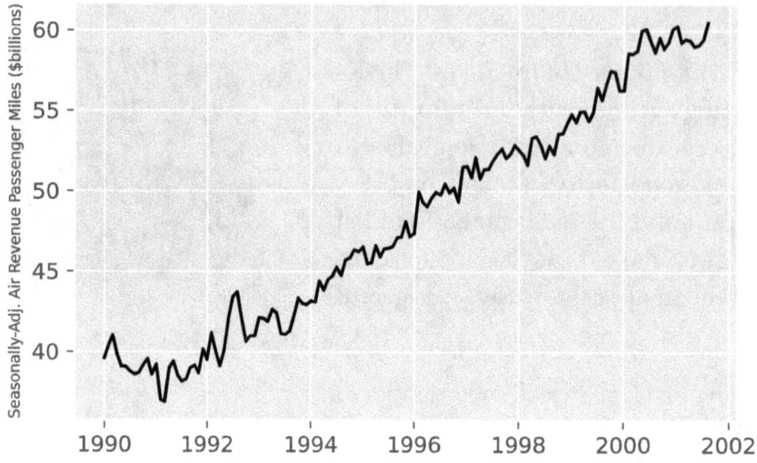

Figure 6.9: Seasonally adjusted pre-September-11 air series.

(c) Specify a linear regression model for the Air series that would produce a seasonally adjusted series similar to the one shown in (b), with multiplicative seasonality. What is the output variable? What are the predictors?[8]

(d) Run the regression model from (c). Remember to use only pre-event data.

i. What can we learn from the statistical significance level of the coefficient for November?

ii. The actual value of Air (air revenue passenger miles) in January 1990 was 35.153577 billion. What is the residual for this month, using the regression model? Report the residual in terms of air revenue passenger miles.

(e) Fit linear regression models to Air, Rail and Auto with additive seasonality and an appropriate trend. For Air and Auto, fit a linear trend. For Rail, use a quadratic trend. Remember to use only pre-event data. Once the models are estimated, use them to forecast each of the three post-event series.

i. For each series (Air, Rail, Auto), plot the complete pre-event and post-event actual series overlaid with the predicted series.

[8] *Hint*: Treat the figure as the residuals plot.

ii. What can be said about the effect of the September 11 terrorist attack on the three modes of transportation? Discuss the magnitude of the effect, its time span, and any other relevant aspects.

2. *Canadian Manufacturing Workers Work-Hours:* The time series plot in Figure 6.10 describes the average annual number of weekly hours spent by Canadian manufacturing workers. The data is available in *CanadianWorkHours.csv*.[9]

   Which one of the following regression-based models would fit the series best?

   - Linear trend model
   - Linear trend model with seasonality
   - Quadratic trend model
   - Quadratic trend model with seasonality

[9] Data courtesy of Ken Black

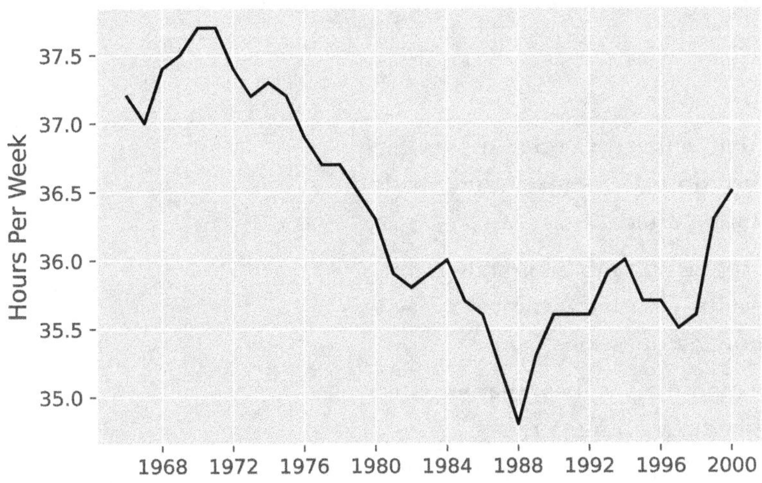

Figure 6.10: Average annual weekly hours spent by Canadian manufacturing workers.

3. *Modeling Toys "R" Us Revenues:* Figure 6.11 is a time plot of the quarterly revenues of Toys "R" Us between 1992 and 1995. The data is available in *ToysRUsRevenues.csv*.[10]

[10] Thanks to Chris Albright for suggesting the use of this dataset

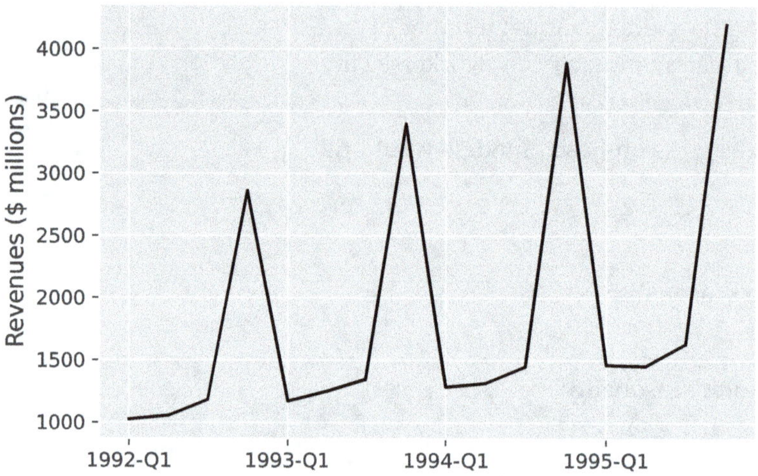

Figure 6.11: Quarterly revenues of Toys "R" Us, 1992-1995.

(a) Fit a regression model with a linear trend and seasonal dummy variables. Use the entire series (excluding the last two quarters) as the training period.

(b) A partial output of the regression model is shown in Table 6.5 (where `s(2,4)` is the Quarter 2 dummy). Use this output to answer the following questions:

i. Mention two statistics (and their values) that measure how well this model fits the training period.

ii. Mention two statistics (and their values) that measure the predictive accuracy of this model.

iii. After adjusting for trend, what is the average difference between sales in Q3 and sales in Q1?

iv. After adjusting for seasonality, which quarter (Q1, Q2, Q3 or Q4) has the highest average sales?

```
                              ARDL Model Results
==============================================================================
Dep. Variable:                      y   No. Observations:                   14
Model:                Seas. ARDL(0,)   Log Likelihood                 -88.547
Method:              Conditional MLE   S.D. of innovations            135.080
Date:               Sat, 19 Apr 2025   AIC                            189.094
Time:                       13:32:00   BIC                            192.929
Sample:                   03-31-1992   HQIC                           188.740
                        - 06-30-1995
==============================================================================
                 coef    std err          z      P>|z|      [0.025      0.975]
------------------------------------------------------------------------------
const        906.7500    115.346      7.861      0.000     645.819    1167.681
trend         47.1071     11.257      4.185      0.002      21.643      72.571
s(2,4)       -15.1071    119.660     -0.126      0.902    -285.796     255.582
s(3,4)        89.1667    128.674      0.693      0.506    -201.914     380.247
s(4,4)      2101.7262    129.165     16.272      0.000    1809.534    2393.919
==============================================================================


                          MAE      ME  MAPE    RMSE
Training set Accuracy   92.53   -0.00  5.01  135.08
Test set     Accuracy  254.67  183.14  7.40  313.68
```

Table 6.5: Regression model fitted to Toys "R" Us time series and its predictive performance in training and test periods.

4. *Forecasting Department Store Sales:* The time series plot shown in Figure 6.12 describes actual quarterly sales for a department store over a 6-year period. The data is available in *DepartmentStoreSales.csv*.[11]

[11] Data courtesy of Chris Albright

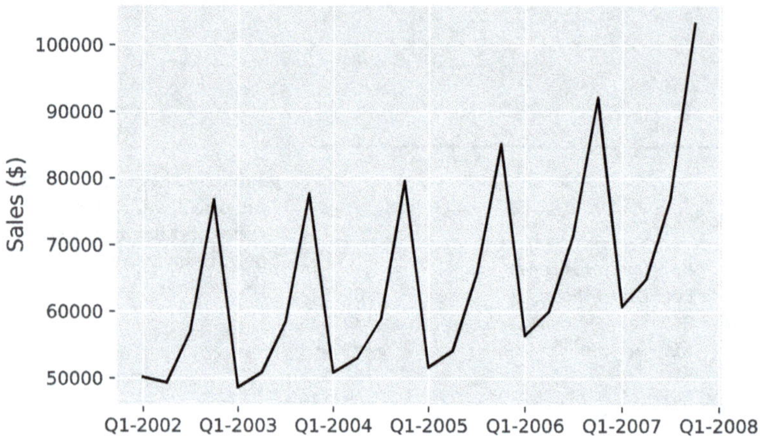

Figure 6.12: Department store quarterly sales series.

(a) The forecaster decided that there is an exponential trend in the series. In order to fit a regression-based model that accounts for this trend, which of the following operations must be performed (either manually or by a function in Python)?

- Take a logarithm of the Quarter index
- Take a logarithm of sales
- Take an exponent of sales
- Take an exponent of Quarter index

(b) Fit a regression model with an exponential trend and seasonality, using only the first 20 quarters as the training period (remember to first partition the series into training and test periods).

(c) A partial output is shown in Table 6.6. From the output, after adjusting for trend, are Q2 average sales higher, lower, or approximately equal to the average Q1 sales?

Table 6.6: Output from regression model fit to department store sales in the training period.

```
sales = pd.read_csv('ptsf-Python/Data/DepartmentStoreSales.csv')
sales['logSales'] = np.log(sales['Sales'])
logSales = sales['logSales'].to_frame()
train, test = temporal_train_test_split(logSales, test_size=4)
exp_seas = ARDL(lags=0, order=0, trend='ct', seasonal=True, auto_ardl=False)
exp_seas.fit(train)
print(exp_seas.summary())
```

```
                              ARDL Model Results
==============================================================================
                 coef    std err          z      P>|z|      [0.025      0.975]
------------------------------------------------------------------------------
const         10.7489      0.019    574.057      0.000      10.709      10.789
trend          0.0111      0.001      8.561      0.000       0.008       0.014
s(2,4)         0.0250      0.021      1.202      0.248      -0.019       0.069
s(3,4)         0.1653      0.021      7.917      0.000       0.121       0.210
s(4,4)         0.4337      0.021     20.572      0.000       0.389       0.479
==============================================================================
```

(d) Use this model to forecast sales in quarters 2007 Q1 and 2007 Q2.

(e) The plots shown in Figure 6.13 describe the fit (top) and forecast errors (bottom) from this regression model.

i. Recreate these plots.

ii. Based on these plots, what can you say about your forecasts for quarters Q21 and Q22? Are they likely to over-forecast, under-forecast, or be reasonably close to the real sales values?

(f) Looking at the residual plot, which of the following statements appear true?

- Seasonality is not captured well.
- The regression model fits the data well.
- The trend in the data is not captured well by the model.

(g) Which of the following is an adequate and parsimonious solution for improving model fit?

- Fit a quadratic trend model to the residuals (with *Quarter* and *Quarter*^{2}).
- Fit a quadratic trend model to Sales (with *Quarter* and *Quarter*^{2}).

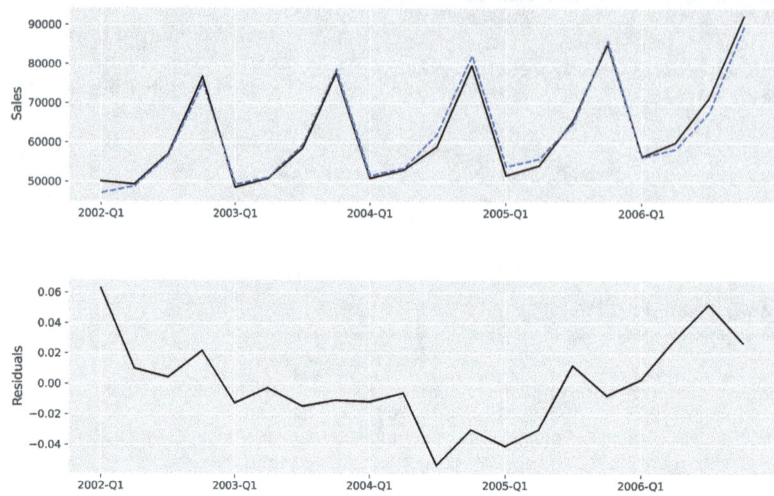

Figure 6.13: Fit of regression model for department store sales.

5. *Souvenir Sales:* The file *SouvenirSales.csv* contains monthly sales for a souvenir shop at a beach resort town in Queensland, Australia, between 1995 and 2001.[12]

Back in 2001, the store wanted to use the data to forecast sales for the next 12 months (year 2002). They hired an analyst to generate forecasts. The analyst first partitioned the data into training and test periods, with the test set containing the last 12 months of data (year 2001). She then fit a regression model to sales, using the training period.

[12] Source: Hyndman and Yang (2018) tsdl: Time Series Data Library. v0.1.0. `github.com/FinYang/tsdl`.

(a) Based on the two time plots in Figure 6.14, which predictors should be included in the regression equation? What is the total number of predictors in the model?

(b) Run a regression model for Sales (in Australian dollars) with a linear trend and additive seasonality. Remember to fit only the training period. Call this model A.

i. Examine the coefficients: Which month tends to have the highest average sales during the year? Why is this reasonable?

ii. What does the trend coefficient of model A mean?

iii. Use this model to forecast the sales in February 2001.

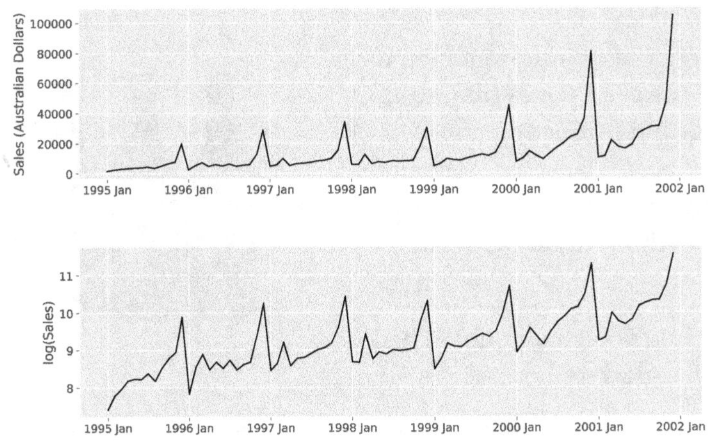

Figure 6.14: Monthly sales at Australian souvenir shop in dollars (top) and in log scale (bottom).

(c) Run a regression model for Sales with an exponential trend and multiplicative seasonality. Remember to fit only the training period. Call this model B.

i. Fitting a model to Sales (in Australian dollars) with with an exponential trend is equivalent to fitting a model to log(Sales) with what type of trend?

ii. What does the estimated trend coefficient of model B mean?

iii. Use this model to forecast the sales in February 2001.

(d) Compare the two regression models (A and B) in terms of forecast performance. Which model is preferable for forecasting? Mention at least two reasons based on the information in the outputs.

(e) Use models A and B to forecast sales in February 2002. What is the extra step needed compared to what you did earlier for forecasting February 2001?

(f) How would you model this data differently if the goal was understanding the different components of sales in the souvenir shop between 1995 and 2001? Mention two differences.

6. *Forecasting Australian Wine Sales:* Figure 6.15 shows time plots of monthly sales of six types of Australian wines (red, rose, sweet white, dry white, sparkling, and fortified) for 1980–1994. The data is available in *AustralianWines.csv*.[13] The units are thousands of liters. You are hired to obtain short-term forecasts (2–3 months ahead) for each of the six series, and this task will be repeated monthly.

   (a) Which forecasting method would you choose if you had to choose the same method for all series? Why?

   (b) Fortified wine has the largest market share of the six types of wine considered. You are asked to focus on fortified wine sales alone and produce as accurate as possible forecasts for the next 2 months.

   - Start by partitioning the data using the period until December 1993 as the training period.
   - Fit a regression model to sales with a linear trend and seasonality.

   i. Create the "actual vs. forecast" plot. What can you say about model fit?

   ii. Use the regression model to forecast sales in January and February 1994.

[13] Source: Hyndman and Yang (2018) tsdl: Time Series Data Library. v0.1.0. `github.com/FinYang/tsdl`.

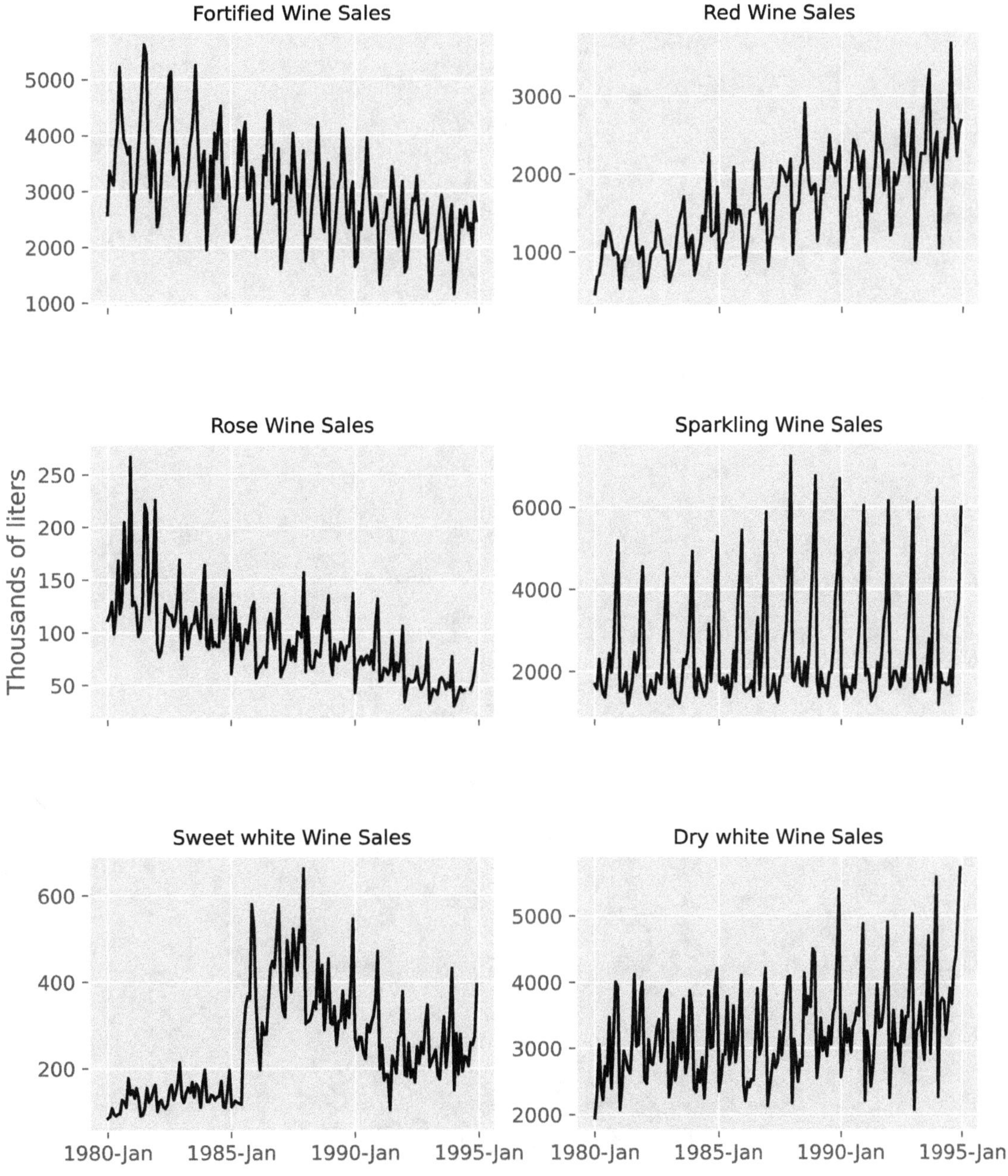

Figure 6.15: Monthly sales of six types of Australian wines between 1980–1994

7
Regression-Based Models: Autocorrelation & External Information

The previous chapter showed how a regression model can capture trend and seasonality. In this chapter we show how a regression model can be used to quantify the correlation between neighboring values in a time series (called *autocorrelation*). This type of model, called an *autoregressive* (AR) model, is useful for improving forecast accuracy by making use of the information contained in the autocorrelation (beyond trend and seasonality). It is also useful for evaluating the predictability of a series (by evaluating whether the series is a "random walk"). We introduce AR models and the larger family of ARIMA models. Secondly, we show how to include information about special events and integrate information from external series. The various steps of fitting linear regression and autoregressive models, using them to generate forecasts, and assessing their predictive accuracy, are illustrated using the Amtrak ridership series.

7.1 Autocorrelation

When we use linear regression for time series forecasting, we are able to account for patterns such as trend and seasonality. However, ordinary regression models do not account for correlation between values in different periods, which in cross-sectional data is assumed to be absent. Yet, in the time series context, values in neighboring periods tend to be correlated. Such correlation, called *autocorrelation*, is informative and can help in improving forecasts. If we know that values tend to be followed by similar values (positive autocorrelation) or by very different values (negative autocorrelation), then we can use that information to adjust forecasts. We will now discuss how to compute the autocorrelation of a series and how best to utilize the information for improving forecasting.

Computing Autocorrelation

Correlation between values of a time series in neighboring periods is called *autocorrelation* because it describes a relationship between the series and itself. To compute autocorrelation, we compute the correlation between the series and a lagged version of the series.[1] Figure 7.1 shows the first 24 months of the Amtrak ridership series, the lag-1 series, and the lag-2 series.

[1] Recall: A lagged series is a "copy" of the original series, which is moved forward one or more time periods. A lagged series with lag-1 is the original series moved forward one time period; a lagged series with lag-2 is the original series moved forward two time periods, and so on.

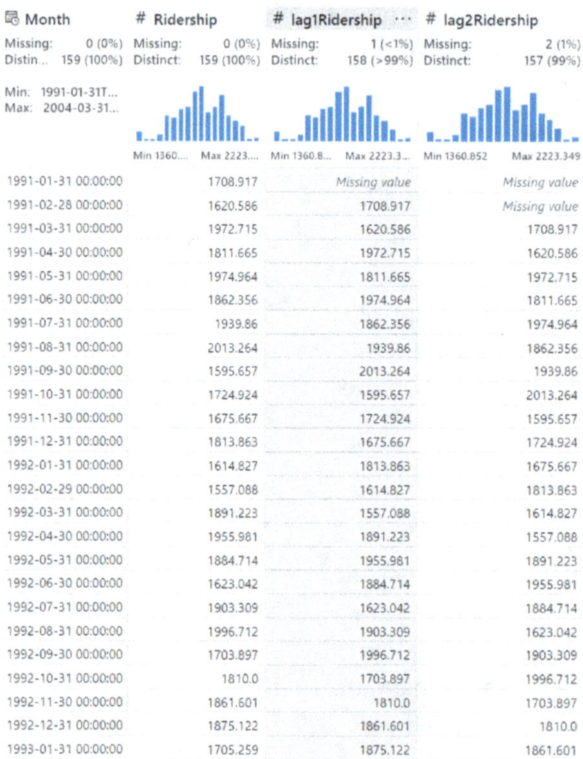

Month	# Ridership	# lag1Ridership	# lag2Ridership
Missing: 0 (0%)	Missing: 0 (0%)	Missing: 1 (<1%)	Missing: 2 (1%)
Distin... 159 (100%)	Distinct: 159 (100%)	Distinct: 158 (>99%)	Distinct: 157 (99%)
Min: 1991-01-31T... Max: 2004-03-31...	Min 1360.... Max 2223....	Min 1360.8... Max 2223.3...	Min 1360.852 Max 2223.349
1991-01-31 00:00:00	1708.917	Missing value	Missing value
1991-02-28 00:00:00	1620.586	1708.917	Missing value
1991-03-31 00:00:00	1972.715	1620.586	1708.917
1991-04-30 00:00:00	1811.665	1972.715	1620.586
1991-05-31 00:00:00	1974.964	1811.665	1972.715
1991-06-30 00:00:00	1862.356	1974.964	1811.665
1991-07-31 00:00:00	1939.86	1862.356	1974.964
1991-08-31 00:00:00	2013.264	1939.86	1862.356
1991-09-30 00:00:00	1595.657	2013.264	1939.86
1991-10-31 00:00:00	1724.924	1595.657	2013.264
1991-11-30 00:00:00	1675.667	1724.924	1595.657
1991-12-31 00:00:00	1813.863	1675.667	1724.924
1992-01-31 00:00:00	1614.827	1813.863	1675.667
1992-02-29 00:00:00	1557.088	1614.827	1813.863
1992-03-31 00:00:00	1891.223	1557.088	1614.827
1992-04-30 00:00:00	1955.981	1891.223	1557.088
1992-05-31 00:00:00	1884.714	1955.981	1891.223
1992-06-30 00:00:00	1623.042	1884.714	1955.981
1992-07-31 00:00:00	1903.309	1623.042	1884.714
1992-08-31 00:00:00	1996.712	1903.309	1623.042
1992-09-30 00:00:00	1703.897	1996.712	1903.309
1992-10-31 00:00:00	1810.0	1703.897	1996.712
1992-11-30 00:00:00	1861.601	1810.0	1703.897
1992-12-31 00:00:00	1875.122	1861.601	1810.0
1993-01-31 00:00:00	1705.259	1875.122	1861.601

Figure 7.1: First 24 months of Amtrak ridership series, lag-1 series, and lag-2 series. The `Pandas DataFrame` is shown using the Data Wrangler extension in VS Code which provides additional information about each of the three columns.

Next, to compute the lag-1 autocorrelation (which measures the linear relationship between values in consecutive time periods), we compute the correlation between the original series and the lag-1 series (e.g., via the `pandas` method `corr`) to be 0.08. Note that although the original series shown in Figure 7.1 has 24 time periods, the lag-1 autocorrelation will only be based on 23 pairs (because the lag-1 series does not have a value for Jan-91). Similarly, the lag-2 autocorrelation—measuring the relationship between values that are two time periods apart—is the correlation between the original series and the lag-2 series (yielding -0.15).

We can use the `plot_acf` function in the `statsmodels` package to compute and plot the autocorrelations of a series at different lags (see Figure 7.2).

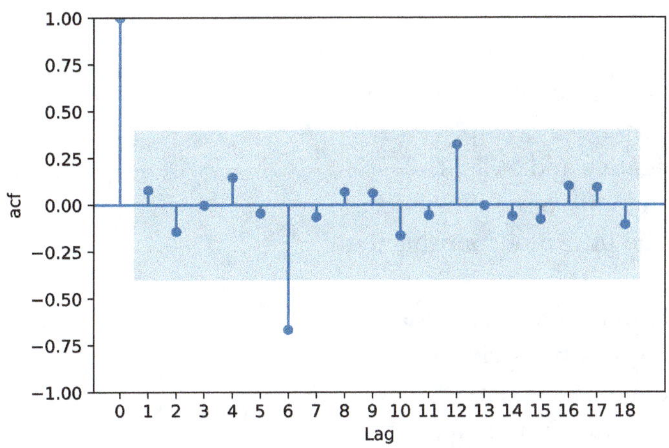

Figure 7.2: `plot_acf` output showing autocorrelations at lags 1–18 for the first 24 months of Amtrak ridership. Autocorrelation values exceeding the blue shaded confidence band (at ±2 standard errors) can be considered non-zero.

Code for creating Figure 7.2

See full code at github.com/gshmueli/ptsf-Python

```
from statsmodels.graphics.tsaplots import plot_acf

y = ridership.copy().iloc[:24,0]

fig, ax = plt.subplots(figsize=(6, 4))
plot_acf(x=y.values, lags=18, title="", bartlett_confint=False, ax=ax)
```

We specify *lags=18* because the default displays fewer lag values.

A few typical autocorrelation behaviors that are useful to explore are:

Strong autocorrelation (positive or negative) at multiples of a lag larger than 1 typically reflects a cyclical pattern. For example, strong positive autocorrelation at lags 12, 24, 36,... in monthly data will reflect an annual seasonality (where values during a given month each year are positively correlated).

Positive lag-1 autocorrelation (called "stickiness") describes a series where consecutive values move generally in the same direction. In the presence of a strong linear trend, we would expect to see a strong positive lag-1 autocorrelation.

Negative lag-1 autocorrelation reflects swings in the series, where high values are immediately followed by low values and vice versa.

Examining the autocorrelation of a series can therefore help to detect seasonality patterns. In Figure 7.2, for example, we see that the strongest autocorrelation is negative and at lag-6. This indicates a biannual pattern in ridership, with 6-month switches from high to low ridership. A look at the time plot confirms the high-summer low-winter pattern.

In addition to looking at autocorrelations of the raw series, it is useful to look at autocorrelations of residual series. For example, after fitting a regression model (or using any other forecasting method), we can examine the autocorrelation of the series of residuals. If we have adequately modeled the seasonal pattern, then the residual series should show no autocorrelation at the season's lag. Figure 7.3 displays the autocorrelations for the residuals from the regression model with seasonality and quadratic trend shown in Figure 6.7. It is clear that the 6-month (and 12-month) cyclical behavior no longer dominates the series of residuals, indicating that the regression model captured them adequately. However, we can also see a strong positive autocorrelation from lag-1 on, indicating a positive relationship between neighboring residuals. This is valuable information, which can be used to improve forecasts.

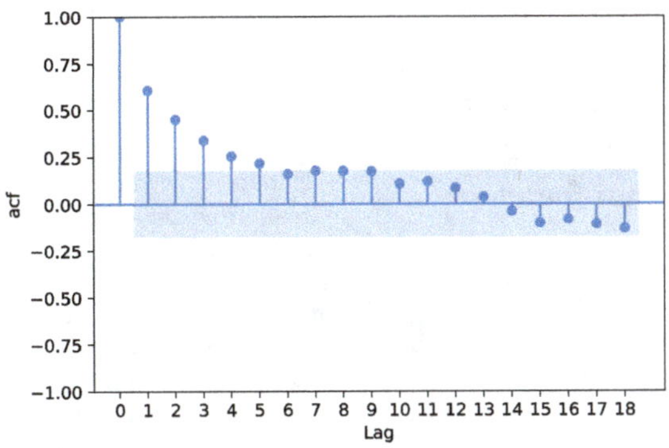

Figure 7.3: `plot_acf` output of autocorrelations of residual series from Figure 6.7.

7.2 *Capturing Autocorrelation: AR and ARIMA Models*

Among regression-type models that directly capture autocorrelation are autoregressive (AR) models and the more general class of models called ARIMA models (AutoRegressive Integrated Moving Average).

Autoregressive (AR) Models

AR models are similar to linear regression models, except that the predictors are the past values of the series. For example, an autoregression model of order 2 (AR(2)), can be written as

$$y_t = \beta_0 + \beta_1 y_{t-1} + \beta_2 y_{t-2} + \epsilon_t. \tag{7.1}$$

Estimating such models is roughly equivalent to fitting a linear regression model with the series as the output, and the lagged series (at lag-1 and 2 in this example) as the predictors. However, it is better to use designated ARIMA estimation methods (e.g., those available in the `sktime` package's *PyFableARIMA* class) over ordinary linear regression estimation in order to produce more accurate results.[2]

[2] ARIMA model estimation differs from ordinary regression estimation by accounting for the dependence between observations.

Evaluating Predictability

Before attempting to forecast a time series, it is important to determine whether it is predictable, in the sense that its past (non-trivially) predicts its future. One useful way to assess predictability is to test whether the series is a *random walk*. A random walk is a series in which changes from one time period to the next are random. According to the efficient market hypothesis in economics, asset prices are random walks and therefore predicting stock prices is a game of chance.[3]

A random walk is a special case of an AR(1) model, where the slope coefficient is equal to 1:

$$y_t = \beta_0 + y_{t-1} + \epsilon_t. \tag{7.2}$$

We see from this equation that the difference $y_t - y_{t-1}$, between the values at periods $t-1$ and t, is random, hence the term *random walk*. Forecasts from such a model are basically equal to the most recent observed value (the naive forecast), reflecting the lack of any other information. Furthermore, with a symmetric distribution for the errors, the forecast that a random walk will go up is always a coin flip (50%). Consequently, economists refer to such time series as "unpredictable". Technically, though, you can make a forecast about a random walk. The trouble is that the forecast is naive, and anyone can do it.

To test whether a series is a random walk, we fit an AR(1) model and test the hypothesis that the slope coefficient is equal to 1 ($H_0 : \beta_1 = 1$ vs. $H_1 : \beta_1 \neq 1$). If the hypothesis is rejected (reflected by a small p-value), then the series is not a random walk, and we can attempt to predict it (with something beyond the naive forecast).

As an example, consider the AR(1) model fitted to the residuals as shown in Figure 7.4. The slope coefficient (0.6042) is more than 5 standard errors away from 1, indicating that this is not a random walk. In contrast, consider the AR(1) model fitted to the series of S&P 500 monthly closing prices between May 1995 and August 2003 (available in *SP500.csv*.) The slope coefficient is 0.9833, with a standard error of 0.0145. The coefficient is sufficiently close to 1 (around one standard error away), indicating that this may be a random walk.[4] Forecasting this series using any of the methods described earlier is therefore not likely to improve over the naive forecast.

Another approach for evaluating predictability, which is math-

[3] There is some controversy surrounding the efficient market hypothesis, claiming that the slight autocorrelation in asset prices does make them predictable to some extent. However, transaction costs and bid-ask spreads tend to offset any prediction benefits.

[4] A more complex statistical approach for testing whether a time series is non-stationary (e.g., a random walk) is using the Augmented Dickey-Fuller test. In `sktime`, the class *StationarityADF* can perform this test. In the case of the S&P 500 monthly closing prices, the test suggests the series is non-stationary and may be a random walk.

ematically equivalent to the above approach, is to examine the series of differences between each pair of consecutive values $(y_t - y_{t-1})$. This is called the *lag-1 differenced series* (see also Section 5.3 in Chapter 5). For example, we can obtain the differenced series for the ridership data by subtracting the third column (lag1Ridership) from the second column (Ridership) in Figure 7.1. Examine equation (7.2), and subtract y_{t-1} from both sides. We see that a random walk is equal to a constant plus a random term. Hence, to test whether a series is a random walk, we compute the differenced series and then examine the ACF plot of the differenced series. If the ACF plot indicates that the autocorrelations at lags 1,2,3, etc. are all approximately zero (all the bars are within the thresholds), then we can infer that the original series is a random walk.

7.3 *Forecasting with ARIMA models*

In general, there are two approaches to taking advantage of autocorrelation. One is by directly building the autocorrelation into the regression model by using ARIMA models, and the other is by constructing a simple second-level forecasting model on the residual series. We first describe the second-level approach and then the more complex ARIMA modeling.

AR as a Second-Layer Model

We start by describing a particular use of AR models that is straightforward to apply in the context of forecasting, and which can provide significant improvement to short-term forecasts. This approach captures autocorrelation by constructing a second-level forecasting model for the residuals, as follows:

1. Generate a k-step-ahead forecast of the series (F_{t+k}), using any forecasting method.
2. Generate a k-step-ahead forecast of the forecast error ($\hat{e}_{t+k}$), using an AR (or other) model.
3. Improve the initial k-step-ahead forecast of the series by adjusting it according to its forecasted error:

Improved $F^*_{t+k} = F_{t+k} + \hat{e}_{t+k}$.

This three-step process means that we fit a low-order AR model to the series of residuals (or forecast errors) that is then used to forecast future residuals. By fitting the series of residuals, rather than the raw series, we avoid the need for initial data transformations (because the residual series is not expected to contain any trends or cyclical behavior besides autocorrelation).

To fit an AR model to the series of residuals, we first examine the autocorrelations of the residual series. We then choose the order of the AR model according to the lags in which autocorrelation appears. Often, when autocorrelation exists at lag-1 and higher, it is sufficient to fit an AR(1) model of the form

$$e_t = \beta_0 + \beta_1 e_{t-1} + \epsilon_t, \qquad (7.3)$$

where e_t denotes the residual (forecast error) at time t. For example, although the autocorrelations in Figure 7.3 appear large from lags 1 to 10 or so, it is likely that an AR(1) would capture all these relationships. The reason is that if neighboring values are correlated, then the relationship can propagate to values that are two periods apart, then three periods apart, and so forth.

An AR(1) model fitted to the Amtrak ridership residual series is shown in Figure 7.4. The corresponding Python code[5] and model output are also shown in Figure 7.4.

The AR(1) coefficient (0.5998) is close to the lag-1 autocorrelation shown in Figure 7.3 (equal to 0.6041). The forecasted residual for April 2001 is computed by plugging in the most recent residual from March 2001 (equal to 12.108) into the AR(1) model: $0.1492 + 0.5998 \times 12.108 = 7.411$. This value is computed directly using the `predict` method (Figure 7.4 bottom). The positive value tells us that the regression model will produce a ridership forecast for April 2001 that is too low and that we should adjust it up by adding 7,411 riders. In this case, the regression model (with quadratic trend and seasonality) produced a forecast of 2,004,271 riders, and the improved two-stage model [regression + AR(1) correction] corrected it by increasing it to 2,011,682 riders. The actual value for April 2001 turned out to be 2,023,792 riders — closer to the improved forecast.

[5] The forecaster `PyFableARIMA` in `sktime` fits and forecasts ARIMA models (which includes as a subset AR models). Argument `pdq(1,0,0)` refers to an AR(1) model.

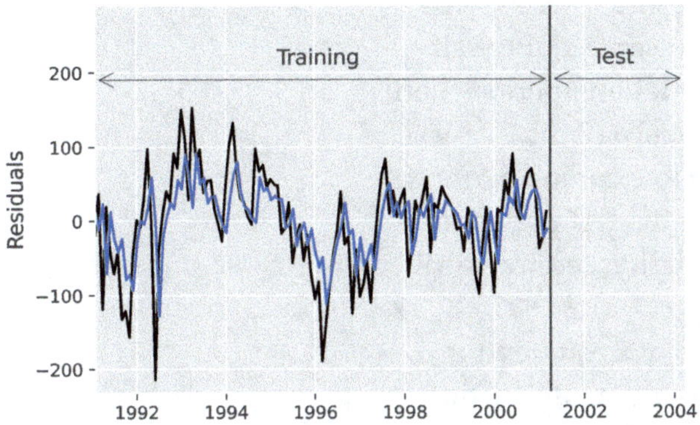

Figure 7.4: Fitting an AR(1) model to the residual series from Figure 6.7.

Code for creating Figure 7.4, AR(1) model summary, and one-step-ahead forecast

See full code at github.com/gshmueli/ptsf-Python

```
quad_seas = ARDL(lags=0, trend='ctt', seasonal=True, auto_ardl=False).fit(train)
fitted = quad_seas.predict(train.index)
resid = pd.Series((train.squeeze() - fitted.squeeze()), index=train.index, name='resid')

resid_ar = PyFableARIMA(formula='resid ~ 1 + pdq(1,0,0)')
        # '1 +' is used to add a constant to the ARIMA model
resid_ar.fit(resid)
resid_ar_fitted = resid_ar.get_fitted_values()

ax = plot_series(resid, resid_ar_fitted, markers=['']*2,
                    labels=None, y_label="Residuals", ax=ax)

resid_ar.PyFableARIMA_report()

          ARIMA Report:
          Series: resid
          Model: ARIMA(1,0,0) w/ mean

          Coefficients:
                   ar1  constant
                0.5998    0.1492
          s.e.  0.0712    4.7389

          sigma^2 estimated as 2876:  log likelihood=-663.54
          AIC=1333.08   AICc=1333.29   BIC=1341.52


print("Residuals forecast:" )
print(resid_ar.predict([1]))

          Residuals forecast:
          2001-04    7.41111
          Freq: M, Name: forecast, dtype: float64
```

From the plot of the actual versus fitted residual series, we can see that the AR(1) model fits the residual series quite well. Note, however, that the plot is based on the training period (until March 2001). To evaluate predictive performance of the two-level model [regression + AR(1)], we would have to examine performance (e.g., via MAPE or RMSE metrics) on the test period, in a fashion similar to the calculation that we performed for April 2001 above.

Finally, to examine whether we have indeed accounted for the autocorrelation in the series, and that no more information remains in the series, we examine the autocorrelations of the series of residuals-of-residuals.[6] This can be seen in Figure 7.5. It is clear that no more autocorrelation remains, and that the addition of the AR(1) model has captured the autocorrelation information adequately.

[6] Residuals-of-residuals here are the residuals obtained after the AR(1) was applied to the regression residuals.

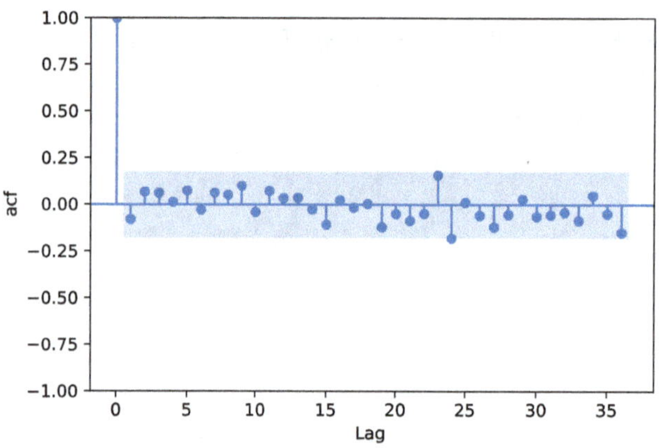

Figure 7.5: Autocorrelations of residuals-of-residuals series.

We mentioned earlier that improving forecasts via an additional AR layer is useful for *short-term forecasting*. The reason is that an AR model of order k will only provide useful forecasts for the next k periods, and after that forecasts will rely on earlier forecasts rather than on actual data. For example, to forecast the residual of May 2001, when the time of prediction is March 2001, we would need the residual for April 2001. However, because that value is not available, it would be replaced by its forecast. Hence, the forecast for May 2001 would be based on the forecast for April 2001.

ARIMA Models

Moving from AR to ARIMA models creates a larger set of more flexible forecasting models but also requires more statistical expertise. Let us briefly describe ARIMA models[7] and then discuss their use for forecasting.

An Autoregressive Integrated Moving Average Model (ARIMA) is one that directly models the autocorrelation of the series values as well as the autocorrelations of the forecast errors. To see the three components of an ARIMA model (AR, I, and MA), let's start with an AR(p) model:

$$y_t = \beta_0 + \beta_1 y_{t-1} + \beta_2 y_{t-2} + \cdots + \beta_p y_{t-p} + \epsilon_t. \quad (7.4)$$

An AR(p) model captures the autocorrelations of the series values at lags $1, 2, \ldots, p$.

Next, we add autocorrelation terms for the forecast errors (called "Moving Average") up to lag q to get an ARMA(p, q) model:

$$\begin{aligned} y_t &= \beta_0 + \beta_1 y_{t-1} + \beta_2 y_{t-2} + \cdots + \beta_p y_{t-p} \\ &+ \epsilon_t + \theta_1 \epsilon_{t-1} + \theta_2 \epsilon_{t-2} + \cdots + \theta_q \epsilon_{t-q}. \quad (7.5) \end{aligned}$$

AR and ARMA models can only be fitted to data without trend or seasonality. Therefore, an ARIMA model incorporates a preliminary step of differencing,[8] which removes trend. This differencing operation is the "I" (Integrated) in ARIMA. The order of differencing, denoted by parameter d, indicates how many rounds of lag-1 differencing are performed: $d = 0$ means no differencing, which is suitable if the series lacks a trend; $d = 1$ means differencing the series once (at lag-1), which can remove a linear trend; $d = 2$ means differencing the series twice (each time at lag-1), which can remove a quadratic trend. Similarly, a seasonal-ARIMA (SARIMA) model incorporates a step of differencing to remove seasonality and/or autocorrelation terms for capturing remaining seasonal effects.[9]

[7] For a detailed description of ARIMA models see classic time series textbooks such as Chapter 4 in

C. Chatfield and H. Xing. *The Analysis of Time Series: An Introduction*. Chapman & Hall/CRC, 7th edition, 2019

[8] Differencing was described in detail in Section 5.3.

[9] See e.g., `people.duke.edu/~rnau/seasarim.htm`.

ARIMA Models in `sktime`: Using Class PyFableARIMA

In general, ARIMA models require selecting the values of p, d, q and then the software estimates the β and θ parameters. The PyFableARIMA class[10] in the `sktime` package allows the user to specify p, d, q values[11] or leave them blank, in which case the software will search for the p, d, q that result in the model with the best AIC, AICc, or BIC.[12]

PyFableARIMA can also fit seasonal ARIMA models. Seasonal ARIMA models contain an extra set of parameters P, D, Q that specify the number of seasonal autoregressive lags (P), seasonal differencing order (D), and number of seasonal moving average lags (Q). If not specified, the software will search for the best model across seasonal and non-seasonal models.[13]

To illustrate the automated search using *AutoARIMA()*, we use the weekly sales at Walmart (available in *Walmart_One_Pair.csv*; see more information about these data in Example 4 in Section 7.4). After splitting the series into training (the first 105 weeks) and test (the remaining 38 weeks), we ran automated ARIMA to search for the best model over the training period. This can be done using a fast "stepwise" approach, where a search algorithm[14] starts with 4 simple ARIMA models and varies p or q by ± 1 at each step until no further improvement is reached. Alternatively, one can search over a larger set of models by setting argument `stepwise = False`.

Figure 7.6 and Table 7.1 show the code and results of running both models. An ARIMA(1,0,0)(0,1,0)[52] model, which means a single seasonal differencing (lag 52), followed by AR(1), was selected by the stepwise search. The non-stepwise approach selected ARIMA (0,0,2)(0,1,0)[52], which means a single seasonal differencing (lag 52) followed by MA(2). Which model is better for forecasting? From comparing the training and test performance metrics and the performance charts we see that the two models perform almost equally on both the training and test periods. In choosing between the models here, we would choose the simpler stepwise model (lag-52 differencing followed by AR(1)), based on model simplicity (ARIMA(1,0,0) has one less parameter than ARIMA(0,0,2)).

[10] The PyFableARIMA class is an API for the `ARIMA` function in the R `fable` package (`https://fable.tidyverts.org`).

[11] `ARIMA` can take long to run if large parameter values are chosen.

[12] AIC, AICc, and BIC are estimates of prediction error based on information theory and can be used with regression, ARIMA, and ETS models (but not neural networks). Similar to R^2-adjusted, they are computed from the training period by measuring fit to the training data along with a penalty for the number of parameters.

[13] For a seasonal model, *AutoARIMA* requires at least 2 full seasons of data; otherwise, a non-seasonal model will be selected.

[14] For details on the stepwise procedure used in `sktime`'s PyFableARIMA, see `otexts.com/fpp3/arima-r.html`.

In closing, we note that automated search routines should be used with caution, as performance is highly sensitive to the algorithmic implementation and might lead to overfitting if not properly used. Moreover, the search routines are limited to certain ranges of p, d, q and P, D, Q. For example, currently the default limit for `ARIMA`[15] is $p + q + P + Q \leq 6$ and constant $+d + D \leq 2$). Due to these issues, we advocate using the two-layer approach described earlier, when relevant.

[15] This default can be changed by modifying the *order_constraint* argument—see `github.com/tidyverts/fable/blob/master/R/arima.R`.

Table 7.1: Summary of output from running two automated ARIMA models on Walmart weekly sales.

```
Narrow search optimal ARIMA
============================
ARIMA Report:
Series: Weekly_Sales
Model: ARIMA(1,0,0)(0,1,0)[52]

Coefficients:
         ar1
      0.3947
s.e.  0.1244

sigma^2 estimated as 40609852:
AIC=1082.1   AICc=1082.34   BIC=1086.04
```

```
Broad search optimal ARIMA
============================
ARIMA Report:
Series: Weekly_Sales
Model: ARIMA(0,0,2)(0,1,0)[52]

Coefficients:
         ma1     ma2
      0.4339  0.3071
s.e.  0.1343  0.1562

sigma^2 estimated as 39967859:
AIC=1082.37   AICc=1082.86   BIC=1088.28
```

```
Accuracy
========
Series               RMSE    MAE  MAPE  MASE
Narrow (training)  4484.6 2179.6  8.28 0.349
Narrow (test)      4872.1 3660.9 15.78 0.587
Broad  (training)  4406.0 2202.8  8.48 0.353
Broad  (test)      4914.6 3679.0 15.82 0.590
```

7.4 *Including External Information*

Thus far we described how linear regression models can capture trend, seasonality, and autocorrelation (via autoregressive and ARIMA models). Regression models can also capture additional types of patterns that are common in real time series data: outliers, special events, interventions and policy changes, and correlations with other series. Let us consider each separately.

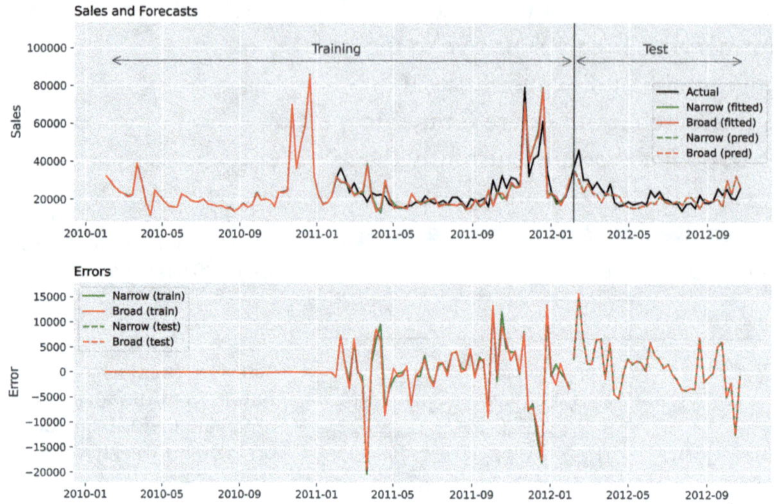

Figure 7.6: Weekly sales at Walmart: automated ARIMA models using a narrower (stepwise) and a broader search.

Code for creating Figure 7.6 and Table 7.1

See full code at `github.com/gshmueli/ptsf-Python`

```
one_pair = pd.read_csv('ptsf-Python/Data/Walmart_One_Pair.csv',
                       parse_dates=['Date'], index_col='Date')
one_pair.index = one_pair.index.to_period('W')
one_pair = one_pair['Weekly_Sales'].to_frame().dropna().squeeze()      # final rows have NA

test_size = len(one_pair.truncate(before='2012-02-06'))
train, test = temporal_train_test_split(one_pair, test_size=test_size)

model = [PyFableARIMA(formula='Weekly_Sales').fit(train),                # narrow search for optimal
         PyFableARIMA(formula='Weekly_Sales', stepwise=False).fit(train)] # broad search for optimal

def calc_residuals(obs, pred):
    return pd.Series(obs.values.flatten() - pred.squeeze().values, index=obs.index)

def apply_model(model, train, test, fitted, pred, resid_train, resid_test):
    fitted.append(model.get_fitted_values())
    pred.append(model.predict(test.index))
    resid_train.append(calc_residuals(train, fitted[-1]))
    resid_test.append(calc_residuals(test, pred[-1]))

fitted, pred, resid_train, resid_test = [], [], [], []
for m in model:
    apply_model(m, train, test, fitted, pred, resid_train, resid_test)

axis[0] = plot_series(one_pair, fitted[0], fitted[1], pred[0], pred[1],
                      markers=['']*5, ax=axis[0], title="Sales and Forecasts", y_label="Sales")

axis[1] = plot_series(resid_train[0], resid_train[1], resid_test[0], resid_test[1],
                      markers=['']*4, title="Errors", labels=None, y_label="Error", ax=axis[1])
```

Outliers

Outliers are extreme data values. As in cross-sectional linear regression, a fitted regression model can be greatly affected or distorted by outliers. Hence, if the training period contains one or more outliers, it is important to carefully assess their effect on the estimated model. To do this, we can fit the model with and without the outliers and see how much the predictive performance is affected. If dropping the outlier(s) does not have much effect, then we can fit the model with the outlier(s).

If the outliers do affect the model, then we should consider removing their effect. We can simply remove these periods from the training data and fit a regression model without them. While regression models can be fitted to series with missing periods, smoothing methods cannot be applied with missing data. Therefore, we might also consider replacing the outliers with forecasts or imputed values (e.g., using a centered moving average).[16]

[16] The same approach can be taken with missing values: either use a regression model or impute/forecast the missing values first, and then fit any forecasting model.

An alternative to removing outliers from the training set is "labeling" them as outliers and incorporating them into the regression model. This is done by using a dummy variable that takes the value 1 for periods with outliers and 0 otherwise, and including it as an additional predictor in the regression model.

Special Events

In some cases, the values in a series are expected to be extreme due to an expected event. Unlike regular patterns such as weekend/weekdays, special events have a known schedule but are less regular than seasonal patterns and are typically shorter. One example of special events is holidays, which affect series such as customer arrivals and sales. Holidays can pose a challenge especially when considering more than a single calendar.[17] Another example is sporting events or music concerts, which affect traffic, accident rates, and more.

[17] For example, lunar calendar holidays (such as Jewish, Muslim, Hindu and Buddhist holidays) fall on different dates of the Gregorian calendar each year.

As with outliers, we can choose to remove these periods from the data (perhaps modeling them separately if we have sufficient instances of the same event), or we can include them in a regression model. Special events can be incorporated into a regression model by using a dummy variable in the model building stage, in the performance evaluation stage, and in the forecasting step. The dummy variable takes the value 1 for periods with special events and 0 otherwise.

During the model building stage, the dummy variable captures special events that took place during the training period and is incorporated as a predictor into the regression model. The same predictor is used to capture special events in the test period for evaluating predictive power. And finally, the dummy variable is used for forecasting future periods that might include special events.

Interventions

In some applications we know that during the training period of our time series there was some intervention or policy change that we think might affect the series' behavior. For example, a special discount that affects sales, or a power cut that affects electricity usage. In such cases, assuming that we know the dates of the intervention, we can either split the series into intervention and non-intervention periods and model each period separately (e.g., a series during discount season and a series during non-discount season), or else we can use one regression model that uses the information on the intervention period timing: create a dummy variable called `Intervention`, which takes the value 1 during periods when the intervention took place, and 0 otherwise. Include this `Intervention` variable in the regression model as a predictor. Note that this type of model assumes that the intervention effect is fixed: it increases or decreases the values of the series by a fixed amount, regardless of other components in the regression model such as trend or seasonality. To capture an intervention with a multiplicative effect, we can use the logarithm of series as the outcome variable.

Correlated External Series

Chapter 4 described the difference between econometric models, where the inclusion of external information is based on a causal theoretical model, and forecasting methods that include external information that improves the accuracy of predictions, regardless of whether a causal model is present. In other words, we include information that is *correlated* with the series of interest, and which shows improved forecast accuracy. Examples of series that correlate with the series of interest include ratings of a TV show that correlate with the social media activity about it; and the so-called "lipstick indicator", whereby lipstick sales appear to go up before economic crises.

The general approach to including external series in a regression model is based on a two-step procedure:

1. Remove trend and seasonality from each of the series (if they exist) — the series of interest (y_t) and the external series (x_t). The result is series y_t^* and x_t^* that contain no trend and no seasonality.

2. Fit a regression model of y_t^* with predictors that are lags of y_t^* and/or x_t^*.

While there might be many external series that are correlated with the series of interest, and multiple lags that we can include as predictors, there are two requirements on what external information to include and how such information is included in the model. One affects the values of the predictors and the other affects the estimated forecasting model itself. We describe each of these considerations next.

Consideration #1: Lagged or Forecasted Predictors Recall that all predictor information must be available at the time of prediction. If the time of prediction is t, then the forecasting model should include either lagged versions of the external information ($x_{t-1}, x_{t-2}, \ldots$) or forecasts of external information that is unavailable at the time of prediction. Availability of information refers not only to past vs. future, but also to delays in acquiring the external data.

Consider the example from Chapter 4 of using information on weekly gas prices for forecasting weekly airfare. While the two series (gas prices and airfare) might be highly correlated, airfare forecasts can only use *already known* gas prices or *forecasted* gas prices. In other words, we can build models of the form

$$(\text{airfare})_t = \beta_0 + \beta_1(\text{gas price})_{t-1} + \epsilon \quad (7.6)$$

and use the already-known gas price from last week, if such data is available in a timely manner. Or, we can build the model

$$(\text{airfare})_t = \beta_0 + \beta_1(\text{forecasted gas price})_t + \epsilon \quad (7.7)$$

which includes an unknown gas price value, and hence requires building a separate model for forecasting weekly gas prices (in itself a harder task, and if the forecast is accurate, a more lucrative one than forecasting airfare).

Consideration #2: Data Availability at Time of Prediction With time series forecasting, it is advantageous to update the model as new information arrives. With regression-type models, updating leads to new β coefficients. Continuous updating requires assuring that the model is trained only on data that is available at the time of prediction. The training period must therefore take into account data availability and the forecast horizon.

For example, forecasting one-week-ahead airfare rates requires the forecasting model to be trained only on data that is available up to the time of prediction. This depends on how quickly we receive prior weekly airfare and gas price figures. Any delay in acquiring the information must be taken into account in choosing the training period. A delay of two weeks requires shifting the training period two weeks back, thereby requiring 3-step-ahead forecasts. In other words, even when training data are available right up to the time of prediction, if in practice we will have a two week delay in getting data, we must not include the last two weeks of training data in the model (though we *can* include forecasts of those data from a separate model).

Careful attention to the choice of training period is needed not only for producing forecasts but also when evaluating predictive performance. Test period forecasts should be based on models that were estimated/trained only on data that was available at the "time of prediction".

Example 1: Forecasting Crop Yield Regression models with external information predictors are common in agriculture for forecasting crop yield. We use one such example to elucidate the issues of predictor choice and training period.

Tannura et al. (2008) developed linear regression models for forecasting annual soybean and corn yield in the United States "Corn Belt" (Iowa, Illinois and Indiana) based on data from 1960–2006.[18] Their forecasting model includes a linear trend to capture technological advances in agriculture as well as external weather predictors: average monthly precipitation ($x_1 = prec$) and average monthly temperature ($x_2 = temp$).[19] The model for yield in year t is:

[18] M. A. Tannura, S. H. Irwin, and D. L. Good. Weather, technology, and corn and soybean yields in the U.S. Corn Belt. Marketing and Outlook Research Report 2008-01, Department of Agricultural and Consumer Economics, University of Illinois at Urbana-Champaign, 2008

[19] The quadratic precipitation terms represent the effect of heavy summer rainfall on yield.

$$\begin{aligned}(yield)_t &= \beta_0 + \beta_1 t + \beta_2(\text{Sept through April prec})_t \\ &+ \beta_3(\text{May prec})_t + \beta_4(\text{June prec})_t + \beta_5(\text{June prec})_t^2 \\ &+ \beta_6(\text{July prec})_t + \beta_7(\text{July prec})_t^2 + \beta_8(\text{Aug prec})_t + \beta_9(\text{Aug prec})_t^2 \\ &+ \beta_{10}(\text{May temp})_t + \beta_{11}(\text{June temp})_t + \beta_{12}(\text{July temp})_t + \beta_{13}(\text{Aug temp})_t + \epsilon.\end{aligned}$$

This model is intended to produce annual forecasts on the first day of June, July, August, September, and October each year (assuming that later forecasts will be more accurate due to increased weather information). To assure that the model is only based on information available at the time of prediction, two steps were taken by the researchers:

1. To produce forecasts in a certain year, the regression model is estimated using data only up to the prior year. For example, to produce forecasts for 2005, the regression model is estimated using weather data only until Dec 2004. This approach was also used for performance evaluation: forecasts for each year in the test period were based on estimating the model on weather data only up to the prior year.

2. On a day when a forecast is generated, actual temperature and precipitation values for that year are entered only for months prior to that date (and hence the subscript t). For later months, the average monthly temperature and precipitation in previous years is used.

Example 2: Forecasting Box-office Revenues In the article "Predicting the Future With Social Media",[20] the authors build a linear regression model for forecasting box-office revenue generated by a movie in its opening weekend. Their predictors are based on tweets that referred to movies prior to their release.[21] The daily tweet rate (TR) from each of the last seven days was included as seven predictors, as well as the number of theaters in which the movie was to be released. Their model for box-office revenues for a movie on the opening week (day t) is given by:

[20] S. Asur and B. A. Huberman. Predicting the future with social media. In *2010 IEEE/WIC/ACM international conference on web intelligence and intelligent agent technology*, volume 1, pages 492–499. IEEE, 2010

[21] Twitter was acquired by Elon Musk in 2022 and renamed as X. The URL is now x.com. A "tweet" is a "post", a "retweet" a "repost", etc.

$$\begin{aligned}(\text{Box-office revenue})_t &= \beta_0 + \beta_1 \text{TR}_{t-1} + \beta_2 \text{TR}_{t-2} + \beta_3 \text{TR}_{t-3} \\ &+ \beta_4 \text{TR}_{t-4} + \beta_5 \text{TR}_{t-5} + \beta_6 \text{TR}_{t-6} + \beta_7 \text{TR}_{t-7} \\ &+ \beta_8 (\text{\# Theaters})_t + \epsilon.\end{aligned}$$

The authors stress two issues related to predictor availability:

1. "In all cases, we are using only data available prior to the release to predict box-office for the opening weekend." This includes the number of theaters, which is known in advance.

2. "Note however, that since historical information on tweets are not available [retroactively], we were able to use data only [for] the movies we have collected"

The latter point relates to practical use of the forecasting model, where the needed predictor information requires special data collection.[22]

[22] One of the most important components of a forecasting project is locating the most informative—and available—data. At the time, Twitter provided exceptional (and free) access to its data. However, X charges for its data and is more limited in what it provides.

Example 3: Forecasting Bike Rentals (regression with external predictors) In Chapter 5 (Section 5.7) we modeled data on hourly rentals at a bike sharing service in Washington, DC. Using the daily data from the same source,[23] we now model the daily counts, but this time we also include external information on whether it is a working day (yes/no) and the type of weather.

In the data set, the variable `workingday` has levels 0 (not working) and 1 (working). We assume this information is known in advance.[24] The variable `weathersit` has levels 1 (clear), 2 (mist), or 3 (rain/snow). Recall that we cannot use weather information on day t as a predictor for bike rentals on day t because that information is unavailable prior to day t. We would therefore

[23] H. Fanaee-T and J. Gama. Event labeling combining ensemble detectors and background knowledge. *Progress in Artificial Intelligence*, pages 1–15, 2013

[24] `workingday` is a combination of day-of-week and holiday dates, which are all known in advance.

need to either use lags of the weather information or else obtain weather forecasts. For illustration purposes, we will assume `weathersit` is a next-day *weather forecast* and that we refresh our bike rental forecasts daily ("roll-forward forecasting"). We partition the series, keeping the final 90 days as the test period.

Our regression model for daily rentals includes terms for trend, day-of-week seasonality, and monthly seasonality. In addition, we incorporate the weather forecast and working-day information as follows: We know from domain expertise that bike rentals are affected by weather differently on working days and non-working days. On non-working days people might choose not to rent bikes on rainy days, whereas on working days there is less choice for commuters. We therefore create an interaction term between `workingday` and `weathersit` and include it as a predictor in our regression model.

Figure 7.7 and Table 7.2 show the code and results of fitting the above regression model to the training period (641 days) and then using it to forecast ridership in the final 90 days. We see in the training period that the model has "dips" on certain days, which are likely non-working days with rain/snow. The coefficient for this combination (-3220) is the largest negative coefficient. We also see that the model misses a few large dips, especially during the test period (over-forecasting on those days). We might need further external information to account for those discrepancies, if such information is available.

Example 4: Forecasting Walmart Sales (ARIMA and External Predictors) In 2014, Walmart ran a competition on Kaggle.com to recruit data scientists.[25] They posted data on weekly sales in 45 stores, by department. In the training set, data was available on 3331 store-department pairs. The training data included weekly sales for 143 weeks and external information for each store about holidays, temperature, fuel price, promotional markdowns, inflation, and unemployment. The test set included external information on only 3169 pairs, some of which were not in the training set. The goal was to forecast sales by store-department pair in each of the test set's 39 weeks.[26]

[25] `www.kaggle.com/c/walmart-recruiting-store-sales-forecasting`.

[26] For this predictive challenge, it is best to use an automated forecasting system. For example, one can construct a "for loop" to fit and make forecasts for the 3169 time series in the test set.

In the following, we illustrate the use of external data for fore-

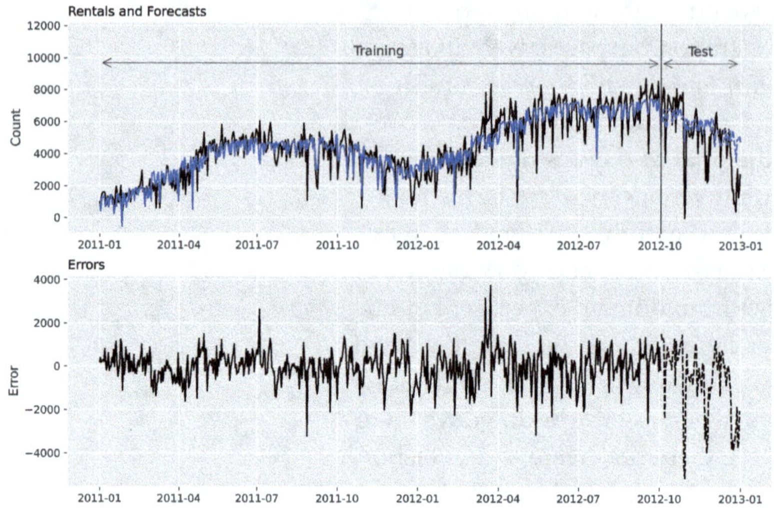

Figure 7.7: Linear regression model fit to the daily Bike Sharing data, including external information on weather and working day.

Code for creating Figure 7.7 and Table 7.2

See full code at github.com/gshmueli/ptsf-Python

```
bike = pd.read_csv('ptsf-Python/Data/BikeSharingDaily.csv',parse_dates=True,index_col=1)

months = pd.get_dummies(bike.index.strftime('%b')).set_index(bike.index).drop(['Jan'], axis=1)
working = pd.get_dummies(bike['workingday'].astype('category'), prefix='Z')
working = working.rename(columns={'Z_0': 'Nonworking', 'Z_1': 'Working'})
weather = pd.get_dummies(bike['weathersit'].astype('category'), prefix='Z')
weather = weather.rename(columns={'Z_1': 'Clear', 'Z_2': 'Mist', 'Z_3': 'RainSnow'})
inter_cols = [f'{col1}_{col2}' for col1 in working.columns for col2 in weather.columns]
tmp_df = pd.concat([working, weather], axis=1)
inter = tmp_df.assign(**{col: tmp_df.eval(col.replace('_', '*')) for col in inter_cols})
X = pd.concat([months[['Feb', 'Mar', 'Apr', 'May', 'Jun', 'Jul', 'Aug', 'Sep', 'Oct', 'Nov', 'Dec']],
    inter[['Working_Clear','Nonworking_Mist','Working_Mist','Nonworking_RainSnow','Working_RainSnow']]
    ], axis=1)

y_train, y_test = temporal_train_test_split(bike['cnt'], test_size=90)
n_train = len(y_train)

mdl = ARDL(lags=0, order=0, trend='ct', seasonal=True).fit(y_train, X=X.iloc[:n_train, :])
fitted = mdl.predict(y_train.index, X=X.iloc[:n_train, :])
pred = mdl.predict(y_test.index, X=X.iloc[n_train:, :])

axis[0] = plot_series(bike['cnt'], fitted, pred, markers=['']*3, ax=axis[0],
            title="Rentals and Forecasts", labels=None, y_label="Count")
axis[1] = plot_series(y_train - fitted, y_test - pred, markers=['']*2, ax=axis[1],
            title="Errors", labels=None, y_label="Error")
print(pd.concat([accuracy_df("Train", y_train, fitted, y_train),
                 accuracy_df("Test", y_test, pred, y_train)]).drop('MASE', axis=1).round(0))
```

Table 7.2: Partial output of the linear model fit to the daily Bike Sharing data (code in Figure 7.7).

```
                              ARDL Model Results
==============================================================================
Dep. Variable:                    cnt   No. Observations:                  641
Model:                      ARDL(...)   Log Likelihood               -5160.270
Method:               Conditional MLE   S.D. of innovations            758.546
Date:                Fri, 11 Apr 2025   AIC                          10370.539
Time:                        19:35:31   BIC                          10482.115
Sample:                    01-01-2011   HQIC                         10413.844
                         - 10-02-2012
===========================================================================================
                              coef    std err          z      P>|z|      [0.025      0.975]
-------------------------------------------------------------------------------------------
const                    1306.3613    135.958      9.609      0.000    1039.365    1573.358
trend                       6.2764      0.180     34.842      0.000       5.923       6.630
s(2,7)                   -364.1915    114.820     -3.172      0.002    -589.677    -138.706
s(3,7)                   -632.8539    207.410     -3.051      0.002   -1040.169    -225.539
s(4,7)                   -492.6959    231.525     -2.128      0.034    -947.369     -38.023
s(5,7)                   -495.5486    229.808     -2.156      0.031    -946.849     -44.249
s(6,7)                   -422.8810    229.569     -1.842      0.066    -873.713      27.951
s(7,7)                   -413.2995    227.781     -1.814      0.070    -860.620      34.021
Feb.L0                    245.9376    142.295      1.728      0.084     -33.503     525.379
Mar.L0                   1126.4496    139.926      8.050      0.000     851.660    1401.239
Apr.L0                   1778.3403    141.550     12.563      0.000    1500.361    2056.319
May.L0                   2385.5309    140.674     16.958      0.000    2109.273    2661.789
Jun.L0                   2484.0938    143.341     17.330      0.000    2202.598    2765.589
Jul.L0                   2109.6485    143.455     14.706      0.000    1827.930    2391.367
Aug.L0                   2025.6225    144.881     13.981      0.000    1741.102    2310.143
Sep.L0                   2121.7471    147.110     14.423      0.000    1832.850    2410.645
Oct.L0                   1419.1817    169.111      8.392      0.000    1087.078    1751.285
Nov.L0                    537.1070    174.663      3.075      0.002     194.101     880.113
Dec.L0                   -296.6630    172.940     -1.715      0.087    -636.284      42.958
Working_Clear.L0          477.0863    204.719      2.330      0.020      75.056     879.117
Nonworking_Mist.L0       -520.3628    122.913     -4.234      0.000    -761.742    -278.984
Working_Mist.L0          -212.2061    208.983     -1.015      0.310    -622.610     198.198
Nonworking_RainSnow.L0 -3220.4817    358.019     -8.995      0.000   -3923.566   -2517.398
Working_RainSnow.L0     -1492.1283    293.087     -5.091      0.000   -2067.696    -916.560
===========================================================================================

Accuracy
--------
         RMSE     MAE   MAPE
Train   759.0   564.0   18.0
Test   1662.0  1176.0  291.0
```

casting weekly sales. Specifically, we examine whether adding holidays information improves forecasts. We analyze the weekly sales from one store-department pair: Store 1 and Department 6. We use the first 105 weeks as training and the final 38 weeks as test. In Section 7.3 we fitted two automated ARIMA models to this training period that had similar performance on the test period. The stepwise procedure yielded the seasonal ARIMA(1,0,0)(0,1,0)[52] model (lag-52 seasonal differencing followed by AR(1)). This model, which we call SAR(1) for short, indicates that once the week-of-year seasonality is accounted for (via differencing), there remains autocorrelation of order 1. We will now see if including external information about holidays improves over this model.

Variable `IsHoliday` is a dummy variable. It equals `TRUE` if the week contains a major US holiday; otherwise, it is `FALSE`. We will include this variable as a predictor in our ARIMA model. Holiday dates are known in advance, so we do not need to use lags.

Using automated stepwise search, we compare two ARIMA models: one model includes only the series itself (as in Section 7.3), and another that includes `IsHoliday` as an additional predictor. We then compare the performance of the two models on the test period to evaluate the effect of `IsHoliday` on forecasts of weekly sales.

Figure 7.8 and Table 7.3 show the code and output comparing the two models. The selected model that includes `IsHoliday` is a regression model with the predictor `IsHoliday` and AR(2) errors. We named this model `AR2_IsHoliday`. This model has worse performance metrics on both the training and test periods compared to the seasonal AR(1), which we named `SAR1`. Examining the performance charts, we see that during the test period both models capture the first holiday peak, but `AR2_IsHoliday` performs poorly on the second holiday as well as the non-holidays compared to the `SAR1` model. In other words, the weekly seasonality appears more informative than the holiday information.[27]

[27] We could also try a SAR(1) model with `IsHoliday` by specifying the model: `PyFableARIMA (Weekly_Sales ~ IsHoliday + 0 + pdq(1,0,0) + PDQ(0,1,0))`. We leave this for the reader to explore.

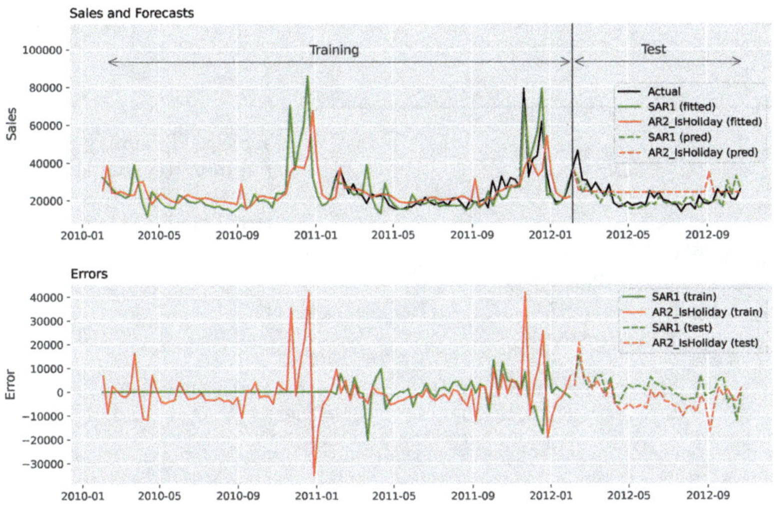

Figure 7.8: Weekly sales at Walmart: Comparing two automated ARIMA models (1) using only the series and (2) with external variable `IsHoliday`.

Code for creating Figure 7.8 and Table 7.3

See full code at `github.com/gshmueli/ptsf-Python`

```
y_train, X_train = train['Weekly_Sales'], train['IsHoliday']
y_test, X_test = test['Weekly_Sales'], test['IsHoliday']

# Automated ARIMA fitted to the training set
SAR1 = PyFableARIMA(formula='Weekly_Sales').fit(y=y_train, X=None)
AR2_IsHoliday = PyFableARIMA(formula='Weekly_Sales ~ IsHoliday').fit(y=y_train, X=X_train)

def apply_model(model, y_train, y_test, X_test, fitted, pred, resid_train, resid_test):
    fitted.append(model.get_fitted_values())
    pred.append(model.predict(fh=test.index, X=X_test))
    resid_train.append(calc_residuals(y_train, fitted[-1]))
    resid_test.append(calc_residuals(y_test, pred[-1]))

fitted, pred, resid_train, resid_test = [], [], [], []

apply_model(SAR1, y_train, y_test, None, fitted, pred, resid_train, resid_test)
apply_model(AR2_IsHoliday, y_train, y_test, X_test, fitted, pred, resid_train, resid_test)

axis[0] = plot_series(one_pair['Weekly_Sales'], fitted[0], fitted[1], pred[0], pred[1],
                      markers=['']*5, ax=axis[0], title="Sales and Forecasts", y_label="Sales")
axis[1] = plot_series(resid_train[0], resid_train[1], resid_test[0], resid_test[1],
                      markers=['']*4, title="Errors", labels=None, y_label="Error", ax=axis[1])
```

Table 7.3: Summary of output from running ARIMA models with and without external predictor `IsHoliday`.

```
print("SAR1")
SAR1.PyFableARIMA_report()

SAR1                                 Coefficients:
ARIMA Report:                                  ar1
Series: Weekly_Sales                        0.3947
Model: ARIMA(1,0,0)(0,1,0)[52]       s.e.   0.1244

                                     sigma^2 estimated as 40609852:  log likelihood=-539.05
                                     AIC=1082.1   AICc=1082.34   BIC=1086.04


print("AR2_IsHoliday")
AR2_IsHoliday.PyFableARIMA_report()

AR2_IsHoliday                      Coefficients:
ARIMA Report:                                ar1     ar2  IsHolidayTRUE  intercept
Series: Weekly_Sales                      0.3891  0.2424      10616.911  24263.028
Model: LM w/ ARIMA(2,0,0) errors   s.e.   0.0963  0.0951       3246.291   2557.851

                                   sigma^2 estimated as 100287084:  log likelihood=-1114.4
                                   AIC=2238.8   AICc=2239.4   BIC=2252.07


pd.concat([accuracy_df("SAR1 (training)", y_train, fitted[0], y_train), \
           accuracy_df("SAR1 (test)", y_test, pred[0], y_train),
           accuracy_df("AR2_IsHoliday (training)", y_train, fitted[1], y_train), \
           accuracy_df("AR2_IsHoliday (test)", y_test, pred[1], y_train)])

Accuracy
========
                   Series   RMSE    MAE  MAPE  MASE
SAR1           (training) 4484.6 2179.6  8.28 0.349
SAR1           (test)     4872.1 3660.9 15.78 0.587
AR2_IsHoliday  (training) 9821.7 5766.7 20.88 0.924
AR2_IsHoliday  (test)     6578.1 5203.9 25.60 0.834
```

7.5 Problems

1. *Canadian Manufacturing Workers Work-Hours:* The time series plot in Figure 7.9 describes the average annual number of weekly hours spent by Canadian manufacturing workers. The data is available in *CanadianWorkHours.csv*.[28]

[28] Data courtesy of Ken Black

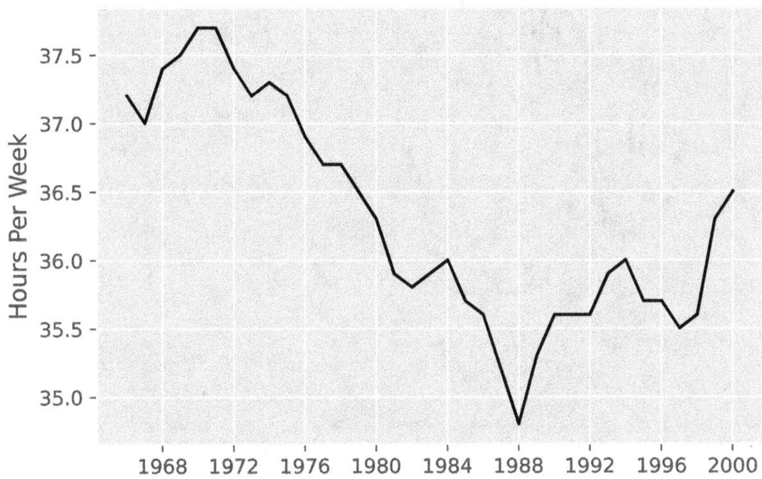

Figure 7.9: Average annual weekly hours spent by Canadian manufacturing workers.

   (a) If we computed the autocorrelation of this series, would the lag-1 autocorrelation exhibit negative, positive, or no autocorrelation? How can you see this from the plot?

   (b) Compute the autocorrelation and produce an ACF plot. Verify your answer to the previous question.

2. *Forecasting Walmart Stock:* Figure 7.10 shows a time plot of Walmart daily closing prices between February 2001 and February 2002. The data is available at `finance.yahoo.com` and in *WalMartStock.csv*.[29] The ACF plots of these daily closing prices and its lag-1 differenced series are in Figure 7.11. Table 7.4 shows the output from fitting an AR(1) model to the series of closing prices and to the series of differences. Use all the information to answer the following questions.

[29] Thanks to Chris Albright for suggesting the use of this data

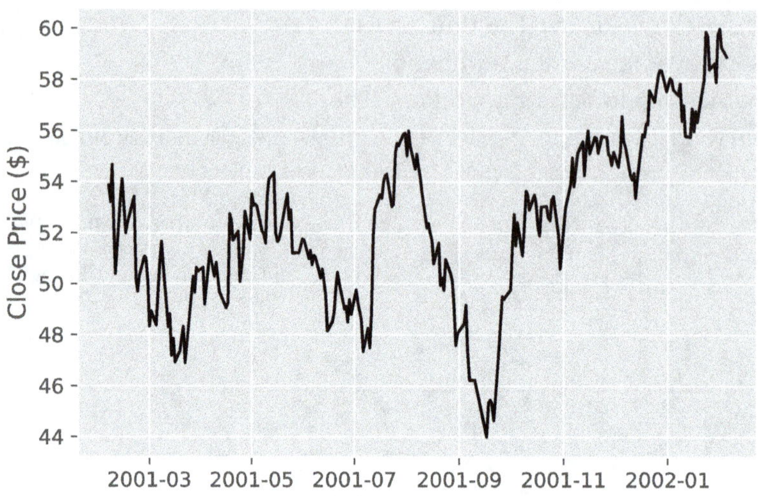

Figure 7.10: Daily closing price of Walmart stock, February 2001–2002.

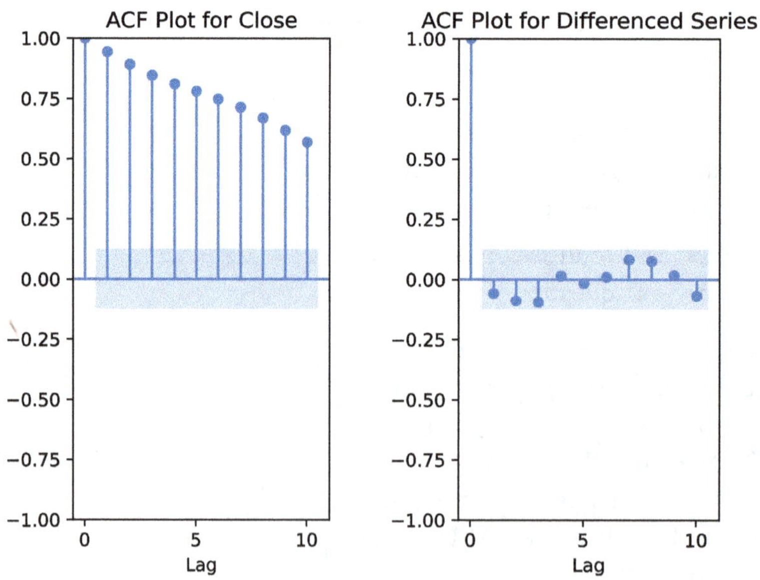

Figure 7.11: ACF plots for the Walmart stock series and its lag-1 differenced series.

```
Series: close                          Series: diff_close
Model: ARDL(1,)                        Model: ARDL(1,)
===============================        ===============================
                coef    std err                        coef    std err
-------------------------------        -------------------------------
const          2.1458     1.037        const          0.0245     0.064
y.L1           0.9594     0.020        y.L1          -0.0581     0.064
===============================        ===============================
```

Table 7.4: Output of fitting AR(1) models to the Walmart stock series and the differenced series. The AR(1) coefficient is labeled `y.L1`.

(a) Create a time plot of the differenced series.

(b) Which of the following is/are relevant for testing whether this stock is a random walk?

- The autocorrelations of the closing price series
- The AR(1) slope coefficient for the closing price series
- The AR(1) constant coefficient for the closing price series
- The autocorrelations of the differenced series
- The AR(1) slope coefficient for the differenced series
- The AR(1) constant coefficient for the differenced series

(c) Recreate the AR(1) model output for the Close price series shown in the left of Table 7.4. Does the AR model indicate that this is a random walk? Explain how you reached your conclusion.

(d) What are the implications of finding that a time series is a random walk? Choose the correct statement(s) below.

- You cannot obtain forecasts better than naive forecasts.
- The series is random.
- The changes in the series from one period to the other are random.

3. *Souvenir Sales:* The file *SouvenirSales.csv* contains monthly sales for a souvenir shop at a beach resort town in Queensland, Australia, between 1995 and 2001.[30]

Back in 2001, the store wanted to use the data to forecast sales for the next 12 months (year 2002). They hired an analyst to generate forecasts. The analyst first partitioned the data into training and test periods, with the test set containing the last

[30] Source: Hyndman and Yang (2018) tsdl: Time Series Data Library. v0.1.0. `github.com/FinYang/tsdl`.

12 months of data (year 2001). She then fit several ARIMA and regression models to sales, using the training period. Let's follow her steps.

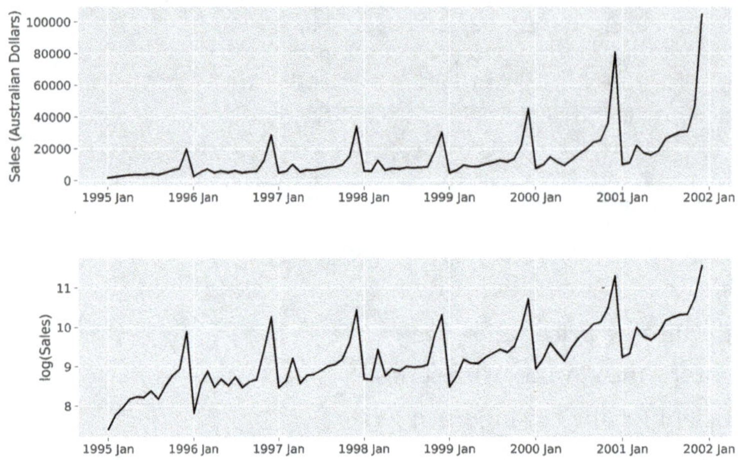

Figure 7.12: Monthly sales at Australian souvenir shop in dollars (top) and in log scale (bottom).

(a) Run ARIMA on the Sales series using *PyFableARIMA*, without specifying any parameters. This will search through a set of ARIMA models and select the "best" one.

i. Look at the selected ARIMA model. What are the values of p, d, q and P, D, Q?

ii. Use the selected model to forecast sales in February 2001.

iii. Now try fitting an ARIMA model to $log(Sales)$, again without specifying any parameters. What model was selected now? (What are the values of p, d, q and P, D, Q?)

iv. Use the selected model to forecast sales in February 2001. Is the forecast substantially different from the first ARIMA model you used?

v. Compare the predictive performance of the two auto-selected ARIMA models, by comparing performance metrics and by examining performance charts. Is one of the models preferable to the other? If so, which one and how have you determined this?

(b) Run a regression model for sales with an exponential trend and multiplicative monthly seasonality. Use this model to forecast the sales in February 2001.

(c) Using the training period, create an ACF plot until lag-15 for the forecast errors. Now fit an AR model with lag-2 [ARIMA(2, 0, 0)] to the forecast errors.

i. Examining the ACF plot and the estimated coefficients of the AR(2) model (and their standard errors), what can we learn about the possibility of improving the regression model's forecasts?

ii. Compute an improved forecast for February 2001, combining the regression and AR(2) models.[31]

iii. How does this improved forecast compare to the forecasts from the regression alone? To the two ARIMA models? (Consider also the actual value in February 2001).

(d) We now want to forecast February 2002 (in the future). Think carefully which data to use for model fitting, and which parameters to set for each model. Compute the forecast using each of the four models: two ARIMA models, a regression model, and a regression model with AR(2) errors.

[31] *Hint*: this can be done with a single *PyFableARIMA* call, or in two steps using *ARDL* and then *PyFableARIMA* as in Figure 7.4.

4. *Shipments of Household Appliances:* The file *ApplianceShipments.csv* contains the series of quarterly shipments (in millions of USD) of U.S. household appliances between 1985 and 1989.[32] The series is plotted in Figure 7.13.

[32] Data courtesy of Ken Black

(a) If we compute the autocorrelation of the series, which lag (> 0) is most likely to have the largest coefficient (in absolute value)?

(b) Create an ACF plot and compare it with your answer.

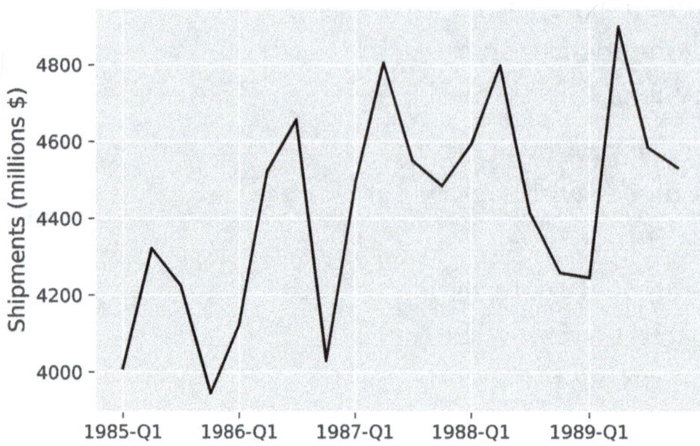

Figure 7.13: Quarterly shipments of U.S. household appliances over five years.

5. *Forecasting Australian Wine Sales:* Figure 7.14 shows time plots of monthly sales of six types of Australian wines (red, rose, sweet white, dry white, sparkling, and fortified) for 1980–1994. The data is available in *AustralianWines.csv*.[33] The units are thousands of liters. You are hired to obtain short-term forecasts (2–3 months ahead) for each of the six series, and this task will be repeated every month.

[33] Source: Hyndman and Yang (2018) tsdl: Time Series Data Library. v0.1.0. `github.com/FinYang/tsdl`.

   (a) Fortified wine has the largest market share of the six types of wine considered. You are asked to focus on fortified wine sales alone and produce as accurate as possible forecasts for the next 2 months.

      - Start by partitioning the data using the period until December 1993 as the training period.
      - Fit a regression model to sales with a linear trend and seasonality.

      i. Create the "actual vs. forecast" plot. What can you say about model fit?

      ii. Use the regression model to forecast sales in January and February 1994.

   (b) Create an ACF plot for the residuals from the above model until lag-12.

      i. Examining this plot, which of the following statements are reasonable?

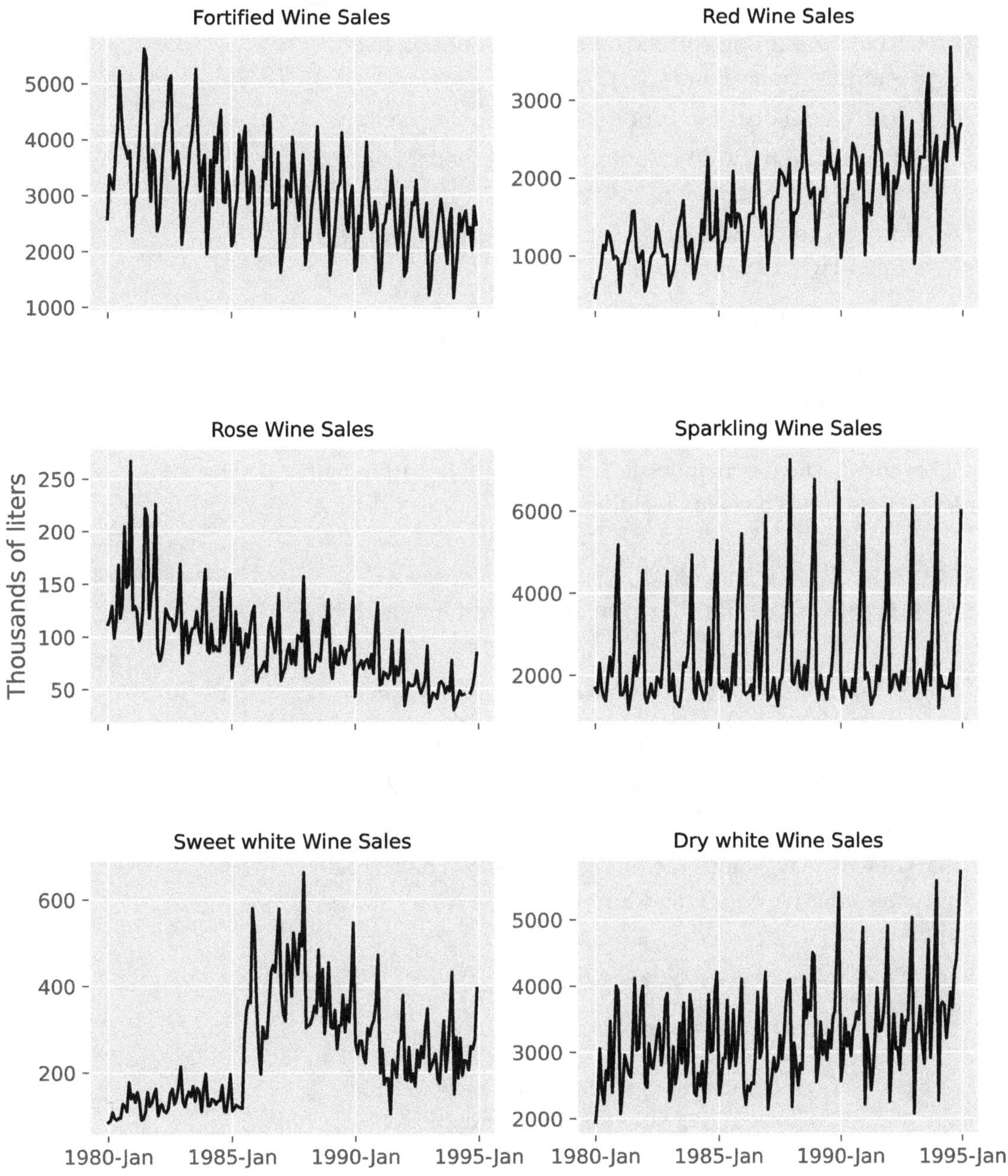

Figure 7.14: Monthly sales of six types of Australian wines between 1980–1994

- Decembers (month 12) are not captured well by the model.
- There is a strong correlation between sales on the same calendar month.
- The model does not capture the seasonality well.
- We should try to fit an autoregressive model with lag-12 to the residuals.

ii. How can you handle the above effect without adding another layer to your model?

6. *Forecasting Weekly Sales at Walmart:* The data in *Walmart-Store1Dept72.csv* is a subset from a larger datasets on weekly department-wise sales at 45 Walmart stores, which were released by Walmart as part of a hiring contest hosted on `kaggle.com`.[34] The file includes data on a single department at one specific store. The fields include:

[34] The full dataset and the contest description are available at `www.kaggle.com/c/walmart-recruiting-store-sales-forecasting`.

- `Date`: The week
- `Weekly_Sales`: Sales for the given department in the given store
- `IsHoliday`: Whether the week is a special holiday week
- `Temperature`: Average temperature in the region
- `Fuel_Price`: Cost of fuel in the region
- `MarkDown1-5`: Anonymized data related to promotional markdowns that Walmart is running. `MarkDown` data is only available after Nov 2011, and is not available for all stores all the time.
- `CPI`: The consumer price index
- `Unemployment`: The unemployment rate

Figure 7.15 shows a time plot of weekly sales in this department. We are interested in creating a forecasting model for weekly sales for the next 52 weeks.

(a) Recreate the time plot of the weekly sales data. Which systematic patterns appear in this series?

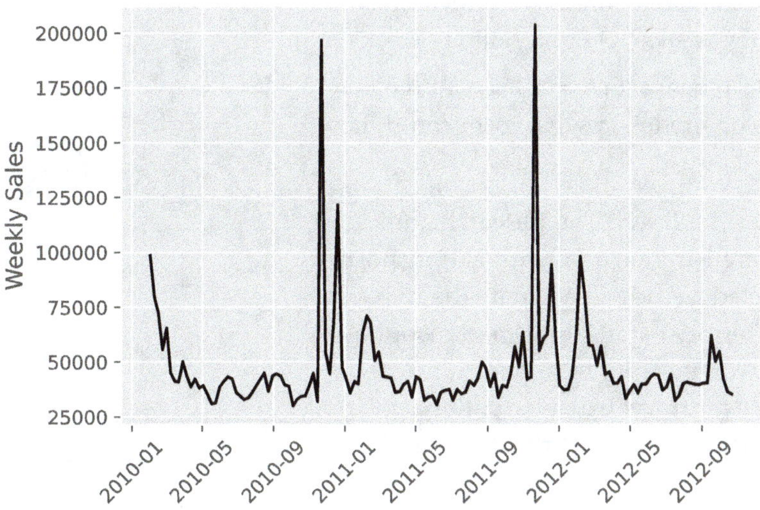

Figure 7.15: Weekly sales at department 72 of Walmart store 1.

(b) Create time plots of the other numerical series (`Temperature`, `Fuel_Price`, `CPI`, and `Unemployment`). Also create scatter plots of the sales series against each of these four series (each point in the scatter plot will be a week). From the charts, which of the four series would potentially be useful as external predictors in a regression model for forecasting sales?[35]

[35] *Hint*: A convenient way to get the scatter plots is to use the `pairplot` function from the `seaborn` package and focus on the column or row with the `Weekly_Sales`. Create a DataFrame `df` with the 5 columns of interest and call `seaborn(df, kind='reg')`.

(c) The period to forecast is November 2, 2012 to July 26, 2013. For which of the series does the file include data for this forecasting period? For which series is there no data for this period? Explain why.

(d) How is it possible that we have `Temperature` for the prediction period?

(e) Treat the first 91 weeks (until Oct 28, 2011) as the training period, and the next 52 weeks as the test period. Create seasonal naive forecasts for the test period. Create a time plot of these forecasts and a plot of the forecast errors series. Compute the average error and RMSE.

(f) Build a regression model for `Weekly_Sales` that includes only `IsHoliday` as a predictor. Compare the performance of this model to the seasonal naive forecasts. Which one performs better on holiday weeks? On non-holiday weeks?

(g) If we wanted to include `Temperature` and `Fuel_Price` as predictors in the regression model, in what form could they be included?

7. *Forecasting Post-September 11 Air Travel:* The Research and Innovative Technology Administration's Bureau of Transportation Statistics (BTS) conducted a study to evaluate the impact of the September 11, 2001, terrorist attack on U.S. transportation. The goal of the study was stated: "to provide a greater understanding of the passenger travel behavior patterns of persons making long distance trips before and after September 11."

   The report analyzes monthly passenger movement data between January 1990 and April 2004. Data on three monthly time series for this period are given in the file *Sept11Travel.csv*: (1) actual airline revenue passenger miles (Air), (2) rail passenger miles (Rail), and (3) vehicle miles traveled (Auto).

   Suppose that instead of assessing the impact of the September 11 terrorist attack, our goal is to forecast future air travel.

   (a) Perform the following steps:

   - Create a dummy variable `afterAttack` (1 = if the month is after the attack).
   - Partition the series so that years 2003–2004 are in the test period.
   - Create a benchmark seasonal naive model (choose an appropriate seasonal cycle).
   - Fit a linear regression model with trend and/or seasonality predictors (as needed for Air). Show the resulting model.[36]
   - Fit a linear regression model with trend and/or seasonality predictors and the new `afterAttack` predictor. Show the resulting model.
   - Fit an ARIMA model with the new `afterAttack` predictor. Show the resulting model.

[36] *Hint*: See the code accompanying Table 6.4.

(b) Compare the performance of the four models in terms of training and test performance. Compute performance metrics and create performance charts. Which model performs best? In what sense?

(c) Since all three series (`Air`, `Rail`, `Auto`) have strong monthly seasonality, let us consider using one series as an external predictor for forecasting `Air`.

- Create lag-12 variables for each of the Rail and Auto series.
- Create scatter plots of the Air and lag(12) variables.

Based on the scatter plots, which series is the most promising external predictor for forecasting `Air`?[37]

[37] *Hint*: Use the `pairplot()` function from the `seaborn` package to plot the scatter plot matrix.

(d) Using your chosen external predictor, fit three models for forecasting `Air`:

- Linear regression with the promising predictor and `afterAttack` (only 2 predictors). Show the resulting model.
- Linear regression with the promising predictor, `afterAttack`, seasonality, and trend. Show the resulting model.
- ARIMA with the promising predictor and `afterAttack`. Show the resulting model.

(e) Compare the performance of the three models from (d) in terms of performance metrics and charts (training and test). Compare them also to the previous three models in (a). Which model would you choose for forecasting future air travel? Why? Consider not only predictive performance but also practical considerations such as simplicity, computation, costs of over/under-forecasting, etc.

8
Neural Networks

8.1 Neural Networks for Forecasting Time Series

Among artificial intelligence algorithms used for predicting cross-sectional data, *neural networks* (also known as *artificial neural networks* or *neural nets*) are commonly used for time series forecasting, especially in financial forecasting, and when external information is useful. Neural networks can be used to generate numerical as well as binary forecasts.

The neural network algorithm is based on a model of biological activity in the brain, where neurons are interconnected and learn from experience. Neural nets are highly data-driven, and can become computationally expensive. Their structure allows us to capture complex relationships between predictors and a response, and setting them up requires little user input. The "price" is that neural nets are considered a blackbox, in the sense that the relationship they capture is not easy to understand. Hence, neural nets are good candidates for automated predictive tasks, where the main goal is generating accurate forecasts, but they are an inadequate choice for descriptive or explanatory tasks.

In terms of performance, the forecasting literature provides inconclusive evidence regarding the performance of neural networks for time series forecasting. In tourism forecasting, for instance, neural networks were found to outperform other methods in a few cases, while producing inferior performance in others.[1] Similar results are reported in financial series and re-

[1] C. J. Lin, H. F. Chen, and T. S. Lee. Forecasting tourism demand using time series, artificial neural networks and multivariate adaptive regression splines: Evidence from Taiwan. *International Journal of Business Administration*, 2(2):14–24, 2011

newable energy forecasting. It appears that the performance of neural networks is more beneficial with high frequency series, such as hourly, daily, or weekly data, compared to low frequency series.[2] And finally, it can be combined with other methods to produce ensemble forecasts.

In this chapter we give a brief overview of neural nets and then focus on their use for time series forecasting.[3]

[2] A performance comparison of neural nets to alternatives is given on the 2008 *NN5 Forecasting Competition for Neural Networks & Computational Intelligence* website `http://neural-forecasting-competition.com/NN5/motivation.htm`.

[3] On neural nets in cross-sectional prediction, see chapter "Neural Nets" in .

G. Shmueli, P. C. Bruce, P. Gedeck, and N. R. Patel. *Machine Learning for Business Analytics: Techniques, Concepts and Applications in Python*. John Wiley & Sons, 2nd edition, 2025

8.2 *The Neural Network Model*

We have seen that linear regression can be used for modeling non-linear relationships between the predictors and the outcome variable by using transformations such as $\log(y)$ or creating *derived variables* from the predictor variables such as t^2 or $\sin(\pi t/365.25)$. A derived variable is a transformation of the original variables. Examples include dummy variables created from a categorical variable and transformations such as $\log(y)$. Neural networks offer a further extension of linear regression by creating *multiple layers of derived variables*.

A neural network links predictors and outcome through a sequence of *layers*. In each layer, some operation is performed on the input information to produce an output (thereby creating a derived variable). The output of one layer is the input into the next layer. A neural network consists of three types of "layers", as illustrated in Figure 8.1:

1. An *input layer* accepts the input values of the predictors (numerical or binary).

2. One or more *hidden layers* create derived variables. A hidden layer receives inputs from the previous layer, performs a calculation on those inputs, and generates an output.

3. An *output layer* receives inputs from the last hidden layer and produces predicted values (numerical or binary).

Each layer contains *nodes*, denoted by circles in Figure 8.1. Each node is a variable. The input layer nodes are the original predictor variables. For example, in Figure 8.1 nodes 1 and 2 take

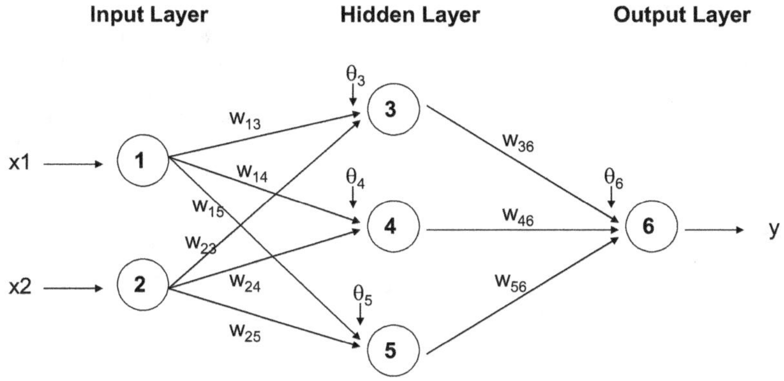

Figure 8.1: Schematic of a neural network with a single hidden layer, for predicting a single outcome (y) from two predictors (x_1, x_2).

as input the values of predictors x_1 and x_2, respectively. Their output is identical to their input.

Hidden layer nodes are derived variables. In particular, they are a *weighted sum of the inputs* to which some monotone function, called an *activation function*, is applied. Common functions are linear, exponential, and s-shaped functions such as the logit and hyperbolic tangent.[4]

[4] s-shaped or *sigmoidal* functions are common because they squash very small and very large values while maintaining near-linearity for mid-range values. The two most common s-shaped functions are the *logit* function $g(s) = \frac{1}{1+e^{-s}}$ and the *hyperbolic tangent* function $g(s) = -1 + \frac{2}{1+e^{-s}}$.

Node Computation in Technical Terms

For a set of input values $x_1, x_2, \ldots, x_p$, the output of node j is the weighted sum $\theta_j + \sum_{i=1}^{p} w_{ij}x_i$, where $\theta_j, w_{1j}, \ldots, w_{pj}$ are weights that are initially set randomly and then adjusted as the network "learns". The constant θ_j controls the level of contribution of node j.

An activation function of choice, $g(s)$, is then applied to the weighted sum to produce the derived variable $g(\theta_j + \sum_{i=1}^{p} w_{ij}x_i)$, which is the output of node j.

In Figure 8.1, for instance, node 3 computes the weighted sum of nodes 1 and 2 as $\theta_3 + w_{13}x_1 + w_{23}x_2$. An activation function is then applied to this weighted sum. Similarly, the output of node 6 is the activation function applied to a weighted sum of θ_6 and the outputs of nodes 3, 4, and 5.

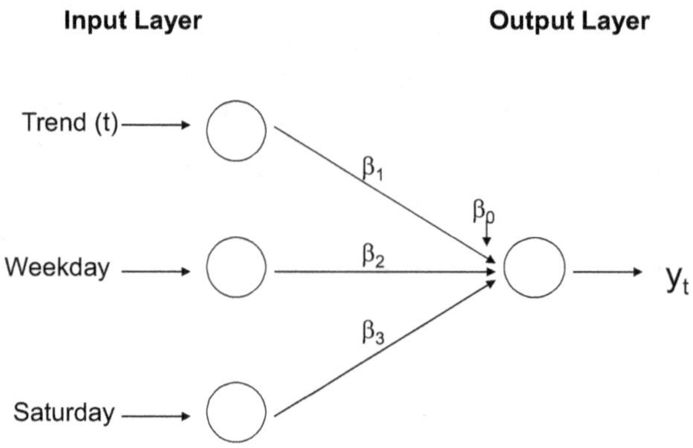

Figure 8.2: Schematic of a neural network reflecting a linear or logistic regression model with trend and weekday/Saturday/Sunday seasonality.

Linear regression, logistic regression,[5] and autoregressive models can be written as neural networks without hidden layers. This is important to notice, because in practice the best performing neural network is often the simplest one: that is, one with no hidden layers.[6] Figure 8.2 displays a neural network diagram for a linear or logistic regression with three predictors: a linear trend and two dummies for capturing an additive weekday/Saturday/Sunday seasonality pattern. Note that:

- A linear activation function corresponds to the linear regression model

$$y_t = \beta_0 + \beta_1 t + \beta_2 Weekday + \beta_3 Saturday + \epsilon.$$

- An exponential activation function $g(s) = e^s$ corresponds to the linear regression model

$$\log(y_t) = \beta_0 + \beta_1 t + \beta_2 Weekday + \beta_3 Saturday + \epsilon.$$

- A logit activation function corresponds to the logistic regression model

$$P(y_t = 1) = \frac{1}{1 + e^{-(\beta_0 + \beta_1 t + \beta_2 Weekday + \beta_3 Saturday)}}.$$

Figure 8.3 shows a neural network schematic for an AR(3) model (using a linear activation function). A general schematic for a neural network used for forecasting a time series is shown in Figure 8.4.

[5] For logistic regression and its use in forecasting, see Section 9.3 in Chapter 9.

[6] N. K. Ahmed, A. F. Atiya, N. El Gayar, and H. El-Shishiny. An empirical comparison of machine learning models for time series forecasting. *Econometric Reviews*, 29:594–621, 2010

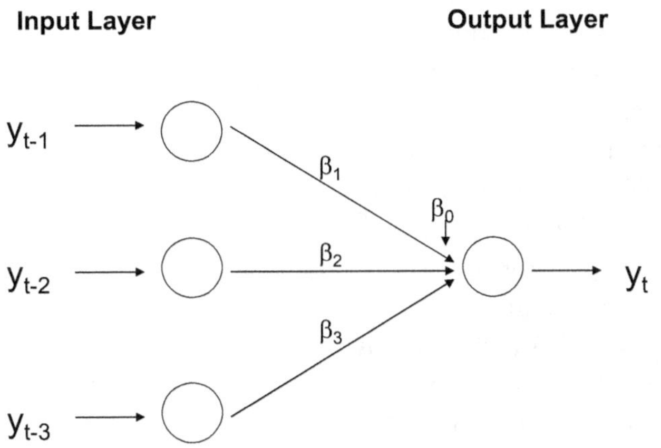

Figure 8.3: Schematic of a neural network reflecting an AR(3) model (assuming a linear activation function).

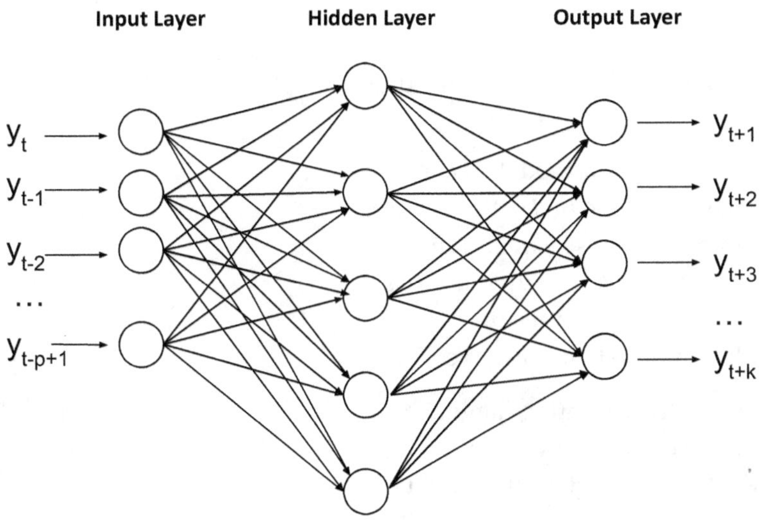

Figure 8.4: Schematic of a forecasting neural network where the inputs are multiple lags. The network includes a hidden layer, and produces forecasts at several horizons. Generalizations of this could include external information (as in Figure 8.2) and additional hidden layers.

Note that a neural net can include multiple output nodes. In the context of time series forecasting, we use this to produce forecasts of different horizons. The schematic in Figure 8.4 is based on roll-forward forecasting, where forecasts for times $t+1, t+2, \ldots$ are based on the series "moving forward" one period at a time. Additional hidden layers can be added in Figure 8.4 to further increase the complexity of the relationship between the inputs and output. The diagram can also be expanded to include external information by specifying additional input nodes. In fact, successful applications of neural networks for time series forecasting are often based on including external information rather than extrapolation. For example, Law and Au[7] found that for forecasting annual Japanese tourist arrivals in Hong Kong, a neural network outperformed naive forecasts, linear regression, moving average, and exponential smoothing. The input layer of their neural network model included six nodes: Service Price, Average Hotel Rate, Foreign Exchange Rate, Population, Marketing Expenses, and Gross Domestic Expenditure. All of these capture external information.

[7] R. Law and N. Au. A neural network model to forecast Japanese demand for travel to Hong Kong. *Tourism Management*, 20:89–97, 1999

8.3 Preprocessing

Four preprocessing issues should be considered prior to running a neural network:

Creating Derived Predictors: As in regression models, we can create predictors such as lagged versions of the time series, lagged versions of external information, seasonal dummies, and a time index to capture trend. These are then used as inputs to the neural network. `sktime` provides utilities to handle lagged variables with a minimal amount of code.

Handling rows with missing values: When creating lagged variables that will be included as predictors, rows with missing values must be handled. Possible treatment would be removal of such rows or imputing the missing values. The choice would depend on the model.

Scaling: Often, neural networks perform best when the predictors and response are on a scale of [0,1] or [-1,1]. Hence, in the time series context, the series itself as well as all predictors should be scaled before running the neural network.

Removing trend and seasonality: There have been mixed reports in the literature regarding the need for removing trend and seasonality prior to using neural networks for forecasting time series. While some researchers claim that neural networks can automatically account for trend and seasonal patterns, substantial empirical evidence has shown that deseasonalization and de-trending improve the performance of neural networks.[8] To deseasonalize and/or detrend a series, use any of the methods described in previous chapters (regression, exponential smoothing, etc.) with the exception of differencing, which has been shown to lead to inferior performance.[9]

[8] G. P. Zhang and D. M. Kline. Quarterly time-series forecasting with neural networks. *IEEE Transactions on Neural Networks*, 18(6):1800–1814, 2007

[9] N. K. Ahmed, A. F. Atiya, N. El Gayar, and H. El-Shishiny. An empirical comparison of machine learning models for time series forecasting. *Econometric Reviews*, 29:594–621, 2010

8.4 User Input

To run a neural network, users must determine the number of input nodes, the number of hidden layers, the number of nodes per hidden layer, the activation function, and the number of output nodes. Let us examine each choice separately:

The number of input nodes is equal to the number of predictors and is therefore problem-dependent. Generally, the more input nodes, the less time periods for the network to train on. Zhang and Kline conducted a large study on neural network forecasting and reached the conclusion that the number of predictors is a critical choice:

> [...] different combinations of input variables can have significant impact on the model performance. Therefore, in applying [neural networks], it is critical to identify a set of important input variables to be included in the modeling process.

The number of hidden layers affects the level of complexity of the relationship between the inputs and outputs. Typically, 1-2 layers are sufficient. Using too many layers can cause overfitting, while too few leads to underfitting.

The number of nodes per hidden layer requires trial and error. Using too few nodes will lead to underfitting, while too many nodes will lead to over-fitting. Comparing the training and test performance can help in determining an adequate number.

Choice of activation function: The most common activation functions for binary inputs/outputs are s-shaped functions (e.g. logistic). For numerical inputs/outputs, common activation functions are linear and rectified linear unit (ReLU) functions.[10]

[10] The ReLU function outputs the same value as the input if the input is positive, and outputs zero otherwise: $ReLU(x) = max(0, x)$.

The number of output nodes depends on the number of forecasts that we want to generate. Some software packages are limited to a single output node.

8.5 Forecasting with Neural Nets in Python using `sktime`

Two widely known Python machine learning ecosystems that implement neural networks include `scikit-learn` (also called `sklearn`) and `tensorflow` with `keras`. One of the goals of `sktime` is to provide time-series analysts easy access to `scikit-learn`.

To see the power this approach might provide, let's consider forecasting models of the form shown in Figure 8.4:

$$F_{t+k} = f(y_t, y_{t-1}, \ldots, y_{t-p+1}).$$

These models use the most recent p values as predictors. The autoregressive $AR(p)$ models from Chapter 7 correspond to the special case where the function f is linear. A much larger class of models is obtained if we allow f to be an (unknown!) nonlinear function, which we try to discover using neural nets. This can be depicted in Figure 8.4, where we would have p values in the input layer, one value in the output layer, and non-linear activation functions linking the nodes in the different layers.

Fitting such a neural network model directly in `sklearn` or `tensorflow` with `keras` would require several operations. First, a preprocessing step to partition the training series into a sequence of p-long sub-series (rolling windows) that serve as predictors. For each sub-series we set the respective output value. Table 8.1 shows the required structure.

Predictor series (X)	Output value (Y)
$y_1, y_2, \ldots, y_p$	y_{p+1}
$y_2, y_3, \ldots, y_{p+1}$	y_{p+2}
$\vdots$	$\vdots$
$y_{t-p}, \ldots, y_{t-1}$	y_t

Table 8.1: Converting a time series of length t into a sequence of sub-series and associated one-step-ahead output values.

Second, preprocessing may also include a step that normalizes the inputs to be in the range [0,1] or [-1,1], or standardizes them to have mean 0 and variance 1.

Third, once we have fit the model in the training period, we need to set up the predictors for the test period. As we discussed in Chapter 7, the challenge when using models based on lagged series (such as AR and ARIMA) is that forecasting beyond one-step ahead requires using forecasted values. For instance, suppose that you want to forecast two months ahead in the test period and you have included the last two months' values as predictors in the training period. Your predictors in the test period for the two-steps-ahead forecast will then need to include the last value in the training period and the one-step ahead forecast.

Fourth, an additional problem when using neural networks is that the fitting stage depends on a choice of random initial weights. This dependence can be mitigated by fitting several neural networks, each with a different choice of initial weights, and averaging the different networks' forecasts into an ensemble forecast.

Finally, to obtain forecasts in the original scale, post-processing may be required to invert the normalization step,

Fortunately, there is a forecaster class in `sktime` that will do all this preprocessing, tabularization, ensembling, and post-processing work for you when working with a time series. The forecaster *NNetAR* fits "neural network autoregression" (NNAR) models.[11] The class *NNetAR* has several main arguments: *n_networks*, *n_nodes*, *p*, *P*, *period*, and *auto*.

[11] NNAR refers to this type of model. In contrast, *NNetAR* refers to the Python forecaster class in the `sktime` package (inspired by the `NNETAR` function in the R `fable` package `https://fable.tidyverts.org`.)

- *n_networks* controls the number of neural networks fit. The default is 20.

- p specifies the order of the non-seasonal autoregressive (AR) terms. For instance, a neural network autoregression with $p = 2$ would include the lag 1 and lag 2 of the series as inputs. If not specified, *NNetAR* chooses p based on the best-fit AR(p) model (see *auto* below).

- P specifies the order of the seasonal autoregressive terms. The number of seasonal lags P is set to 1 as its default. A seasonal lag is the last observed value from the same season. For example, with monthly data, a neural network autoregression with $p = 2$ and $P = 1$ would include lag-1, lag-2, and lag-12 of the series as inputs.

- *period* specifies the periodic nature of the seasonality (e.g., 4 for quarterly data and 12 for monthly data).

- *NNetAR* only fits a neural network with a single hidden layer. *n_nodes* refers to the number of nodes in the hidden layer. Its default setting is the number of input nodes plus one ($p + P + 1$) divided by two and rounded to the nearest integer.

- *scale_inputs* controls scaling of the predictors. If `True`, inputs are scaled by subtracting the column means and dividing by their respective standard deviations (i.e., normalized to zero mean and unit variance). The inverse transformation is done automatically for outputs. The default is `True`.

- *auto* allows automated search for p and P. If `auto=True`, p and P are ignored, and optimal values for p and P are determined via AIC. For seasonal time series, this will be computed on the seasonally-adjusted data (via STL decomposition).

NNetAR uses the logistic activation function to map the input value into the hidden node(s) values. To go from the hidden nodes' values to the output value, a linear activation function is used.

8.6 *Example: Forecasting Amtrak Ridership*

To illustrate the use of neural networks for forecasting a time series, we return to the Amtrak ridership example, using *NNetAR*. Suppose that we are interested again in producing one-month-ahead, two-month-ahead,..., 36-month-ahead forecasts.

Preparing the Data

The annual seasonality that characterizes the monthly ridership series can be addressed in several ways in the neural network:

1. include 11 non-seasonal lags and 1 seasonal lag as predictors (done by the *NNetAR* forecaster), or
2. include 11 dummy variables, or
3. deseasonalize the series using some method.

While each avenue can be investigated, we illustrate the results for the first option, which is a common choice in neural network forecasting. As usual, we partition the data into training and test periods, such that the last 36 months are the test period. Note that there are 159 months in the ridership time series. After dropping the first 12 months due to the lag variables and the 36 months for the test period, the training period contains 111 months of data.

Neural Network Output

The result from running a neural network autoregression for forecasting monthly ridership is shown in Figure 8.5. Forecasts for the test period are obtained, as usual, using `predict()`. The code for creating the time plot and for computing performance measures is shown below the plot. The fitted NNAR$(11,1,7)_{12}$ model is a neural network with the last 12 months as predictors (11 from the non-seasonal lags and 1 from the seasonal lag), 7 hidden nodes, and a seasonal period of 12 (monthly data). Because each neural network's parameters are initialized randomly before they are optimized, we set a specific seed using `np.random.seed(RANDOM_SEED)` so that we can replicate our results. Otherwise, the neural network would be different each time we run *NNetAR*.

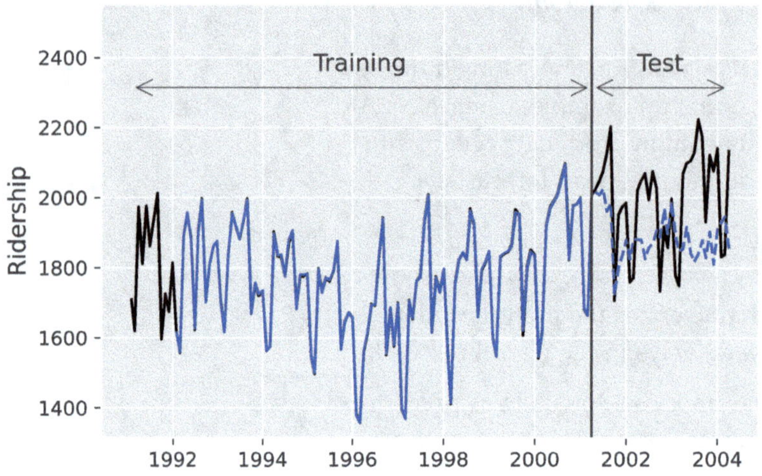

Figure 8.5: Neural network autoregression fitted to the Amtrak ridership data in the training period and forecasted in the test period.

Code for creating Figure 8.5 and Table 8.2

See full code at github.com/gshmueli/ptsf-Python

```
RANDOM_SEED = 43
np.random.seed(RANDOM_SEED)

ridership = pd.read_csv('ptsf-Python/Data/Amtrak.csv', parse_dates=['Month'],
                        date_parser=lambda x: pd.to_datetime(x, format='%Y %b')).set_index('Month')
ridership.index = ridership.index.to_period('M').to_timestamp('M')  # Convert to month-end frequency

TRAIN_SIZE = len(ridership.index) - 36
TEST_SIZE = 36
p, P, SP, SCALE_INPUTS = 11, 1, 12, True
train = ridership.iloc[0:TRAIN_SIZE,:]
test = ridership.iloc[TRAIN_SIZE:(TRAIN_SIZE+TEST_SIZE),:]

nnetar = NNetAR(p=p, P=P, period=SP, n_nodes=7, n_networks=20, scale_inputs=SCALE_INPUTS, auto=False)
nnetar.fit(train)
pred = nnetar.predict(test.index)
fitted = nnetar.predict(train.index[SP:])

fig, ax = plt.subplots(figsize=(6, 4))
ax = plot_series(ridership, fitted, pred, markers=['']*3, y_label='Ridership',ax=ax)

print(pd.concat([accuracy_df('Train', train[SP:], fitted, train[SP:]),
    accuracy_df('Test', test, pred, train)]).round(3))
```

	RMSE	MAE	MAPE	MASE
Train	3.173	2.348	0.134	0.019
Test	177.586	152.136	7.458	1.214

Model	Scale Inputs	Dataset	RMSE	MAE	MAPE
NNetAR p=11,P=1	No	Training	156	128	7.45
		Test	264	230	11.1
NNetAR p=11,P=1	Yes	Training	3.17	2.35	0.13
		Test	178	152	7.46
NNetAR p=2,P=1	No	Training	144	117	6.79
		Test	257	224	10.8
NNetAR p=2,P=1	Yes	Training	53.8	42.6	2.44
		Test	161	130	6.85
Holt-Winters MNA	N/A	Training	55.9	44.3	2.52
		Test	88.0	73.2	3.67

Table 8.2: Performance metrics for *NNetAR* under different settings: manual parameters (p=11, P=1) vs. automated search result (p=2, P=1) and scaling of inputs.

NNetAR provides a lot of flexibility. Table 8.2 shows the training and test performance metrics using different settings. The first two models use $p = 11$ and $P = 1$ that we chose manually, followed by two models with $p = 2$ and $P = 1$ that were chosen by calling *NNetAR* with argument `auto=True`. The table also compares scaled and unscaled inputs. For comparison, we also show the Holt-Winters ETS model from Chapter 5 (see Table 5.4 and Table 5.5).

The table captures three striking features of the *NNetAR* model. The first lesson from this table is that scaling the inputs has a significant effect. The neural net has a much easier time fitting the training data when the data has been normalized. All other things being equal, the performance metrics are better where the inputs have been scaled.

The second observation is that the out-of-sample (test) performance is better when using 3 lags (P=1, p=2) rather than 12 lags (P=1, p=11). This was discovered by setting `Auto=True`, and is confirmed by the metrics displayed in the table.

A third, related, conclusion is that all models, and especially the p=11 cases, exhibit overfitting. This is evident from the large deviations between the training and test performance metrics in Table 8.2 (e.g., compare with the Holt-Winters results). An extreme example is seen in Figure 8.5, both in the chart and in the performance metrics shown below it (for example, MAPE = 0.134 for the training data and MAPE = 7.458 for the test data).

8.7 Deep Learning for Forecasting

Up to this point, we described a neural network with a single hidden layer. The data-driven toolkit for forecasting time series has recently been supplemented with deep learning methods, neural networks with several hidden layers. Recurrent neural networks (RNN) are a type of deep learning method suited for temporal data such as time series or other sequential data such as music, text, and speech.

Compared to the network shown in Figure 8.4, the RNN in Figure 8.6 has two differences. First, the network has more hidden layers. Here we include only two hidden layers, but an RNN can include many hidden layers. The second difference is an additional arrow within each hidden layer. This allows the network to "remember" the information it learned in the previous epoch (iteration through the data). In other words, RNNs incorporate a looping mechanism that allows information to flow from one epoch to the next.

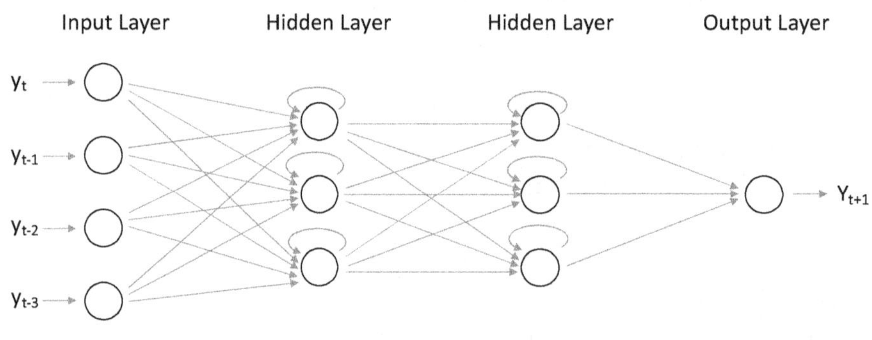

Figure 8.6: Schematic of a recurrent neural network (RNN) with two hidden layers.

Training a RNN on a time series requires partitioning the training series into a sequence of "rolling windows" (sub-series) of width w. Each sub-series serves as the predictor series and has an associated future period that serves as the output value. For example, for one-step-ahead forecasts, we convert the training series $y_1, y_2, \ldots, y_t$ into the set shown in Table 8.1. These sub-series are then fed into the RNN sequentially (into the input layer in Figure 8.6). The arrow from each hidden node to itself then "remembers" the information learned from the previous sub-series.

A simple RNN, however, suffers from "short-term memory" in the sense that it remembers information from very recent periods, but not from longer history. This results from the so-called "vanishing gradient problem". Gradients are values computed to update the neural network weights during backpropagation.[12] The vanishing gradient problem occurs because the gradient updates become small over time, and the earlier layers that receive a small gradient update stop learning. Because these layers don't learn, a simple RNN can forget what it saw much earlier in the sequence, thus having a short-term memory.

[12] Backpropagation is a fine-tuning of the weights of a neural net based on the error rate obtained in the previous epoch.

To overcome the short-term memory issue, a variant of RNN called Long Short-Term Memory (LSTM) was developed. LSTM adds special mechanisms called *gates* to each hidden node that can regulate the information flow by learning which data in a sequence is important to keep (remember) or throw away (forget). Through this process, it can relay relevant information down the long chain of sequences to make predictions. We set the gate to remember a greater or lesser portion of the old information.

Example: Forecasting Amtrak Ridership Using Deep Learning

To illustrate forecasting a series with LSTM using `sktime`, we use the Amtrak ridership data. The analysis is broken into three steps.

1. Create a scikit-learn regressor (Table 8.3).

2. Convert the regressor into a time-series forecaster (Table 8.4).

3. Run the model (code accompanying Figure 8.7).

The architecture of the model (Table 8.3) consists of a sequence of two LSTM layers followed by a dense[13] linear layer. The first LSTM layer expands the input data to a 12×50 tensor,[14] which is passed into the second LSTM layer. The output of the second LSTM layer is converted into a vector using a dense linear layer which is then mapped onto a single output value. *Dropout* means randomly dropping a proportion of nodes from

[13] In a dense layer, each node is fully connected to all the nodes in the previous layer.

[14] A *tensor* is a generalized and computationally efficient representation of matrix data in higher dimensions. A scalar is a rank 0 tensor, a vector is a rank 1 tensor, and a matrix is a rank 2 tensor.

```
from tensorflow.keras.models import Sequential
from tensorflow.keras.layers import Input, LSTM, Dense
from scikeras.wrappers import KerasRegressor

# Define the model creation function
def create_lstm_model(look_back, batch_size=1):
    model = Sequential()
    model.add(Input(batch_shape=(batch_size, look_back, 1)))
    model.add(LSTM(units=50, dropout=0.01, recurrent_dropout=0.01,
                   stateful=True, return_sequences=True))
    model.add(LSTM(units=50, dropout=0.01, recurrent_dropout=0.01,
                   stateful=True, return_sequences=False))
    model.add(Dense(1))
    model.compile(loss='mean_absolute_error', optimizer='adam')
    return model

# Custom callback to reset states
class ResetStatesCallback(tf.keras.callbacks.Callback):
    def on_epoch_end(self, epoch=None, logs=None):
        for layer in self.model.layers:
            if hasattr(layer, 'reset_states'):
                layer.reset_states()

SP = 12 # Seasonal Period
BATCH_SIZE = 1
regressor = KerasRegressor(build_fn=create_lstm_model, batch_size=BATCH_SIZE,
                           look_back=SP, epochs=400, verbose=2, shuffle=False,
                           callbacks=[ResetStatesCallback()])
```

Table 8.3: Defining an LSTM model as a `scikit-learn` object.

the network (here 1% of nodes is dropped) to reduce the risk of over-fitting.

The model specifications are captured in the function `create_lstm_model`, defined in Table 8.3. The `LSTM` layers use default activation functions which are hyperbolic tangent (tanh) for the forward step and sigmoid (logistic) for the recurrent step. The final executable statement of this function specifies how the model is to be fitted. The network weights will be chosen to minimize the mean absolute error (MAE) using the `adam` optimizer (`adam` stands for Adaptive Moment Estimation).

The network also needs instructions on how states should be initialized between epochs. This is done in the code block that defines the class *ResetStatesCallback*, a derived class of *tf.keras.callbacks.Callback*.

These building blocks are combined in the final code block which creates an instance of the *KerasRegressor* class. The class constructor arguments include the model and the callback described above, as well as the batch size and the number of epochs to use for training.

In Step 1, we defined the `scikit-learn` LSTM model *regressor* without reference to any dataset. In particular, the model is not yet ready to take a time series as input. As we saw in Table 8.1, we need to create a sequence of rolling windows of appropriate size to feed *regressor*. This is accomplished by the call to *RecursiveReductionForecaster* in Table 8.4, yielding a time-series forecaster we call `lstm_fc`.

The final code block in Table 8.4 combines `lstm_fc` with a preprocessing step that scales the data to be in the range $[0, 1]$. The resulting pipeline will automatically invert the preprocessing step when producing model outputs.

```
from sklearn.preprocessing import MinMaxScaler
from sktime.forecasting.compose import TransformedTargetForecaster
from sktime.transformations.series.adapt import TabularToSeriesAdaptor
from sktime.forecasting.compose._reduce import RecursiveReductionForecaster

lstm_fc = RecursiveReductionForecaster(regressor, window_length=SP)

pipe = TransformedTargetForecaster( [
    ("standardize", TabularToSeriesAdaptor(MinMaxScaler())),
    ("LSTM", lstm_fc)
    ])
```

Table 8.4: Converting the `scikit-learn` model into a time series forecaster.

Finally, the code in Figure 8.7 fits the LSTM model to the Amtrak data and generates the forecasts. Note that the first code block specifies several random seeds to guarantee reproducibility.

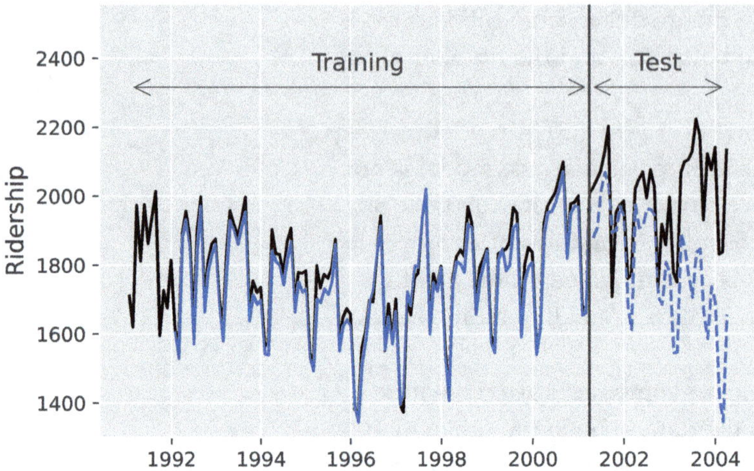

Figure 8.7: Actual and forecasted values using the deep learning LSTM model for Amtrak ridership series.

Code for creating Figure 8.7

See full code at `github.com/gshmueli/ptsf-Python`

```
# Set random seeds for reproducibility
RANDOM_SEED = 48
np.random.seed(RANDOM_SEED)
tf.random.set_seed(RANDOM_SEED)
random.seed(RANDOM_SEED)

ridership = pd.read_csv('ptsf-Python/Data/Amtrak.csv')
ridership['Month'] = pd.to_datetime(ridership['Month'], format='%Y %b')
ridership.set_index('Month', inplace=True)
ridership.index = ridership.index.to_period('M').to_timestamp('M')  # Convert to month-end frequency

TEST_SIZE = 36
train, test = temporal_train_test_split(ridership, test_size=TEST_SIZE)

pipe.fit(train)
pred = pipe.predict(ForecastingHorizon(test.index, is_relative=False))
fitted = pipe.predict(train.index[SP:])

fig, ax = plt.subplots(figsize=(6, 4))
ax = plot_series(ridership, fitted, pred, markers=['']*3,
                 colors=['black','blue','blue'],
                 y_label='Ridership',ax=ax)
plt.show()
```

Model performance: Table 8.5 summarizes the model performance measures. We see from both Figure 8.7 and Table 8.5 that the performance of the LSTM model is significantly worse for the test period compared to the training period. This difference indicates potential over-fitting. In fact, the test performance (e.g., RMSE = 258) is also worse than the Holt-Winters model (RMSE = 76) from Chapter 5 (see Figure 5.6 and Table 5.5). Interestingly, we see in the plot that performance during the first few test months is reasonable, while for longer-term forecasts (more than one year ahead), predictive performance degrades. This means the LSTM model might be more suitable for applications where the model can be updated month by month.

Series	RMSE	MAE	MAPE	MASE
Training	33.59	28.65	1.61	0.24
Test	257.88	209.48	10.43	1.67

Table 8.5: Performance measures for the LSTM model.

Code for creating Table 8.5

See full code at github.com/gshmueli/ptsf-Python

```
from sktime.performance_metrics.forecasting import
        mean_absolute_error, mean_squared_error,
        mean_absolute_percentage_error,
        mean_absolute_scaled_error

def accuracy_df(method, y, y_pred, y_train):
    metrics = {
        'RMSE': np.sqrt(mean_squared_error(y, y_pred)),
        'MAE': mean_absolute_error(y, y_pred),
        'MAPE': mean_absolute_percentage_error(y, y_pred) * 100,
        'MASE': mean_absolute_scaled_error(y_true=y, y_pred=y_pred, y_train=y_train)
    }
    return pd.DataFrame(metrics, index=[method])

print(pd.concat([accuracy_df('Train', train[SP:], fitted, train[SP:]),
    accuracy_df('Test', test, pred, train)]).round(3))
```

Model stability: Our LSTM model was created with some parameter settings that affect how the model learns from the training data. One of these parameters is `epochs`, the maximum number of passes through the data (see bottom-most code block in Table 8.3). Another is the initial weights used for the first iteration. These weights are chosen randomly based on several internal (pseudo) random number generators.[15] We can get different initial weights by changing the seed value (`RANDOM_SEED`) used for these generators (see first code block in Figure 8.7).

[15] See the Wikipedia page *Pseudorandom number generator* for more information.

To illustrate the effect of these two parameters on the resulting forecasts, we ran a few more LSTM models, modifying the random seed number and the number of epochs. The results are shown in Table 8.6 and Figure 8.8. We see that the number of epochs and the initial weights can have a considerable effect on the model forecasts. For example, the MAPE for the test period improved from 10.43% to 4.26% when the seed changed from 48 to 49 and the epochs increased from 400 to 1,000.

How can one avoid the variability inherent in the initial weights and the number of epochs? One approach is to use an ensemble method, taking an average over many instances of the model, using different initial weights and a large enough number of epochs. The price for such an improvement is computation power and time, which might require fast, specialized hardware.

Seed	Epochs	Dataset	RMSE	MAE	MAPE
48	400	Train	33.59	28.65	1.61
		Test	257.88	209.48	10.43
48	1000	Train	13.40	10.78	0.61
		Test	174.04	146.79	7.27
49	400	Train	23.70	17.69	1.01
		Test	114.60	96.67	4.84
49	1000	Train	19.89	13.76	0.81
		Test	105.91	85.39	4.26

Table 8.6: Performance measures for different seeds and different number of epochs.

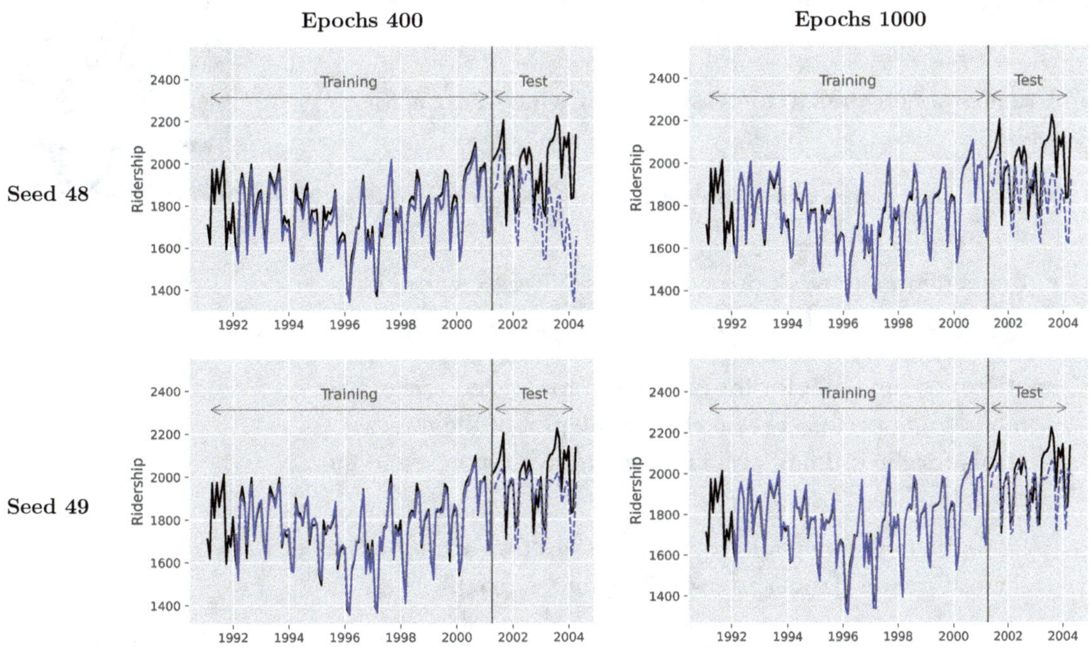

Figure 8.8: LSTM models with different seeds and different number of epochs.

8.8 Problems

Forecasting Australian Wine Sales: Figure 8.9 shows time plots of monthly sales of six types of Australian wines (red, rose, sweet white, dry white, sparkling, and fortified) for 1980–1994. Data available in *AustralianWines.csv*.[16] The units are thousands of liters. You are hired to obtain short-term forecasts (2–3 months ahead) for each of the six series, and this task will be repeated every month.

[16] Source: Hyndman and Yang (2018) tsdl: Time Series Data Library. v0.1.0. `github.com/FinYang/tsdl`.

1. Would you consider neural networks for this task? Explain why.

2. Use neural networks to forecast fortified wine sales, as follows:

   - Partition the data using the period until December 1993 as the training period.
   - Run a neural network using `sktime`'s *NNetAR* with 11 non-seasonal lags ($p = 11$).

   (a) Create a time plot for the actual and forecasted series over the training period. Create also a time plot of the forecast errors for the training period. Interpret what you see in the plots.

   (b) Use the neural network to forecast sales for each month in the test period (January 1994 to December 1994).

3. Compare your neural network to an exponential smoothing model used to forecast fortified wine sales.

   (a) Use `sktime`'s *AutoETS* class to automatically select and fit an exponential smoothing model to the training period until December 1993. Which model did *AutoETS* fit?

   (b) Use this exponential smoothing model to forecast sales for each month in 1994.

   (c) How does the neural network compare to the exponential smoothing model in terms of predictive performance in the training period? In the test period?

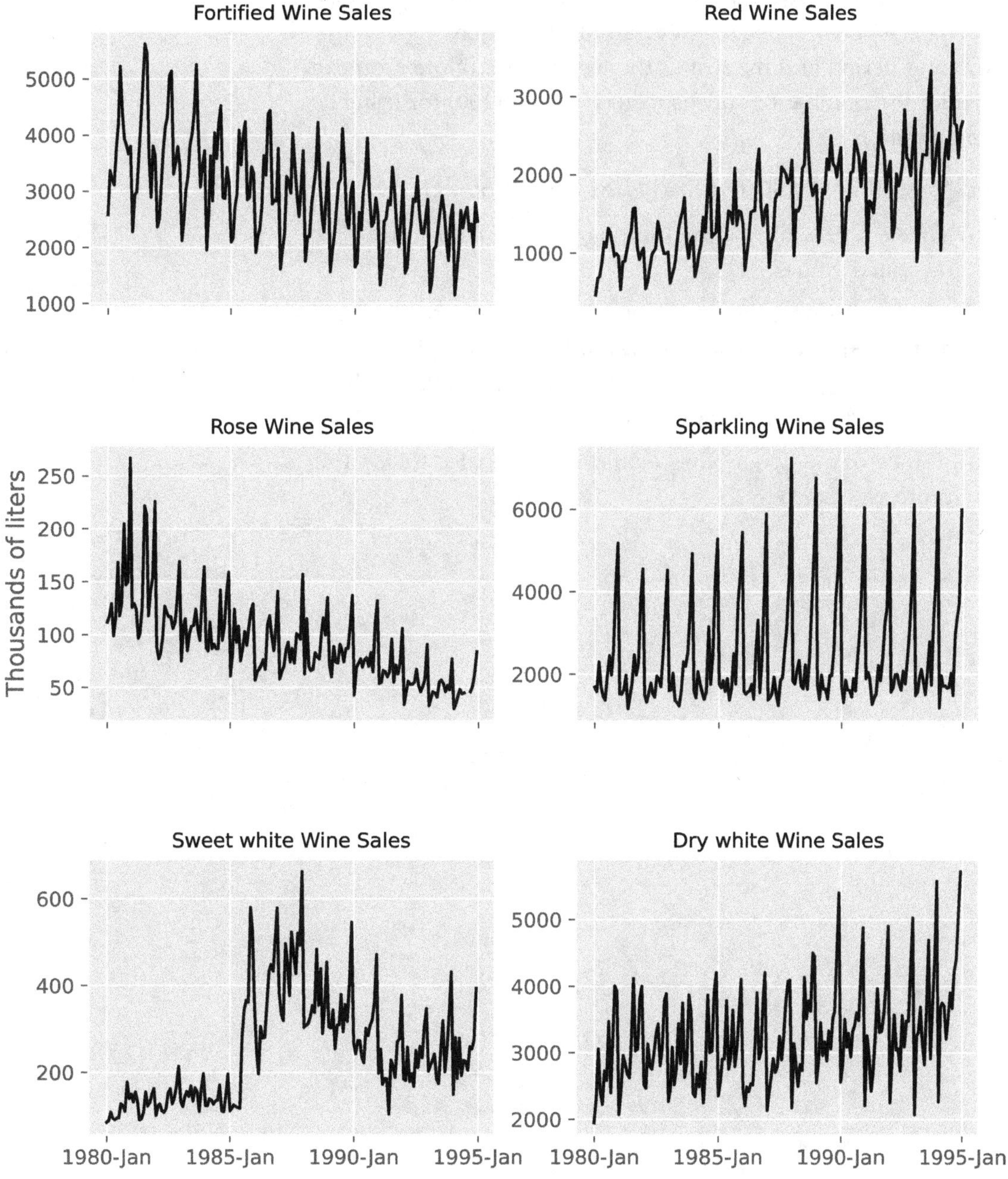

Figure 8.9: Monthly sales of six types of Australian wines between 1980–1994

4. Use the LSTM deep learning technique to forecast the fortified wine series. Use the settings shown in Section 8.7 (Tables 8.3-8.4). As before, use the period until December 1993 as the training period and the rest as the test period. [Note: You can reduce the number of epochs to 100 (`epochs=100`) for faster computation.]

   (a) Report the RMSE and MAPE for the test period.

   (b) Create a time plot of the training and test actual and forecasted values.

   (c) Change the deep learning network architecture by replacing the `LSTM` layers with `RNN` layers[17] while keeping the prepocessing step as is. Report the `RMSE` and `MAPE` for the test period and the performance chart.

   (d) Which of the two models would you select for forecasting future values? Why?

[17] In the model definition, replace `LSTM` with `SimpleRNN`.

9
Forecasting Binary Outcomes

In the previous chapters, we focused on models and performance metrics suitable for generating numerical forecasts. Numerical forecasts are extremely popular in business forecasting. In this chapter, we expand the discussion of forecasting to *binary forecasts* (event/no-event).

Section 9.1 describes the context of binary forecasting, where the goal is to forecast whether an event or non-event will occur in future periods. In Section 9.2 we discuss naive forecasts and performance evaluation in the context of binary outcome forecasting. Section 9.3 introduces logistic regression, which is a model-based method that can be used for forecasting binary outcomes. Like linear regression, logistic regression can be used for extrapolation as well as inclusion of external information. In Section 9.4 we illustrate the process of forecasting a binary outcome and the use of logistic regression using the example of forecasting rainy days in Melbourne, Australia.

9.1 Forecasting Binary Outcomes

While classic time series forecasting deals with numerical data, there is often a need to forecast series of binary events. Three scenarios can lead to the need for binary forecasts:

1. We want to predict whether or not an event will occur in a future time period (e.g., if a recession will take place next year).

2. We are interested in the direction of a measurement in a future time period (e.g., the direction of stock price movements (up/down) in the next five minutes).

3. We are interested in whether or not a numerical measurement (e.g., blood sugar level, air pollution level, or credit card spending) will cross a given threshold in a future time period.

In all three scenarios it is likely that the binary outcome of interest is related to measurements in previous periods. Hence, as in numerical forecasting, we aim to capture systematic components such as trend, seasonality, and autocorrelation. In this chapter, we describe a popular forecasting method for binary outcomes called *logistic regression*. In Chapter 8 the forecasting method of neural networks was introduced, which is also suitable for forecasting binary outcomes. We illustrate how both methods are used for forecasting a binary event in this chapter.

9.2 *Naive Forecasts and Performance Evaluation*

As in numerical forecasting, a naive forecast can simply be the binary value in the previous period. An alternative naive benchmark is the "majority-class" forecast, which is the most popular outcome in the training period: event or non-event. When more than 50% of the training period outcomes are "events", then a naive majority-class forecast is "event". When fewer than 50% of the training period outcomes are "events", then the majority-class forecast is "non-event".

The performance of a binary outcome forecasting method is evaluated by comparing the binary forecasts to the actual binary events. This comparison is commonly presented in a 2×2 table, called a *confusion matrix* (or *classification matrix*). The table shows the correct and erroneous forecasts of events and of non-events, as illustrated in Table 9.1. As in numerical forecasting, we evaluate performance using the test period.

Various performance measures are computed from the confusion matrix values. In addition, costs can be attached to missed events or non-events.[1]

[1] For predictive measures and cost functions derived from the confusion matrix, see the case in Section 11.3 and chapter Performance Evaluation in
G. Shmueli, P. C. Bruce, P. Gedeck, and N. R. Patel. *Machine Learning for Business Analytics: Techniques, Concepts and Applications in Python*. John Wiley & Sons, 2nd edition, 2025

	Predicted	
Actual	**Event**	**Non-Event**
Event	# correctly forecasted events	# missed events
Non-Event	# false alarms	# correctly forecasted non-events

Table 9.1: Confusion matrix for evaluating predictive performance of binary outcome forecasts (computed on the test period).

9.3 *Logistic Regression*

The linear regression methods described in Chapters 6–7 are not suitable for modeling time series of binary values. If the series is numerical but the outcome of interest is binary ("will next month's demand exceed 500 units?"), then we could potentially use linear regression to model the numerical series and then compare the numerical forecast to the threshold to create a binary forecast.

A popular alternative is to model the *probability* of the outcome of interest. In particular, a regression-type model suited for modeling a binary y variable is *logistic regression*. Logistic regression is commonly used for predicting cross-sectional data. It is less common in time series forecasting, perhaps because forecasting binary data is less common in general. When used with time series, logistic regression can incorporate trend, seasonality, lag variables, and external information. In a 2010 forecasting contest of stock price movements (up/down), logistic regression was the main tool used by the first and second place winners.[2]

In this section, we briefly introduce logistic regression and then consider it in the time series context.[3]

In logistic regression, we model the relationship between the probability of the event of interest and the predictors using a nonlinear function called the *logistic* function that guarantees the resulting probabilities remain between 0 and 1.

For predictors $x_1, x_2, \ldots, x_p$ the logistic regression model is given by

$$p = \frac{1}{1 + e^{-(\beta_0 + \beta_1 x_1 + \ldots + \beta_p x_p)}}. \tag{9.1}$$

[2] For details and data on the 2010 INFORMS stock price movement forecasting contest see the case in Section 11.3.

[3] For a detailed description of logistic regression in the context of cross-sectional prediction, see the chapter on Logistic Regression in

G. Shmueli, P. C. Bruce, P. Gedeck, and N. R. Patel. *Machine Learning for Business Analytics: Techniques, Concepts and Applications in Python*. John Wiley & Sons, 2nd edition, 2025

Note that, as in linear regression:

- Logistic regression is a model-based forecasting method (with all the implied advantages and weaknesses).
- The model can include different types of predictors (numerical, dummies, interactions, etc.), including seasonal dummies, trend terms (such as t), and lagged variables (such as y_{t-1}).
- All predictors should be available at the time of prediction.
- Variable selection methods (such as stepwise, forward selection and backward elimination) can be used.[4]

[4] For more on variable selection in linear and logistic regression models, see:
G. Shmueli, P. C. Bruce, P. Gedeck, and N. R. Patel. *Machine Learning for Business Analytics: Techniques, Concepts and Applications in Python*. John Wiley & Sons, 2nd edition, 2025

Lagged Predictors (y_{t-k})

When the binary data is the result of thresholding a continuous measurement (e.g., a thresholded blood sugar count), consider including lagged versions of the *actual measurements* rather than the binary values. For example, include the previous blood sugar count itself rather than whether it exceeded the threshold. Past actual measurements might be more predictive, assuming that they are available at the time of prediction.

Generating Binary Forecasts

Once we estimate the model in equation (9.1), we can obtain the predicted probability for each time period of interest. A binary forecast (event/non-event) is obtained by comparing the predicted probability to 0.5. A higher value leads to an "event" forecast, while a lower value leads to a "non-event".

To put in another way, to convert a forecasted probability into a binary forecast ("will the stock move up (1) or down (0)?"), we must choose a *cutoff value* or threshold on the probability. If the probability exceeds the cutoff, the prediction is "1". Otherwise it is "0". A popular default cutoff value is 0.5: if the "1" event is more likely (probability > 0.5), we assign a "1" label. If the "1" event is less likely (probability ≤ 0.5), we assign a "0" label. While 0.5 is a popular probability threshold, choosing a different value can sometimes improve predictive performance.

9.4 Example: Rainfall in Melbourne, Australia

To illustrate the use of logistic regression for forecasting, consider the example of forecasting rainy days (yes/no) in Melbourne, Australia.[5] Data on daily rainfall amounts in Melbourne are publicly available at `www.bom.gov.au/climate/data/`. We use data on rainfall between Jan 1, 2000 and Oct 31, 2011 (available in *MelbourneRainfall.csv*). The series includes the daily rainfall amount (in mm), as reported by the Melbourne Regional Office station (station number 086071).

[5] Many thanks to Rob J Hyndman for pointing out the data source and his paper (which inspired this example):

R. J. Hyndman. Nonparametric additive regression models for binary time series. In *Proceedings of the Australasian Meeting of the Econometric Society*, 1999

We start by partitioning the series: here we use years 2000–2009 as the training period and years 2010–2011 as the test period.[6] Next, we explore the series.

[6] This partitioning is useful for evaluating predictive performance of up to two years ahead.

Visualizing Binary Series

Time plots of the binary daily data are not very informative. We therefore look at aggregated plots. Specifically, this is done by using some relevant temporal cycle (e.g., day of week, month of year) on the x-axis, and then computing the percentage of 1's on the y-axis. This will show the percentage of 1's in each season. We then use the temporal cycle to create multiple lines, one for each cycle (e.g., one line per week, or one line per year). Figure 9.1 shows a monthly aggregated time plot that displays annual seasonality. The x-axis shows month of year (January to December) and the y-axis is the percent of rainy days in each month. Each line corresponds to a particular year. Finally, we add an overall average line (averaging over the 12 years) to highlight the annual seasonal pattern.

Logistic Regression Model

Based on the annual seasonality observed in the chart, we model annual seasonality by including sine and cosine terms in the logistic regression model. We also include a lag-1 predictor to capture day-to-day rainfall correlation. For the lag variable, we can either include actual rainfall amount, or rain/no-rain. While both options should be considered, we display the results for

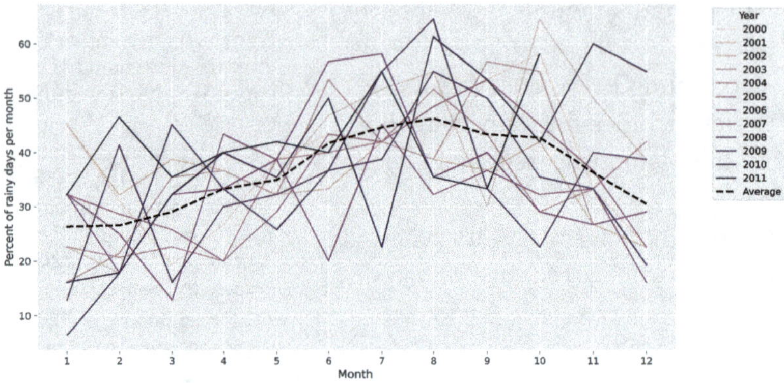

Figure 9.1: Percent of rainy days per month-of-year in Melbourne, Australia. Lines correspond to different years. Black dashed line corresponds to the monthly averages.

Code for creating Figure 9.1

See full code at github.com/gshmueli/ptsf-Python

```
import seaborn as sns # the seaborn package makes it easier to produce a seasonal plot

rain = pd.read_csv('ptsf-Python/Data/MelbourneRainfall.csv', parse_dates=['Date'], index_col='Date')
rain.index = pd.to_datetime(rain.index, format='%d/%m/%Y')

# Create additional columns: 'rainy', 'Year', 'Month'
rain['rainy'] = np.where(rain['RainfallAmount_millimetres'] > 0, 1, 0)
rain['Year'] = rain.index.year
rain['Month'] = rain.index.month

# Calculate monthly and "month-year" rain percentages
month_rain = pd.DataFrame({'pct': rain.groupby('Month')['rainy'].mean() * 100}).reset_index()
month_year_rain = \
     pd.DataFrame({'pct': rain.groupby(['Year', 'Month'])['rainy'].mean() * 100}).reset_index()

plt.figure(figsize=(12, 6))
sns.lineplot(data=month_year_rain, x='Month', y='pct', hue='Year', marker='', legend='full')

# Overlay the monthly average rain
sns.lineplot(data=month_rain, x='Month', y='pct', color='black', linestyle='--', \
             linewidth=2, label='Average')
```

using a lag-1 rainfall binary predictor. Our model is therefore:

$$P(rainy_t = 1) = \frac{1}{1 + e^{-(\beta_0 + \beta_1 rainy_{t-1} + \beta_2 \sin(2\pi t/365.25) + \beta_3 \cos(2\pi t/365.25)}}. \tag{9.2}$$

A sample of the data after creating the derived variables[7] is shown in Figure 9.2. Next, we demonstrate fitting a logistic regression model to time series in Python using the *LogisticRegression* class from `scikit-learn`, and then using the model to predict the probability of rain for each day in the training and test periods. The code and results are shown in Table 9.2.

[7] A derived variable is a transformation of an original variable. Here *rainy*, *Lag*1, *Seasonal_sine* and *Seasonal_cosine* are derived variables.

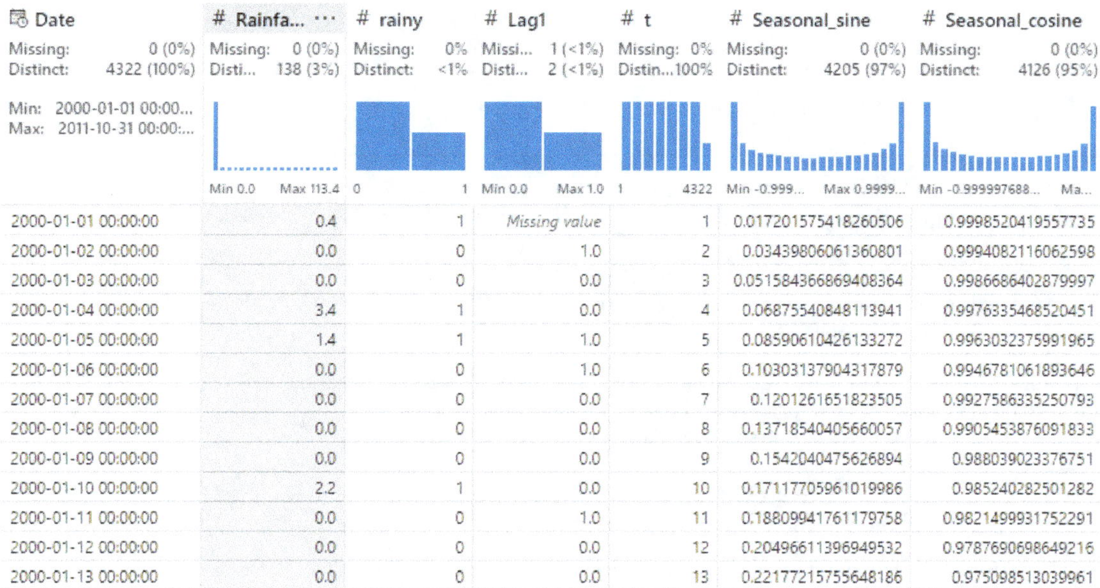

Date	# Rainfa...	# rainy	# Lag1	# t	# Seasonal_sine	# Seasonal_cosine
Missing: 0 (0%) Distinct: 4322 (100%)	Missing: 0 (0%) Disti... 138 (3%)	Missing: 0% Distinct: <1%	Missi... 1 (<1%) Disti... 2 (<1%)	Missing: 0% Distin...100%	Missing: 0 (0%) Distinct: 4205 (97%)	Missing: 0 (0%) Distinct: 4126 (95%)
Min: 2000-01-01 00:00... Max: 2011-10-31 00:00:...	Min 0.0 Max 113.4	0 1	Min 0.0 Max 1.0	1 4322	Min -0.999... Max 0.9999...	Min -0.999997688... Ma...
2000-01-01 00:00:00	0.4	1	*Missing value*	1	0.017201575418260506	0.9998520419557735
2000-01-02 00:00:00	0.0	0	1.0	2	0.03439806061360801	0.9994082116062598
2000-01-03 00:00:00	0.0	0	0.0	3	0.051584366869408364	0.9986686402879997
2000-01-04 00:00:00	3.4	1	0.0	4	0.06875540848113941	0.9976335468520451
2000-01-05 00:00:00	1.4	1	1.0	5	0.08590610426133272	0.9963032375991965
2000-01-06 00:00:00	0.0	0	1.0	6	0.10303137904317879	0.9946781061893646
2000-01-07 00:00:00	0.0	0	0.0	7	0.1201261651823505	0.9927586335250793
2000-01-08 00:00:00	0.0	0	0.0	8	0.13718540405660057	0.9905453876091833
2000-01-09 00:00:00	0.0	0	0.0	9	0.1542040475626894	0.988039023376751
2000-01-10 00:00:00	2.2	1	0.0	10	0.17117705961019986	0.985240282501282
2000-01-11 00:00:00	0.0	0	1.0	11	0.18809941761179758	0.9821499931752291
2000-01-12 00:00:00	0.0	0	0.0	12	0.20496611396949532	0.9787690698649216
2000-01-13 00:00:00	0.0	0	0.0	13	0.22177215755648186	0.975098513039961

Figure 9.2: Sample of the rainfall dataset after creating the derived predictors. `rainy` is the binary variable to be forecast with 1 denoting a rainy day.

```
            Coef  Estimate
0      Intercept -1.050897
1           Lag1  1.136513
2   Seasonal_sine -0.222010
3 Seasonal_cosine -0.284394
```

Table 9.2: Logistic regression model for daily rain in Melbourne, using *LogisticRegression* from `scikit-learn`. Top: estimated coefficients. Bottom: Predicted rain/no-rain probabilities in the training and test periods.

Train			Test		
Date	Prob no rain	Prob rain	Date	Prob no rain	Prob rain
2000-01-02	0.55	0.45	2010-01-01	0.79	0.21
2000-01-03	0.79	0.21	2010-01-02	0.55	0.45
2000-01-04	0.79	0.21	2010-01-03	0.55	0.45
2000-01-05	0.55	0.45	2010-01-04	0.79	0.21
...	....	....	...	....	....

Code for creating Table 9.2

See full code at `github.com/gshmueli/ptsf-Python`

```
from sklearn.linear_model import LogisticRegression

rainfall = rainfall.assign(t = np.arange(1,len(rainfall)+1,1),
    Seasonal_sine = lambda x: np.sin(2*np.pi*x['t']/365.25),
    Seasonal_cosine = lambda x: np.cos(2*np.pi*x['t']/365.25)
    )
rainfall['rainy'] = np.where(rainfall['RainfallAmount_millimetres'] > 0, 1, 0)
rainfall = rainfall.assign(Lag1=rainfall['rainy'].shift(1))
rainfall = rainfall.iloc[1:,:] ## drop first row that has NA in lag

rain_train = rainfall.truncate(after='2009-12-31')
rain_test = rainfall.truncate(before='2010-01-01')

exog_train = rain_train[['Lag1','Seasonal_sine','Seasonal_cosine']]
exog_test = rain_test[['Lag1','Seasonal_sine','Seasonal_cosine']]

lr_model = LogisticRegression(random_state=0, fit_intercept=True, penalty=None)
lr_model.fit(exog_train, rain_train['rainy'])

print(pd.DataFrame({'Coef': ['Intercept'] + exog_train.columns.tolist(),
              'Estimate':np.append(lr_model.intercept_, lr_model.coef_[0])}))

fitted_probs = lr_model.predict_proba(exog_train)
pred_probs = lr_model.predict_proba(exog_test)
```

Predictive Performance

The *confusion matrix*, based on a threshold[8] of 0.5, is shown in Table 9.3. For the test period it shows a predictive accuracy of 63%. In particular, the model predicts no-rain days with 81% accuracy (specificity) and rainy days with 37% accuracy (sensitivity). Let us compare to a naive majority-class forecast. Because the training period contains 36% of rainy days, a naive majority-class forecast of "no rain" on every day in the test set would have a 59% accuracy rate (394 non-rainy days out of 669). Hence, the logistic regression outperforms this naive benchmark. Note that if incorrect prediction of rainy days was very costly, then the logistic regression would have a substantial cost reduction compared to the naive majority-class rule.

[8] In the Python code for generating the confusion matrix in Table 9.3, a threshold of 0.5 was implicitly used to classify the event of rain ("TRUE") or no rain ("FALSE").

```
Training Confusion Matrix
        Prediction
Actual      0     1
  0      1981   374
  1       807   490

Accuracy : 0.6766
Sensitivity : 0.3778
Specificity : 0.8412
```

```
Test Confusion Matrix
        Prediction
Actual      0     1
  0       320    74
  1       174   101

Accuracy : 0.6293
Sensitivity : 0.3673
Specificity : 0.8122
```

Table 9.3: Summary of logistic regression's predictive performance in the training and test periods.

Code for creating Table 9.3

See full code at github.com/gshmueli/ptsf-Python

```
from sklearn.metrics import confusion_matrix

def performance_summary(label, pred, actual):
    print(f"{label} Confusion Matrix")
    columns = pd.MultiIndex.from_product([['Prediction'], [0, 1]])
    Z = pd.DataFrame(confusion_matrix(actual, pred), index=[0, 1], columns=columns)
    Z.index.name = 'Actual'
    tn, fp, fn, tp = confusion_matrix(actual, pred).ravel()  # tn=true neg, fp=false pos, ...
    metrics = pd.Series({"Accuracy": (tp + tn) / len(actual),"Sensitivity": tp / (tp + fn),
                         "Specificity": tn / (tn + fp)})
    print(f"{Z}\n\n{metrics.to_string(float_format='{:.4f}'.format)}")

performance_summary("Training", lr_model.predict(exog_train), rain_train['rainy'])
performance_summary("Test", lr_model.predict(exog_test), rain_test['rainy'])
```

9.5 *Neural Networks*

In Chapter 8 we described how neural networks can be used for forecasting time series, and illustrated them with a numerical series. Neural nets can also be used to forecast binary series. We use the *MLPClassifier* from the `scikit-learn` package.

To illustrate the use of *MLPClassifier*, we applied it to the Melbourne rainfall example, using the same predictors used in the logistic regression model. The code and results of applying *MLPClassifier* are shown in Table 9.4. The fitted model is an average of 20 networks, each with a single hidden layer with two hidden nodes. The model uses one lagged value of *rainy* as a predictor in addition to the seasonal sine and cosine predictors.

In terms of performance, the neural network is very similar to the logistic regression on both the training and test data when considering accuracy, sensitivity and specificity.

Table 9.4: Fitting a neural net to Melbourne rainfall using *MLPClassifier* from `scikit-learn`.

```
X_train = rain_train[['Lag1', 'Seasonal_sine', 'Seasonal_cosine']]
X_test = rain_test[['Lag1', 'Seasonal_sine', 'Seasonal_cosine']]
y_train = rain_train['rainy']
y_test = rain_test['rainy']

NETWORKS = 20   # Number of MLPClassifiers
HIDDEN_NODES = 2

# Create an ensemble of MLPClassifier models
estimators = [(f'mlp{i}',
               MLPClassifier(hidden_layer_sizes=(HIDDEN_NODES,), random_state=42+i, max_iter=1000))
              for i in range(NETWORKS)]
ensemble = VotingClassifier(estimators=estimators, voting='soft')

ensemble.fit(X_train, y_train)
train_pred = ensemble.predict(X_train)
test_pred = ensemble.predict(X_test)

performance_summary("Training", train_pred, y_train)
performance_summary("Test", test_pred, y_test)
```

```
Training Confusion Matrix                  Test Confusion Matrix
        Prediction                              Prediction
Actual     0     1                         Actual      0     1
  0      2033   322                          0       331    63
  1       852   445                          1       182    93

Accuracy : 0.6785                          Accuracy : 0.6338
Sensitivity : 0.3431                       Sensitivity : 0.3382
Specificity : 0.8633                       Specificity : 0.8401
```

9.6 *Problems*

For predicting whether the agricultural epidemic of *powdery mildew in mango* will erupt in a certain year in the state of Uttar Pradesh in India, Misra et al. (2004)[9] used annual outbreak records during 1987–2000. The epidemic typically occurs in the third and fourth week of March, and hence outbreak status is known by the end of March of a given year. The authors used a logistic regression model with two weather predictors (maximum temperature and relative humidity) to forecast an outbreak. The data is shown in the table below and are available in *PowderyMildewEpidemic.csv*.

[9] A. K. Misra, O. M. Prakash, and V. Ramasubramanian. Forewarning powdery mildew caused by Oidium mangiferae in mango (Mangifera indica) using logistic regression models. *Indian Journal of Agricultural Science*, 74(2):84–87, 2004

Year	Outbreak?	Max temperature	Relative humidity
1987	Yes	30.14	82.86
1988	No	30.66	79.57
1989	No	26.31	89.14
1990	Yes	28.43	91.00
1991	No	29.57	80.57
1992	Yes	31.25	67.82
1993	No	30.35	61.76
1994	Yes	30.71	81.14
1995	No	30.71	61.57
1996	Yes	33.07	59.76
1997	No	31.50	68.29
2000	No	29.50	79.14

Table 9.5: Data on Powdery Mildew in Mango outbreaks in Uttar Pradesh, India.

1. In order for the model to serve as a forewarning system for farmers, what requirements must be satisfied regarding data availability?

2. Write an equation for the model fitted by the researchers in the form of equation (9.1). Use predictor names instead of x notation.

3. Create a scatter plot of the two predictors, using different hue for epidemic and non-epidemic markers. Does there appear to be a relationship between epidemic status and the two predictors?

4. Compute roll-forward naive forecasts of epidemic status for years 1995–1997 using previous-year data (assume every year at the time of prediction we have last year's data). What is the naive forecast for year 2000? Summarize the results for these four years in a confusion matrix.

5. Partition the data into training and test periods, so that years 1987–1994 are the training period. Fit a logistic regression to the training period using the two predictors, and report the outbreak probability as well as a forecast for year 1995 (use a threshold of 0.5).

6. Generate outbreak forecasts (and predicted probabilities) for years 1996, 1997, and 2000 by repeatedly moving the training period forward. For example, to forecast year 1996, partition the data so that years 1987–1995 are the training period. Then fit the logistic regression model and use it to generate a forecast (use threshold 0.5).

7. Summarize the logistic regression's predictive accuracy for these four years (1995–1997, 2000) in a confusion matrix.

8. Does the logistic regression outperform the naive forecasts?

9. For year 1997, there is some uncertainty regarding the data quality of the outbreak status.[10] According to the logistic regression model, is it more likely that an outbreak occurred or not?

10. If we fit a logistic regression with a lag-outbreak predictor such as $P(Outbreak_t) = \frac{1}{1+e^{-(\beta_0+\beta_1 Outbreak_{t-1})}}$ to years 1987–1997, how can this model be used to forecast an outbreak in year 2000?

[10] Different researchers report different outbreak status. See, for example `goo.gl/qcq93e` vs. the last page of `goo.gl/9C4KKh`.

10 Communication and Maintenance

10.1 Presenting Forecasts

Once a forecasting model is finalized and forecasts are produced, a critical step is presenting the forecasts to management or other stakeholders. Without proper presentation, the entire effort invested in the forecasting process can be lost. This section focuses on oral presentation, which is typically accompanied by slides. In Section 10.3 we discuss presentation in written reports.

Proper presentation is audience-dependent. For managerial audiences it is better to avoid too much technical detail and keep the focus on the forecasts, their uncertainty level, and various factors affecting them. For more technical audiences, one can include a high-level description of the forecasting method, the data used for generating forecasts, and the performance evaluation approach and results.

In what form should forecasts be presented? For presentation of the big picture and the forecasts in context, and especially for oral presentations, charts are a more appropriate choice than tables. For a single series, a time plot that includes both existing data and forecasts is commonly used. An example is shown in Figure 10.1, where the monthly series of search volume for the keywords "business analytics" on Google is displayed, alongside forecasts for the next 12 months (represented by a dashed line on a gray background). The choice of scale on the y-axis of the time plot should be carefully considered. An overly-fine scale will magnify meaningless differences in values, while an overly-crude

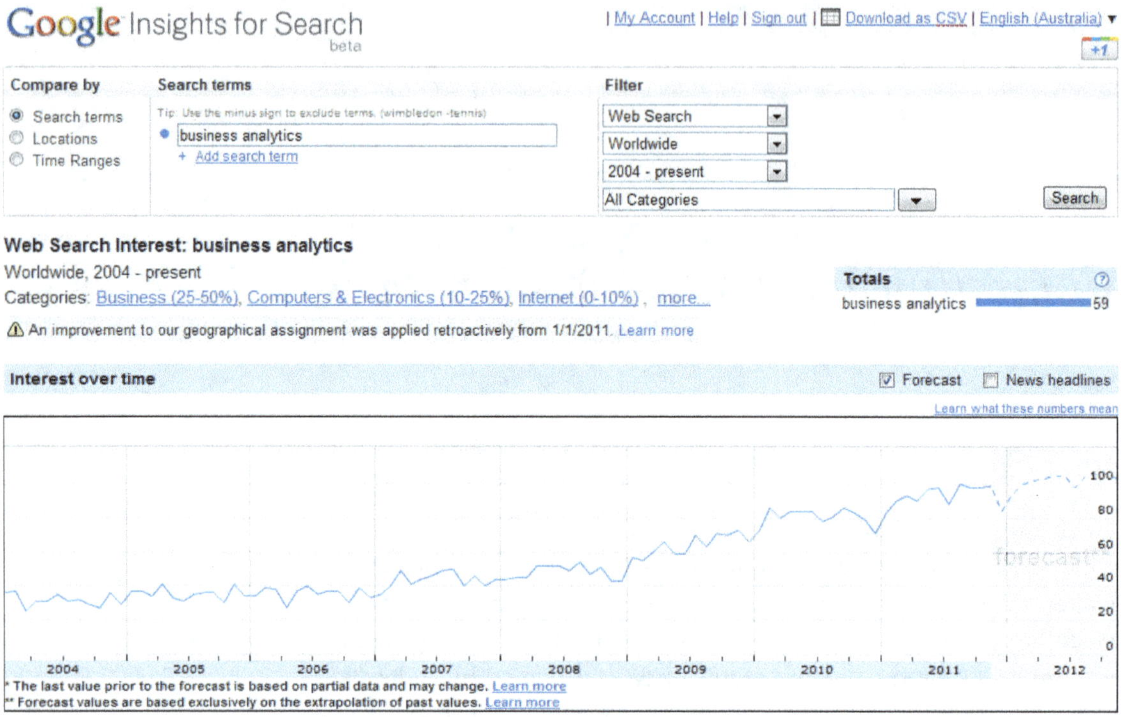

Figure 10.1: Time plot including forecasts for monthly search volume of keywords "business analytics" on Google (from Google Insights for Search service, the precursor to Google Trends).

scale will mask meaningful differences. If existing forecasting methods are being used or considered, the charts should include them as well, allowing an easy comparison with the new forecasting method. In cases where the presentation is aimed at choosing one forecasting method among a few alternatives (for reasons such as data or software availability, interpretability, or simplicity of application), the alternatives should be displayed on the same chart for ease of comparison. If only a few forecasted numbers are of interest, these numbers can be added to the chart using annotation.

Charts can also include intervals or shaded areas to display prediction intervals, as illustrated in Figure 10.2. In fact, displaying prediction intervals is highly desirable because forecasts are often perceived by users to be more certain than they really are.

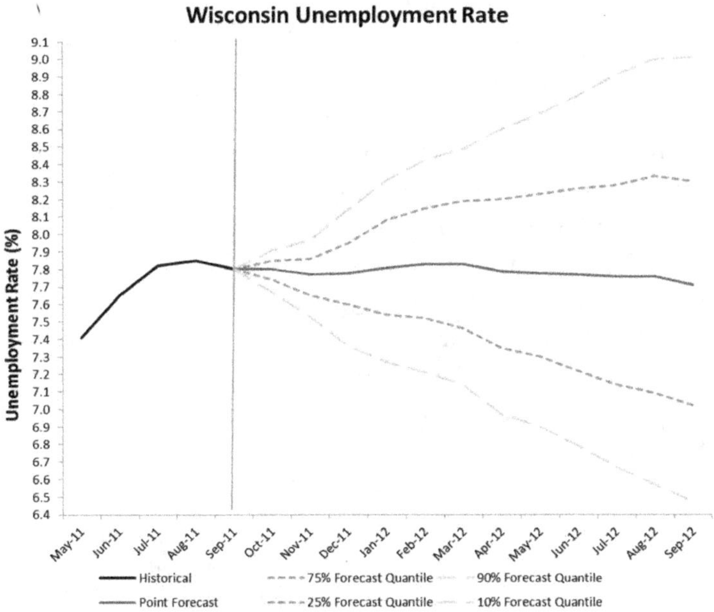

Figure 10.2: Presenting point forecasts and prediction intervals (adapted from www.ssc.wisc.edu/~bhansen/forecast with permission from Bruce Hansen).

10.2 *Monitoring Forecasts*

When forecasts are generated on an ongoing basis, it is imperative to occasionally re-assess performance. Extrapolation methods are based on the assumption that the conditions under which the forecasting takes place are identical to those occurring during the modeled period. However, conditions might change either gradually or drastically, thereby requiring the re-assessment of forecasts under the new conditions and perhaps even updating the forecasting method.

Monitoring forecasting performance can be achieved by plotting two charts: one displaying the actual and forecasted series and the other displaying the forecast errors. Although both charts are based on the same information, displaying the information from the two angles is complementary; it is easier to detect deterioration in forecast precision by examining the forecast error chart, while the actual/forecasted chart is more intuitive for grasping the direction of the deviations and their magnitude in the larger context.

Some experts advocate using *control charts* for monitoring forecast errors.[1] Control charts are time plots that also include lower and upper thresholds, as illustrated in Figure 10.3. If a threshold is exceeded, it is an indication that performance is "out of control" and action is needed. In the forecasting context, "out of control" means a change in the conditions affecting the series.

[1] For more information on control charts see the NIST/SEMATECH e-Handbook of Statistical Methods (`itl.nist.gov/div898/handbook/pmc/section3/pmc31.htm`).

Standard control charts assume that the forecast error distribution is normal and stable over time. However, we have seen that the normality assumption is often violated (see Section 3.3). An alternative is to use the empirical distribution of forecast errors, as estimated from existing (past and present) data. The thresholds can be set, for example, as the 1st and 99th percentiles of the empirical distribution (see Section 3.3).

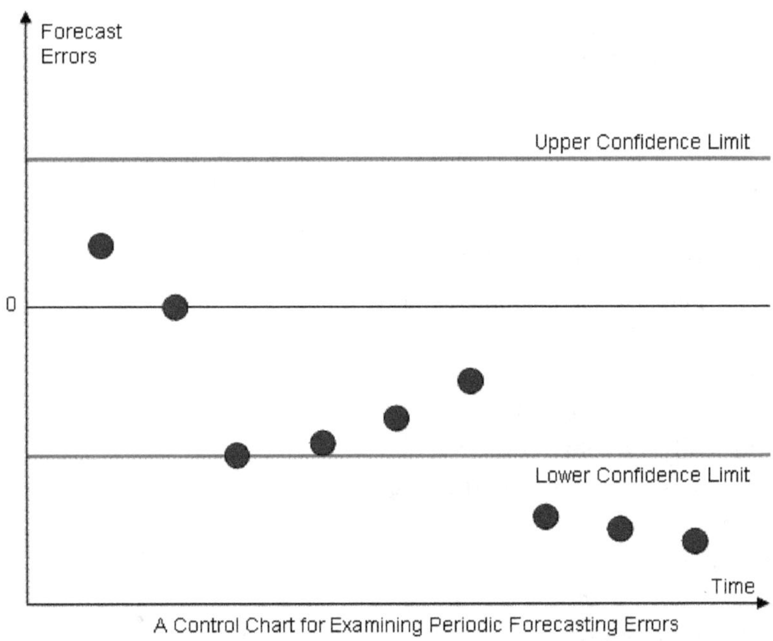

Figure 10.3: Control chart for monitoring forecast errors. Image from `home.ubalt.edu/ntsbarsh/stat-data/forecast.htm`, reproduced with permission from Hossein Arsham.

10.3 *Written Reports*

Providing clear written reports about the forecasting process and the resulting forecasts is crucial to gain the confidence of different stakeholders. The following two quotes illustrate the role of written documentation in light of skeptic audiences:

> Forecasters should document exactly what they do. Even with very clear documentation, some skeptics will assume that the forecasters have fiddled with the numbers.[2]

> Lack of understanding of NASS methodology and/or the belief in a hidden agenda can prevent market participants from correctly interpreting and utilizing the acreage and yield forecasts.[3]

[2] U.S. National Research Council. Forecasting demand and supply of doctoral scientists and engineers: Report of a workshop on methodology. National Academies Press, 2000

[3] See Section 1.4

As in oral presentation, written reports of forecasting projects must cater to their audiences. An *executive summary* should include a high-level description of the problem, the data used, the method(s) used, the forecasts, and their expected precision. A time plot of the series and its forecasts is useful if the number of forecasted series is reasonably small. For a large number of series, a few examples can suffice along with a complete set of plots either in the appendix or in an online appendix. A *technical summary* can include further details about data processing (such as handling missing values), the motivation for choosing particular forecasting methods, the performance evaluation approach, and results from several approaches including benchmark models and any currently used methods.

Charts of the time series and their forecasts should be well formatted and easily readable. If the report is likely to be printed in black and white, it is better to use grayscale or other line differentiators in charts. For time plots, grayscale is typically preferable to different line types, as human perception of continuity over time is lost with broken lines.

If the number of forecasted values is large, tables can supplement charts for displaying the forecasted values. When reporting numerical forecasts, the level of rounding should be carefully considered. If the forecasts from the written report will be used as-is in practice, a sufficient number of decimals (depending on the problem at hand) should be supplied. If the reported numbers are only used for information, and the actual forecasts will be taken from an electronic source, then the level of rounding should be geared towards readability.

10.4 *Keeping Records of Forecasts*

When the forecasting task is an ongoing task, it is imperative to keep a record of forecasts and actual values, or, equivalently, of forecasts and forecast errors. Such record-keeping allows evaluation of the forecasting method over time, its improvement when needed, and comparison of the performance of the forecasting method with competing or alternative forecasting methods. Gathering sufficient forecast histories is also useful for quantifying the distribution of the forecast error, which can be used to generate predictive intervals. From a managerial point of view, records of forecasts and forecast errors provide "hard data" regarding performance that can be conveyed to stakeholders and used for planning as well as obtaining a level of comfort with the forecasting method. In the next section we consider another important use of record keeping, related to imposed "forecast adjustments".

10.5 *Addressing Managerial "Forecast Adjustment"*

"Forecast Analyst" is a job title for an expert who produces forecasts for a company. Forecast analysts work in a wide variety of organizations and provide forecasts for various purposes. For example, a job posting for a "Senior Forecast Analyst" at Johnson & Johnson Consumer Companies, Inc. included the following description:[4]

> The Senior Forecast Analyst is responsible for working with Marketing, Sales, and Operations to develop monthly and annual sales forecasts for J&J Consumer Company franchises. Specific responsibilities will include:
>
> - Influencing business decisions based on insight to market dynamics, category share, and the sales forecast.
> - Quantifying and influencing decisions on brand level risks and opportunities.
> - Developing and updating complex forecasting models.
> - Sharing insights and challenging assumptions at the monthly forecast meetings.

[4] Job post available at `web.archive.org/web/20111110131519/www.ibf.com/bo/jnj.htm`.

- Providing input to Sales & Marketing regarding predicted effectiveness of multiple promotional scenarios and their impact to the sales forecast.
- Identifying the drivers of variance in monthly forecasts.
- Analyzing data to quantify anticipated incremental sales from marketing events and new product launches.
- Composing and distributing monthly forecasting highlight reports.
- Developing sales forecast estimates for new products.
- Performing various ad hoc analyses and producing materials for senior level presentations.
- Representing the Forecasting department on cross-functional teams addressing new brand launches.
- Leading cross-company and cross-functional projects to create transformational improvement in forecast accuracy and process efficiency.

The inter-organizational role of a forecast analyst requires an understanding of how forecasts are used by different stakeholders and how those stakeholders are affected by the forecast values. In particular, a challenge to the successful implementation of forecasting into decision making is the widespread practice of "adjusting" forecasts by management or other decision makers in the organization.

One motivation for adjustment is specific agendas of different stakeholders, where costs or gains associated with over- or under-forecasting have different value to different stakeholders. An example is adjustments by different departments in the same organization. The marketing department might try to "adjust down" sales forecasts to emphasize the effectiveness of a new marketing strategy to be deployed, while the operations department might try to "adjust up" the same forecasts for inventory management purposes. Another example is adjustments by different levels of management. In an international pharmaceutical company, a country manager may want product sales forecasts to be as low as possible when bonuses are tied to exceeding that estimate, while a brand director at headquarters level may want as high a forecast as possible so as to secure the optimal level of resources for the product.[5]

[5] "When forecasters take the floor: 6 tips on presenting a forecast" by Peter Mansell, blog post on `eyeforpharma.com`, Jun 28, 2011 (available at `bit.ly/forecast6tips`).

Another motivation for forecast adjustment is knowledge of events that are not accounted for in the model. Research on whether such adjustments improve or degrade the final performance is inconclusive.

No matter the motivation behind the adjustments, a practical strategy is to keep a record of the forecasts before and after adjustment in order to accumulate objective data. Once actual data arrives, the information on forecasts and forecast errors should be reviewed to determine which approach is best. Obviously, "best" depends on the final goal of the forecasting task.

11
Cases

11.1 Forecasting Public Transportation Demand

Background

Forecasting transportation demand is important for multiple purposes such as staffing, planning, and inventory control. The public transport system in Santiago de Chile has gone through a major effort of reconstruction. In this context, a business intelligence competition took place in October 2006, which focused on forecasting demand for public transportation. This case is based on the competition, with some modifications.

Problem Description

A public transportation company is expecting increased demand for its services and is planning to acquire new buses and extend its terminals. These investments require a reliable forecast of future demand. To create such forecasts, one can use data on historic demand. The company's data warehouse has data on each 15-minute interval between 6:30 and 22:00, on the number of passengers arriving at the terminal. As a forecasting consultant, you have been asked to create a forecasting method that can generate forecasts for the number of passengers arriving at the terminal.

Vicente Valdes metro station, Santiago de Chile.

Available Data

Part of the historic information is available in the file *bicup2006.csv*. The file contains the demand for a 3-week period, separated into 15-minute intervals.

Assignment Goal

Your goal is to create a model/method that produces accurate forecasts. To evaluate your accuracy, partition the given historic data into two periods: a training period (the first two weeks) and test period (the last week). Models should be fitted only to the training data and evaluated on the test data.

Although the competition winning criterion was the lowest Mean Absolute Error (MAE) of forecasts for March 22–24, the next 3 days beyond the data period, this is not the goal for this assignment. Instead, if we consider a more realistic business context, our goal is to create a model that generates reasonably good forecasts on any time/day of the week. Consider not only predictive metrics such as MAE, MAPE, and RMSE, but also look at actual and forecasted values, overlaid on a time plot.

Assignment

For your final model, present the following summary:

1. Name of the method/combination of methods
2. A brief description of the method/combination
3. All estimated equations associated with constructing forecasts from this method
4. The MAPE and MAE for the training period and the test period
5. Forecasts for the future period (March 22–24), in 15-minute intervals
6. A single chart showing the fit of the final version of the model to the entire period (including training, test, and future). Note that this model should be fitted using the combined training + test data

Tips and Suggested Steps

1. Use exploratory analysis to identify the components of this time series. Is there a trend? Is there seasonality? If so, how many "seasons" are there? Are there any other visible patterns? Are the patterns global (the same throughout the series) or local?[1]
2. Consider the frequency of the data from a practical and technical point of view. What are some options?
3. Compare the weekdays and weekends. How do they differ? Consider how these differences can be captured by different methods.
4. Examine the series for missing values or unusual values. Suggest solutions.
5. Based on the patterns that you found in the data, which models or methods should be considered?
6. Consider how to handle actual counts of zero within the computation of MAPE.

[1] Obtaining the day of week in `Python`: If `X` is a `pandas` `DataFrame` or `Series` with a `datetime` index, then `X.index.dayofweek` will return values in the range 0 (Monday) to 6 (Sunday).

11.2 *Forecasting Tourism (2010 Competition, Part I)*

Background

Tourism is one of the most rapidly growing global industries and tourism forecasting is becoming an increasingly important activity in planning and managing the industry.

Problem Description

The 2010 tourism forecasting competition had two parts. In part I, competitors were tasked with producing forecasts for the next four years, given 518 series of annual tourism data.

Available Data

The data consists of 518 annual series, each related to some (undisclosed) tourism activity. Tourism activities include inbound tourism numbers to one country from another country, visitor nights in a particular country, tourism expenditure, etc. The series differ in length, ranging from 7-year series to 43-year series. They also differ in the order of magnitude of values.

The data is available at `www.kaggle.com/c/tourism1/Data` (download the file "tourism_data.csv").[2]

[2] Downloading the data requires creating a free account on `kaggle.com`.

Assignment Goals

This case will give you experience with forecasting a large number of series. While the competition goal was to achieve the highest predictive accuracy, the goal of this case is to highlight different aspects of the forecasting process that pertain to forecasting a large number of series. For example, easy-to-use visualization tools have a significant advantage for visualizing a large number of series.

Note that the multiple series in this case are not likely to be forecasted together. However, it is common to forecast the demand for a large number of series, such as products in a supermarket chain.

Another aspect of this case is the use of different predictive measures, and handling practical issues such as zero counts and summarizing forecast accuracy across series.

The assignment provides guidelines for walking you through the forecasting process. Remember that the purpose is not winning the (already completed) contest, but rather learning how to approach the task of forecasting a large number of series.

Assignment

Note: the series in `tourism_data.csv` are organized so that each series is in a separate column. To effectively handle and model these series, first convert the data into long format using the `pandas` method `melt`. This means that one column will include the values from all series, another will include the time stamp, and a third, new column will include the series name.[3]

[3] See `pandas.pydata.org/docs/reference/api/pandas.melt.html`.

1. Plot all the series. What type of components are visible? Are the series similar or different? Check for problems such as missing values and possible errors. (For plotting tips, see *Tips and Resources* at the end of the Assignment.)

2. Partition the series into training and test periods, so that the last 4 years are in the test period for each series. What is the logic of such a partitioning? What is the disadvantage?

3. Generate naive forecasts for each series for the test period. For each series, create forecasts with horizons of 1,2,3, and 4 years ahead ($F_{t+1}, F_{t+2}, F_{t+3}$, and F_{t+4}).

4. Which measures are suitable if we plan to combine the results for the 518 series? Consider MAE, average error, MAPE and RMSE.

5. For each series, compute MAPE of the naive forecasts once for the training period and once for the test period.

6. The performance measure used in the competition is *Mean Absolute Scaled Error* (MASE). Explain the advantage of MASE and compute the training and test MASE for the naive forecasts.

7. Create a scatter plot of the MAPE pairs, with the training MAPE on the x-axis and the test MAPE on the y-axis. Create a similar scatter plot for the MASE pairs. Now examine both plots. What do we learn? How does performance differ between the training and test periods? How does performance range across series?

8. The competition winner, Lee Baker, used an ensemble of three methods:

   - Naive forecasts multiplied by a constant trend (justified because "globally tourism has grown at a rate of 6% annually").
   - Linear regression.
   - Exponentially-weighted linear regression.

   (a) Write the exact formula used for generating the first method, in the form $F_{t+k} = \ldots$ $(k = 1, 2, 3, 4)$.

   (b) What is the rationale behind *multiplying* the naive forecasts by a constant? (*Hint*: think empirical and domain knowledge).

   (c) What should be the dependent variable and the predictors in a linear regression model for this data? Explain.

   (d) Fit the linear regression model to the first five series and compute forecast errors for the test period.

   (e) Before choosing a linear regression, the winner described the following process:

   > I examined fitting a polynomial line to the data and using the line to predict future values. I tried using first through fifth order polynomials to find that the lowest MASE was obtained using a first order polynomial (simple regression line). This best fit line was used to predict future values. I also kept the $[R^2]$ value of the fit for use in blending the results of the predictor.

   What are two flaws in this approach?

   (f) If we were to consider exponential smoothing, what particular type(s) of exponential smoothing are reasonable candidates?

(g) The winner concludes with possible improvements, one being "an investigation into how to come up with a blending [ensemble] method that doesn't use as much manual tweaking would also be of benefit". Can you suggest methods or an approach that would lead to easier automation of the ensemble step?

(h) The competition focused on minimizing the average MAPE of the next four values across all 518 series. How does this goal differ from goals encountered in practice when considering tourism demand? Which steps in the forecasting process would likely be different in a real-life tourism forecasting scenario?

Tips and Resources

- **Tip 1 for plotting many series:** To plot the series in groups of, say, 50 series at a time: create a long-format DataFrame `df_plot` with a 'Series' column. Then select the first 50 series using `df_plot['Series'].unique()[:50]`. You can then use the `pandas` method `isin()`. Then modify the selection `[:50]` for a different choice of series.

- **Tip 2 for plotting many series:** To create a multi-panel plot with one panel per each time series, use the `FacetGrid()` function from the `seaborn` package. The `col_wrap` argument controls the number of columns. The `height` and `aspect` arguments control the shape of each individual plot.

- The winner's description of his approach and experience: `medium.com/kaggle-blog/how-i-did-it-lee-baker-on-winning-tourism-forecasting-part-one-d427e6221d5`.

- Article: "The tourism forecasting competition", by Athanasopoulos, Hyndman, Song and Wu, *International Journal of Forecasting*, April 2011. `robjhyndman.com/publications/the-tourism-forecasting-competition/`.

11.3 Forecasting Stock Price Movements (2010 INFORMS Competition)

Background

Traders, analysts, investors and hedge funds are always looking for techniques to better predict stock price movements. Knowing whether a stock will increase or decrease allows traders to make better investment decisions. Moreover, good predictive models allow traders to better understand what drives stock prices, supporting better risk management.[4]

[4] From `kaggle.com`.

Problem Description

The 2010 INFORMS Data Mining Contest challenged participants to generate accurate forecasts of 5-minute stock price movements (up/down) for a particular stock over a forecast horizon of 60 minutes.

Available Data

The data to be forecasted, named `TargetVariable`, is a time series of intraday trading data, showing stock price movements at five minute intervals. Values of this series are binary (1/0) to reflect up/down movements in the next 60 minutes.

Additional external data include sectoral data, economic data, experts' predictions and indexes. This data is in the form of 609 time series named `Variable...`. The first column in the file is the timestamp. The length of all series is 5922 periods.

The data is available at `www.kaggle.com/c/informs2010/Data`. Download the file "TrainingData.zip" (the other file "TestData.zip" contains the template for submitting forecasts and is not needed for this case).[5]

[5] Downloading the data requires creating a free account on `kaggle.com`.

Assignment Goals

This assignment will give you experience with forecasting binary outcomes for high-frequency data and with integrating external data into a forecasting method. In particular, this task highlights the difficulty of searching for useful external information among a large number of potential external variables.

While the winning criterion in the competition was a particular predictive measure on a test set, the purpose of this case is not focused on achieving the highest predictive accuracy but rather to to come up with practical solutions that can then be implemented in practice. Another goal is to evaluate whether a series (in this case stock price movements) can be forecasted at better-than-random accuracy.

Assignment

Read the data into Python.[6]

[6] Note that variable `Timestamp` uses Microsoft Excel's date/time format that counts days since 1/1/1970. See *Tips and Resources* at the end of this assignment for code that converts it to a `Pandas DatetimeIndex`.

1. **Data visualization:** Create the following three charts and then examine them.

   (a) Create a time plot of the target variable using temporal aggregation as follows: the x-axis should show the time of day, and the y-axis should compute the mean of `TargetVariable` (this will show the proportion of 1's during different 5-min periods in a day, aggregated across all days).[7]

   (b) Create a similar chart, with separate lines for each month.

   (c) Create a similar chart, with separate lines by day of week.

   (d) Examine the charts for patterns and extreme values. Notice the 3:55pm time slot. Some competitors noticed that this period always had larger gains/losses, suspecting that it represents the start/end of a trading day, and therefore more than 5 minutes. This is an example where a competition differs from real life forecasting: in real life, we would know exactly when the trading day starts and ends. How can this information help improve forecasts for these periods?

[7] Refer to Figure 9.1 for an example.

2. **Missing data:** Find the three dates when there were weekdays with no data at all.[8] What are solutions for dealing with these missing values?

[8] *Hint*: create a list of all the dates of weekdays during this period and filter this list by the dates that appear in the data.

3. **Exploring external predictors**: Among all the variables in the contest, the Variable74 columns appeared the most useful. We expect a useful numerical predictor to distinguish between `TargetVariable=1` and `TargetVariable=0`.

   (a) Create side-by-side boxplots of `Variable74OPEN` by `TargetVariable`. Create similar charts for `Variable74HIGH`, `Variable74LOW`, and `Variable74LAST_PRICE`. Does any of these four predictors seem useful for predicting `TargetVariable`?

   (b) One participant reported that differencing the four `Variable74` variables at lag 12 was useful for predicting `TargetVariable`. Create the four lag-12 differenced predictors, and for each create a side-by-side boxplot by `TargetVariable`. Does any of these appear useful? Do the differenced predictors appear more useful than the original predictors?

4. Partition the data into training and test, so that the last 2539 periods are in the test period.

   (a) How many minutes does the test period contain?

   (b) What is the percentage of periods in the training period where `TargetVariable` has a value of 1?

5. **Benchmark 1: majority class.** Report the confusion matrix for using majority-class forecasts on the test period.[9]

6. **Benchmark 2: naive forecasts.** Generate naive forecasts for the test period, using the most recent training value. Report the confusion matrix for the naive forecasts.

7. One of the top performing competitors used logistic regression with `Variable74` variables (high, low, open, and last price) as external predictors and their lag-12 differenced versions that you created in (3). He also lagged the target variable by 13 periods. Fit this regression model: the model should include the lagged target variable as the output, and the original `Variable74` columns and their differenced versions as predictors (eight predictors in total). Report the estimated regression model.

[9] *Hint*: create a vector of predicted values all equal to 1. Use the custom function `performance_summary()` defined in Table 9.3.

8. Use the logistic regression model to forecast the test period. Report the confusion matrix. How does the logistic model perform compared to the two benchmark forecast approaches?

9. The winning criterion in this contest was the highest *Area Under the Curve* (AUC)[10] averaged across the results database. Recall that most forecasting methods for binary outcomes generate an event *probability*. The probability is converted to a binary forecast by applying a threshold. The AUC measure is computed from the confusion matrix by considering all possible probability thresholds between 0 and 1. Consider the following confusion matrix, where $a, b, c,$ and d denote the counts in each cell:

[10] See also the evaluation section on the contest website `www.kaggle.com/competitions/informs2010/overview`.

	Predicted	
Actual	**Event**	**Non-Event**
Event	a	b
Non-Event	c	d

The AUC is computed as follows:

- Obtain the confusion matrix for a particular probability threshold (recall that the default is a threshold of 0.5).
- Compute the two measures *sensitivity*= $\frac{a}{a+b}$ (also called *true positive rate* (TPR)) and *specificity*= $\frac{d}{c+d}$ (also called *true negative rate* (TNR)).
- Repeat the last two steps for probability thresholds ranging from 0 to 1 in small steps (such as 0.01).
- Plot the pairs of *sensitivity* (on the y-axis) and *1-specificity* (x-axis) on a scatterplot, and connect the points. The result is a curve called a *ROC Curve*.
- The area under the ROC curve is called the *AUC*. Computing this area is typically done using an algorithm.

High AUC values indicate better performance, with 0.5 indicating random performance and 1 denoting perfect performance.

(a) Plot the ROC curve for the logistic regression model.[11]

(b) Compute the AUC.

[11] See *Tips and Resources* at the end of this Assignment for tips on using `roc_curve` and `auc` from the `sklearn` package.

10. While AUC is a popular performance measure for comparing models, especially when there are many models considered, it has been criticized for various reasons.[12] One criticism is that in practice, a single probability threshold is typically used rather than a range of thresholds. Daniel Rice suggests:[13]

> Instead of picking a model winner in what could be a random AUC lottery, apparently more accurate measures - straight classification error rate and average squared error — with much better statistical and external validity should probably now be considered.

Compute the classification accuracy rate $\left(\frac{a+d}{a+b+c+d}\right)$ for the logistic regression model, using the test period.

[12] A major criticism is that AUC considers misclassification of 1's and 0's equally. For more about AUC and its flaws, see Chapter 5 in

G. Shmueli, P. C. Bruce, P. Gedeck, and N. R. Patel. *Machine Learning for Business Analytics: Techniques, Concepts and Applications in Python*. John Wiley & Sons, 2nd edition, 2025

[13] `www.kdnuggets.com/2010/09/pub-is-auc-the-best-measure.html`.

11. The same competitor, Christopher Hefele, then added more predictors to his model: `Variable167` and `Variable55` (each consisting of four series). His AUC was increased by 0.0005. Is this additional complexity warranted in practice? Fit a logistic regression with the additional predictors (taking appropriate differences), generate forecasts for the test period, and compare the confusion matrix and classification accuracy rate to that of the simpler model (with `Variable74` predictors only).

12. Use a neural network with the three sets of differenced and original variables (74, 167, and 55) as predictors. Generate forecasts and report the confusion matrix and classification accuracy rate. How does the neural network's performance compare to the two benchmark methods and the logistic regression model?

13. Which of the different models that you fitted would you recommend a stock trader use for forecasting stock movements on an ongoing basis? Explain.

Tips and Resources

- Tip for reading `Timestamp`: The variable `Timestamp` uses Microsoft Excel's date/time format, which counts days since 1/1/1970. The following code converts it to a `Pandas DatetimeIndex`:

```
stock['Timestamp'] = pd.to_datetime((stock['Timestamp'] - 25569) *
                                     86400, unit='s', utc=True)
stock['Timestamp'] = stock['Timestamp'].dt.round('min') # rounded to minute
stock.set_index('Timestamp', inplace=True)
```

- Tip for ROC and AUC: The following code produces and plots the ROC curve. It also computes and prints the AUC (area under the curve). The x-axis for the plot is the FPR = false positive rate. The y-axis for the plot is the TPR = true positive rate. The dashed line (y=x) represents what you would expect from random guessing. The area under the dashed line is 1/2. i.e., random guessing of a binary variable would be expected to be correct 50% of the time.

```
from sklearn.metrics import roc_curve, auc
fpr, tpr, thresholds = roc_curve(actual, prob_preds)
roc_auc = auc(fpr, tpr)
plt.plot(fpr, tpr, label=f"AUC = {roc_auc:.2f}")
```

- The top three performers' description of their approaches and experience: `medium.com/kaggle-blog/how-i-did-it-the-top-three-from-the-2010-informs-data-mining-contest-5267983308dd`.

- Forum with postings by top performers and other contestants after the close of the contest: `www.kaggle.com/c/informs2010/forums/t/133/and-the-winner-is`.

Data Resources, Competitions, and Coding Resources

To further assist readers and students with hands-on learning, below is a list of several publicly available, online sources of time series data that can be used for further study, projects, or otherwise.

Publicly Available Time Series Data

- Google Trends: `googletrends.github.io/data/`
- Time Series Data Library: `github.com/FinYang/tsdl`
- Financial Time Series: `finance.yahoo.com`
- Data used in the book *Forecasting: Principles and Practice* (3rd edition) by Rob J Hyndman and George Athanasopoulos is accessible in Python via the `sktime` package. Here is an example:

  ```
  from sktime.datasets import load_fpp3
  global_economy = load_fpp3("global_economy")
  ```

  This creates a `Pandas` DataFrame `global_economy` with a MultiIndex identifying each of the many time series contained in this one data set. The MultiIndex plays the role of the *key* in an R *tsibble* object.

- US Census Bureau business and industry series: `www.census.gov/econ/currentdata/datasets/`

Forecasting Competitions

Engaging in a competition is another good and exciting way to learn more about forecasting. However, remember that competitions are "sanitized" environments and lack the real challenges of determining the goal, cleaning the data, evaluating performance in a business-relevant way, and implementing the forecasting system in practice.

Many of the competitions listed below are annual, and open to anyone interested in competing. Some are recent one-time competitions. Some competition websites make data from past competitions available, including reports by the winners.

- The Time Series Forecasting Grand Competition for Computational Intelligence: `www.neural-forecasting-competition.com`
- The North American collegiate weather forecasting competition: `wxchallenge.com`
- Tourism Forecasting: `www.kaggle.com/c/tourism1` and `www.kaggle.com/c/tourism2`
- The M4 Competition: `https://www.sciencedirect.com/science/article/pii/S0169207019301128`

Coding Resources

There is an abundance of material online to learn Python, including tutorials. Also, all the leading LLM's will provide excellent code to accomplish any standard Python task. In addition to introductory Python tutorials you would benefit from reading up on the following:

- Vectorized calculations in Python via `numpy`
- The Python package `Pandas` with special attention to *DataFrame*, *Series* and *index* objects.
- The Python package `datetime`

Bibliography

[1] N. K. Ahmed, A. F. Atiya, N. El Gayar, and H. El-Shishiny. An empirical comparison of machine learning models for time series forecasting. *Econometric Reviews*, 29:594–621, 2010.

[2] R. R. Andrawis, A. F. Atiya, and H. El-Shishiny. Forecast combinations of computational intelligence and linear models for the NN5 time series forecasting competition. *International Journal of Forecasting*, 27:672–688, 2011.

[3] S. Asur and B. A. Huberman. Predicting the future with social media. In *2010 IEEE/WIC/ACM international conference on web intelligence and intelligent agent technology*, volume 1, pages 492–499. IEEE, 2010.

[4] R. Batchelor. Accuracy versus profitability. *Foresight: The International Journal of Applied Forecasting*, 21:10–15, 2011.

[5] BBC News Europe. Italy scientists on trial over L'aquilla earthquake, 2011. `www.bbc.com/news/world-europe-14981921` Accessed Feb 11, 2024.

[6] BBC News Science & Environment. Can we predict when and where quakes will strike?, 2011. `www.bbc.co.uk/news/science-environment-14991654` Accessed Feb 11, 2024.

[7] R. M. Bell, Y. Koren, and C. Volinsky. All together now: A perspective on the Netflix Prize. *Chance*, 23:24–29, 2010.

[8] H. S. Burkom, S. P. Murphy, and G. Shmueli. Automated time series forecasting for biosurveillance. *Statistics in Medicine*, 26:4202–4218, 2007.

[9] C. Chatfield. *The Analysis of Time Series: An Introduction.* Chapman & Hall/CRC, 6th edition, 2003.

[10] C. Chatfield and H. Xing. *The Analysis of Time Series: An Introduction.* Chapman & Hall/CRC, 7th edition, 2019.

[11] H. Fanaee-T and J. Gama. Event labeling combining ensemble detectors and background knowledge. *Progress in Artificial Intelligence*, pages 1–15, 2013.

[12] E. J. Gardner. Exponential smoothing: The state of the art - Part II. *International Journal of Forecasting*, 22:637–666, 2006.

[13] R. J. Hyndman. Nonparametric additive regression models for binary time series. In *Proceedings of the Australasian Meeting of the Econometric Society*, 1999.

[14] R. J. Hyndman. Another look at forecast-accuracy metrics for intermittent demand. *Foresight: The International Journal of Applied Forecasting*, 4:43–46, 2006.

[15] R. Law and N. Au. A neural network model to forecast Japanese demand for travel to Hong Kong. *Tourism Management*, 20:89–97, 1999.

[16] C. J. Lin, H. F. Chen, and T. S. Lee. Forecasting tourism demand using time series, artificial neural networks and multivariate adaptive regression splines: Evidence from Taiwan. *International Journal of Business Administration*, 2(2):14–24, 2011.

[17] A. K. Misra, O. M. Prakash, and V. Ramasubramanian. Forewarning powdery mildew caused by Oidium mangiferae in mango (Mangifera indica) using logistic regression models. *Indian Journal of Agricultural Science*, 74(2):84–87, 2004.

[18] G. Shmueli, P. C. Bruce, P. Gedeck, and N. R. Patel. *Machine Learning for Business Analytics: Techniques, Concepts and Applications in Python.* John Wiley & Sons, 2nd edition, 2025.

[19] S. S. Soman, H. Zareipour, O. Malik, and P. Mandal. A review of wind power and wind speed forecasting methods

with different time horizons. In *Proceedings of the 42nd North American Power Symposium (NAPS), Arlington, Texas, USA*, 2010.

[20] M. A. Tannura, S. H. Irwin, and D. L. Good. Weather, technology, and corn and soybean yields in the U.S. Corn Belt. Marketing and Outlook Research Report 2008-01, Department of Agricultural and Consumer Economics, University of Illinois at Urbana-Champaign, 2008.

[21] J. W. Taylor. Smooth transition exponential smoothing. *Journal of Forecasting*, 23:385–394, 2004.

[22] J. W. Taylor and R. D. Snyder. Forecasting intraday time series with multiple seasonal cycles using parsimonious seasonal exponential smoothing. *Omega*, 40(6):748–757, 2012.

[23] C. Tofallis. A better measure of relative prediction accuracy for model selection and model estimation. *Journal of the Operational Research Society*, 66:1352–1362, 2015.

[24] U.S. National Research Council. Forecasting demand and supply of doctoral scientists and engineers: Report of a workshop on methodology. National Academies Press, 2000.

[25] G. P. Zhang and D. M. Kline. Quarterly time-series forecasting with neural networks. *IEEE Transactions on Neural Networks*, 18(6):1800–1814, 2007.

Index